MW01715038

ExamView® Pro Testmaker

Human Heritage

A World History

Print Existing Glencoe Tests

- Section Quizzes
- Chapter Tests

Create Customized Tests

- One or more sections
- One or more chapters

For Macintosh and IBM PC (or 100% Compatible) Computers

Glencoe McGraw-Hill

New York, New York   Columbus, Ohio   Woodland Hills, California   Peoria, Illinois

This ExamView® Pro Testmaker for *Human Heritage: A World History* was developed by FSCreations, Inc., 621 Mehring Way, Suite 228, Cincinnati, OH 45202.

Windows is a registered trademark of the Microsoft Corporation.
Macintosh is a registered trademark of Apple Computer, Inc.

Glencoe/McGraw-Hill

A Division of The ***McGraw-Hill*** *Companies*

Send all inquiries to:
Glencoe/McGraw-Hill
8787 Orion Place
Columbus, OH 43240-4027

ISBN 0-07-822545-0

Printed in the United States of America

1 2 3 4 5 6 7 8 9 10 **069** 06 05 04 03 02 01 00

CONTENTS

TO THE TEACHER

This test bank contains multiple choice, matching, completion, and short answer questions covering all 39 chapters of the *Human Heritage: A World History* text. The questions are grouped by type (short answer, multiple choice, etc.) within each chapter. These questions and the test generator software have been prepared to assist you in developing tests for your students.

LEVELS OF DIFFICULTY

Each test question is designated with one of three levels of difficulty. Questions are designated as easy (E), average (A), or challenging (C). Below each question is a code that gives you the level of difficulty for that question. Use this information when you select questions to help you tailor your test to the exact needs and abilities of your students.

COMPONENTS

- *Human Heritage: A World History* Question Bank
- ExamView® Pro Testmaker User's Guide (Windows/Macintosh)
- ExamView® Pro Diskettes (Windows/Macintosh)
- ExamView® Pro Test Player (Windows/Macintosh)
- ExamView® Pro Hybrid CD-ROM (Windows/Macintosh)

The *Human Heritage: A World History* test generator consists of a User's Guide, a set of floppy disks, and a CD-ROM. The *User's Guide* contains instructions for the setup and use of the software. It also contains a printed listing of all the questions that accompany the test generator software. Use this guide to preview the available questions and to make your choices for inclusion on tests; or, if you prefer, you may view and select questions on-screen using the included computer program. The test generator software lets you retrieve the questions you want and then print tests. It also lets you edit and add questions as needed.

In the Windows version, if you have already installed the test generator program for other textbooks, you may have to select the folder named ***Human Heritage*** to locate the question bank files that accompany the *Human Heritage: A World History* textbook.

SITE LICENSE

By installing this software, you accept the terms and conditions of *The McGraw-Hill Companies End User Software License Agreement.* A copy of this agreement can be found on our Web site at www.epgtech.com, on the CD-ROM or diskette under the filename LICENSE.TXT, or can also be obtained by contacting our Software Support Hotline at 1-800-437-3715.

SOFTWARE SUPPORT HOTLINE
Should you encounter any difficulty when setting up or running the programs, contact the Software Support Center at Glencoe Publishing between 8:30 A.M. and 6:00 P.M. Eastern Time. The toll-free number is 1-800-437-3715. Customers with specific questions can contact us via the Internet at the following e-mail address: **epgtech@mcgraw-hill.com**

SECTION 1 — INTRODUCTION

This user's guide accompanies a test generator program called *ExamView® Pro 3.0 Testmaker*—an application that enables you to quickly create printed tests, Internet tests, and computer tests. Computer tests can be on a stand-alone computer or on a local area network (LAN). You can enter your own questions and customize the appearance of the tests you create. The *ExamView* Test Generator program offers many unique features. Numerous options are included that allow you to customize the content and appearance of the tests you create.

The *ExamView* Test Generator provides the following features:

- **an interview mode or "wizard" to guide you through the steps to create a test in less than five minutes**
- **five methods to select test questions**
  - random selection
  - from a list
  - while viewing questions
  - by criteria (including difficulty code, objective, topic, if available)
  - all questions
- **the capability to edit questions or to add an unlimited number of questions**
- **online (Internet-based) testing**
  - create a test that students can take on the Internet using a browser
  - receive instant feedback via e-mail
  - create online study guides with student feedback for incorrect responses
  - include any of the 12 question types
- **Internet test-hosting** *
  - instantly publish a test to the *ExamView* Web site
  - manage tests online
  - allow students to access tests from one convenient location
  - receive detailed reports
  - download results to your grade book or spreadsheet
- **online (stand-alone or LAN-based) testing**
  - allow students to take a test on a stand-alone computer or your school's local area network
  - schedule tests
  - create online study guides with student feedback for incorrect responses
  - incorporate multimedia links (movies and audio)
  - export student test results to a grade book or spreadsheet
- **a sophisticated word processor**
  - streamlined question entry with spell checker
  - tabs, fonts, symbols, foreign characters, and text styles
  - tables with borders and shading
  - full-featured equation editor
  - pictures or other graphics within a question, answer, or narrative
- **numerous test layout and printing options**
  - scramble the choices in multiple choice questions
  - print multiple versions of the same test with corresponding answer keys
  - print an answer key strip for easier test grading
- **link groups of questions to common narratives**

* The Internet test-hosting service must be purchased separately. Visit www.examview.com to learn more.

SECTION 2 — INSTALLATION AND STARTUP INSTRUCTIONS

The *ExamView* Test Generator software is provided on a CD-ROM and floppy disks. The disc includes the program and all of the questions for the corresponding textbook. The *ExamView* Test Player is also included. This Test Player can be used by your students to take tests on a computer.

Before you can use the software, you must install it on your hard drive. The system requirements, installation instructions, and startup procedures are provided below.

SYSTEM REQUIREMENTS

To use the *ExamView* Test Generator or the Test Player, your computer must meet or exceed the following minimum hardware requirements:

Windows

- Pentium computer
- Windows 95, Windows 98, Windows 2000 (or a more recent version)
- color monitor (VGA-compatible)
- CD-ROM and/or high-density floppy disk drive
- hard drive with at least 7 MB space available
- 8 MB available memory (16 MB memory recommended)
- an Internet connection to access the Internet test-hosting features

Macintosh

- PowerPC processor, 100 MHz computer
- System 7.5 (or a more recent version)
- color monitor (VGA-compatible)
- CD-ROM and/or high-density floppy disk drive
- hard drive with at least 7 MB space available
- 8 MB available memory (16 MB memory recommended)
- an Internet connection with System 8.6 (or more recent version) to access the Internet test-hosting features

INSTALLATION INSTRUCTIONS

Follow these steps to install the *ExamView* Test Generator software. The setup program will automatically install everything you need to use *ExamView*. **Note:** A separate Test Player setup program is also included for your convenience. [See Online (Stand-Alone/LAN-based) Testing on page 9 for more information.]

Windows

Step 1
Turn on your computer.

Step 2
Insert the *ExamView* disc into the CD-ROM drive. If you are using floppy disks, insert Disk 1 into Drive A.

Step 3
Click the **Start** button on the *Taskbar* and choose the *Run* option.

Step 4
If you are installing *ExamView* using a CD-ROM, use the drive letter that corresponds to the CD-ROM drive on your computer (e.g., **d:\setup.exe**). The setup program, however, may be located in a subfolder on the CD-ROM if the *ExamView* software is included on the disc with other resources. In this case, click the **Browse** button in the Run dialog box to locate the setup program (e.g., **d:\evpro\setup.exe**).

If you are installing the software from floppy disks, type **a:\setup** and press **Enter** to run the installation program.

Step 5
Follow the prompts on the screen to complete the installation process.

If the software and question banks are provided on more than one floppy disk, you will be prompted to insert the appropriate disk when it is needed.

Step 6
Remove the installation disc when you finish.

Macintosh

Step 1
Turn on your computer.

Step 2
Insert the *ExamView* installation disc into your CD-ROM drive. If you are using floppy disks, insert Disk 1 into a disk drive.

Step 3
Open the installer window, if necessary.

Step 4
Double-click the installation icon to start the program.

Step 5
Follow the prompts on the screen to complete the installation process.

If the software and question banks are provided on more than one floppy disk, you will be prompted to insert the appropriate disk when it is needed.

Step 6
Remove the installation disc when you finish.

GETTING STARTED

After you complete the installation process, follow these instructions to start the *ExamView* Test Generator software. This section also explains the options used to create a test and edit a question bank.

Startup Instructions

Step 1
Turn on the computer.

Step 2

Windows: Click the **Start** button on the *Taskbar.* Highlight the **Programs** menu and locate the *ExamView Test Generator* folder. Select the *ExamView Pro* option to start the software.

Macintosh: Locate and open the *ExamView* folder. Double-click the *ExamView Pro* program icon.

Step 3
The first time you run the software, you will be prompted to enter your name, school/institution name, and city/state. You are now ready to begin using the *ExamView* software.

Step 4
Each time you start *ExamView,* the **Startup** menu appears. Choose one of the options shown in Figure 1. **Note:** All of the figures shown in this user's guide are taken from the Windows software. Except for a few minor differences, the Macintosh screens are identical.

Step 5
Use *ExamView* to create a test or edit questions in a question bank.

ExamView includes three components: Test Builder, Question Bank Editor, and Test Player. The Test Builder includes options to create, edit, print, and save tests. The Question Bank Editor lets you create or edit question banks. The Test Player is a separate program that your students can use to take online (stand-alone/LAN-based) tests/study guides.

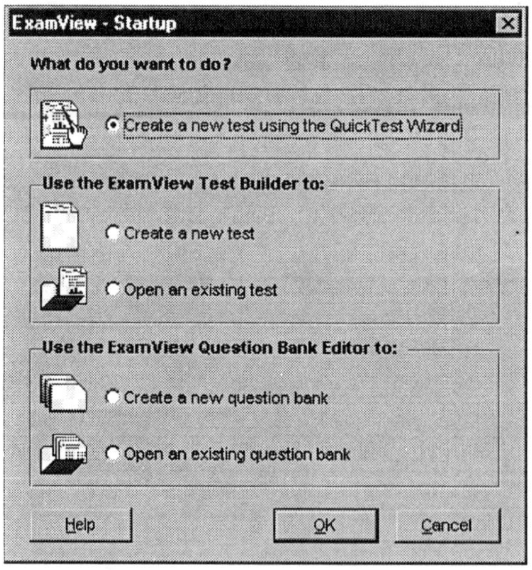

Figure 1 – ExamView Startup Menu

Using The Help System

Whenever you need assistance using *ExamView,* access the extensive help system. Click the **Help** button or choose the *Help Topics* option from the **Help** menu to access step-by-step instructions from more than 150 help topics. If you experience any difficulties while you are working with the software, you may want to review the troubleshooting tips in the user-friendly help system.

Test Builder

The Test Builder allows you to create tests using the QuickTest Wizard, or you can create a new test on your own. (See the sample test in Figure 2.) Use the Test Builder to prepare both printed and online tests/study guides.

- ***If you want ExamView to select questions randomly from one or more question banks,*** choose the *QuickTest Wizard* option to create a new test. (Refer to Figure 1 on page 4.) Then, follow the step-by-step instructions to (1) enter a test title, (2) choose one or more question banks from which to select questions, and (3) identify how many questions you want on the test. The QuickTest Wizard will automatically create a new test and use the Test Builder to display the test on screen. You can print the test as is, remove questions, add new questions, or edit any question.
- ***If you want to create a new test on your own,*** choose the option to create a new test. (Refer to Figure 1 on page 4.) Then, identify a question bank from which to choose questions by using the *Question Bank* option in the **Select** menu. You may then add questions to the test by using one or more of the following selection options: *Randomly, From a List, While Viewing, By Criteria,* or *All Questions.*

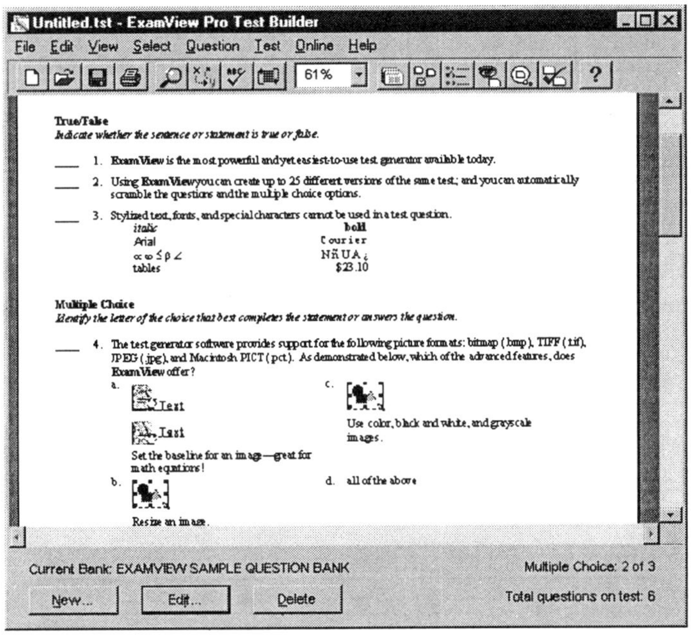

Figure 2 – Sample Test

IMPORTANT: The Test Builder and the Question Bank Editor systems are integrated in one program. As you work with *ExamView*, you can easily switch between the Test Builder and Question Bank Editor components using the *Switch to...* option in the **File** menu.

To create a new test:

Step 1
Start the *ExamView* software.

Step 2
At the Startup window, choose the *Create a new test* option.

Step 3
Enter a title for the new test.

After you enter the title, the program will automatically display the option for you to select a question bank.

Step 4
Choose a question bank.

Step 5
Select the questions you want to include on the test.

Use the question selection options that appear in the **Select** menu. Or, click the corresponding buttons on the toolbar. A description for each of the question selection toolbar buttons appears below.

Click the **Question Bank** toolbar button to select a question bank.

You can create a test using questions from one question bank or from multiple banks. Choose a bank, select the questions you want, and then choose another bank to select more questions.

Click the **Select Randomly** toolbar button when you want the program to randomly select questions for you.

Use the **Select from a List** command to choose questions if you know which ones you want to select. Identify the questions you want by reviewing a question bank printout.

Click the **Select while Viewing** button to display a window that shows all of the questions in the current question bank. Click the check boxes to select the questions you want.

You can use the **Select by Criteria** command to choose questions based on question type, difficulty, and objective (if available).

Click the **Select All** button to choose all of the questions in the current question bank.

Step 6
Save the test.

Step 7
Print the test.

You can use the options in the **Test** menu to customize the appearance of a test, edit test instructions, and choose to leave space for students to write their answers. When you print a test, you may choose how many variations of the test you want, whether you want all the versions to be the same, and whether you want to scramble the questions and the multiple choice options. If you choose to scramble the questions, *ExamView* will print a custom answer sheet for each variation of the test.

If you want your students to take a test online, first create the test. Then, publish the test as an Internet test/study guide (see page 15) or use the Online Test Wizard (see page 10) to create a test for a stand-alone computer or delivery over a LAN (local area network). The software will walk you through the steps to turn any test into an online (Internet or stand-alone/LAN-based) test.

IMPORTANT: You may edit questions or create new questions as you build your test. However, those questions can be used only as part of the current test. If you plan to create several new questions that you would like to use on other tests, switch to the Question Bank Editor to add the new questions.

Question Bank Editor

The Question Bank Editor allows you to edit questions in an existing publisher-supplied question bank or to create your own new question banks. Always use the Question Bank Editor if you want to change a question permanently in an existing question bank. If you want to make a change that applies only to a particular test, create a new question or edit that question in the Test Builder.

A question bank may include up to 250 questions in a variety of formats, including multiple choice, true/false, modified true/false, completion, yes/no, matching, problem, essay, short answer, case, and numeric response. You can include the following information for each question: difficulty code, reference, text objective, state objectives, topic, and notes.

Step 1

Start the *ExamView* software.

Step 2

At the Startup window as illustrated in Figure 1 on page 4, choose to *Create a new question bank* or *Open an existing question bank.*

If you are working in the Test Builder, click the **File** menu and choose *Switch to Question Bank Editor* to edit or create a new question bank.

Step 3

Click the **New** button to create a new question or click the **Edit** button to modify an existing question. Both of these buttons appear at the bottom of the Question Bank Editor window. (See Figure 3.)

You may add new questions or edit questions in a question bank by using the built-in word processor. The word processor includes many features commonly found in commercially available word processing applications. These features include the following: fonts, styles, tables, paragraph formatting, ruler controls, tabs, indents, and justification.

Step 4

Save your work. Then, exit the program or switch back to the Test Builder.

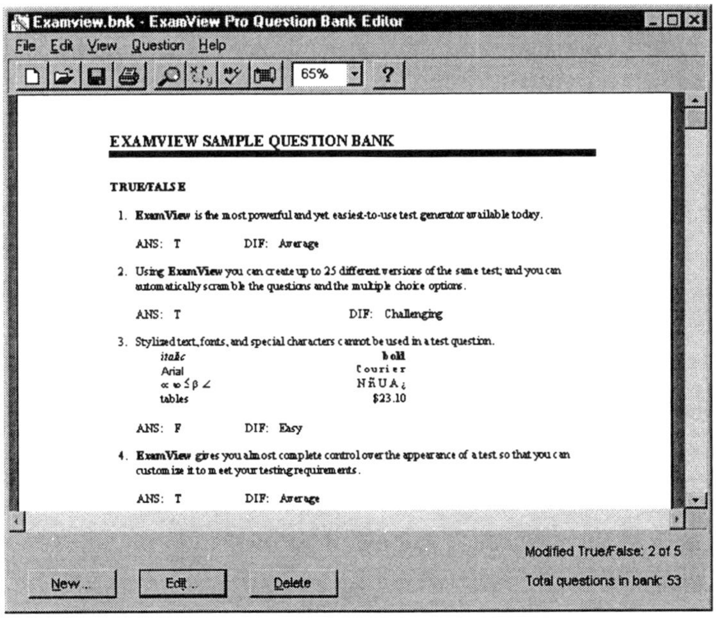

Figure 3 – Question Bank Editor

Online Testing (Stand-Alone/LAN-based vs. Internet)

The *ExamView* software allows you to create paper tests and online tests. The program provides two distinct online testing options: **stand-alone/LAN-based** testing and **Internet** testing. The option you choose depends on your particular testing needs. You can choose either option to administer online tests and study guides.

The **stand-alone/LAN-based** testing option is designed to work on a single computer or a local area network server. That is, you can copy the test/study guide along with the Test Player software onto your computer or local area network. Then students can take the test at the single computer or those computers connected to your server.

To take a stand-alone/LAN-based test, your students must have access to the Test Player program included with the *ExamView* software. The Test Player is a separate program that lets your students take a test/study guide at a computer. You can store the Test Player program and the test on a single computer or a local area network for easy access by your students.

The **Internet** testing option provides a computerized testing solution for delivering tests via the Internet or an Intranet. This option is great for distance learning environments or simply to make a sample test/study guide available to students at home. Students do not need any other program (unlike the stand-alone/LAN-based option). When your students take a test, the results are automatically sent to you via e-mail.

You can publish an Internet test to your own Web site, or you can use the *ExamView* Internet test-hosting service. If you subscribe to the *ExamView* test-hosting service, you can publish a test directly to the Internet with just a few simple steps. Students will have immediate access to the tests that you publish, and you can get detailed reports. For more information on the Internet test-hosting service, visit our Web site at www.examview.com.

SECTION 3 — ONLINE (STAND-ALONE/LAN-BASED) TESTING

Online testing features are seamlessly integrated into the *ExamView* software. If you want to take advantage of these capabilities, simply create a test and then use the Online Test Wizard to set up the testing parameters. Students can then take the test at the computer using the Test Player program.

IMPORTANT: If you want to prepare a test/study guide for delivery via the Internet, use the *Publish Internet Test* option as described on page 16.

ExamView includes many features that let you customize an online (stand-alone/LAN-based) test. You can create a test for a specific class, or you can prepare a study guide for anyone to take. Using the Online Test Wizard, you can schedule a test or allow it to be taken anytime. As your students work on a test, *ExamView* will scramble the question order, provide feedback for incorrect responses, and display a timer, if you selected any of these options.

ONLINE (STAND-ALONE/LAN-BASED) TESTING OVERVIEW

Refer to the steps below for an overview of the online (stand-alone/LAN-based) testing process. Specific instructions for creating a test, taking a test, and viewing results are provided on the following pages.

Step 1
Talk with your network administrator to help you set up a location (folder) on your computer or local area network where you can install the Test Player software and copy your tests/study guides.

If you are using a network, make sure that the administrator gives you and your students full access to the designated folders on the server. You may also want your network administrator to install the Test Player software.

Step 2
Create a test/study guide, and then use the Online Test Wizard to set up the online (stand-alone/LAN-based) test. Save your work and exit the *ExamView* software.

Step 3
If you are using a network, transfer the test/study guide file [e.g., chapter1.tst (Windows) or Chapter 1 (Macintosh)] and any accompanying multimedia files from your computer to the local area network server.

Copy the files from your hard drive to the folder set up by your network administrator. You need only copy the test file unless you linked an audio or video segment to one or more questions.

Step 4
Instruct your students to complete the test/study guide.

Students must have access to a computer connected to the local area network on which the Test Player and test/study guide are stored.

Step 5
After all students finish taking the test, copy the test/study guide file back to your hard drive. It is recommended that you copy the test to a different location from the original test file. The new test file contains all of the students' results.

Note: If you set up a class roster, the test file will contain item analysis information and the results for each student. If you did not set up a roster, no results are recorded, so you do not have to complete this step or the next.

Step 6
Start the *ExamView* software and open the test file to view your students' results.

CREATING AN ONLINE (STAND-ALONE/LAN-BASED) TEST

Follow the steps shown below to create an online (stand-alone/LAN-based) test or study guide. Depending on the options you set, you can create a test or study guide. Before you begin, make sure that you installed the *ExamView* Test Generator and Test Player software. **Note**: See the next section (page 12) for instructions to set up the Test Player. (See page 15 for Internet testing features.)

Step 1
Start the *ExamView* software.

Step 2
Create or open a test/study guide.

Select the questions you want to include on the test. You can include any of the following types: True/False, Multiple Choice, Yes/No, Numeric Response, Completion, and Matching.

Step 3
Select the *Online Test Wizard* option from the **Online** menu.

ExamView presents step-by-step instructions to help you prepare the online (stand-alone/LAN-based) test/study guide. (See Figure 4.) Read the instructions provided and complete each step. **Note**: Click the **Help** button if you need more assistance.

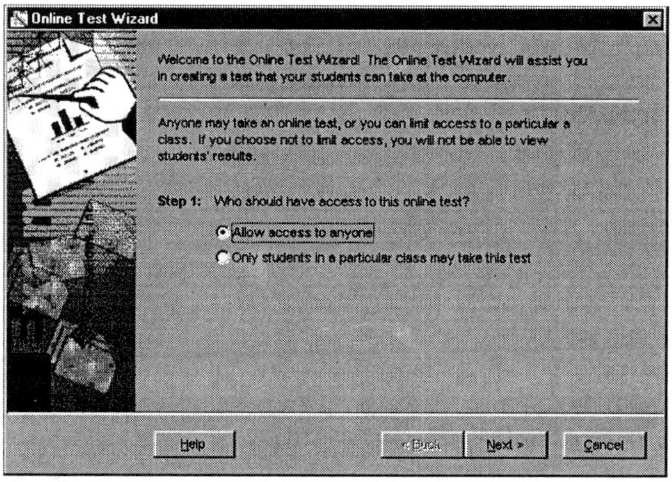

Figure 4 – Online Test Wizard (Step 1)

Step 4
Click the **Finish** button after you complete the last step using the Online Test Wizard. As you can see in Figure 5 on page 11, *ExamView* shows a summary that describes the settings for the online test.

Step 5
Save the test/study guide to a location where your students can easily access it. For example, save it in the same location where you installed the Test Player program.

If you are using a network, it is recommended that you save the test/study guide to a location on a network server where students have read/write access. The Test Player will store all of your students' results (if you entered a class roster) in the test file itself. You can copy the test to individual computers, but this configuration takes more time to gather the results.

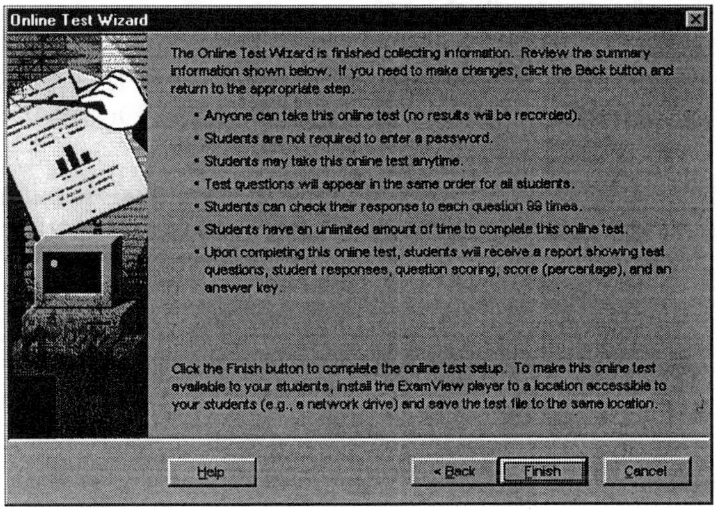

Figure 5 – Online Test Wizard (Summary)

Step 6

If you included multimedia links in any of the questions, copy those files to the same location where you saved the test/study guide.

If the multimedia files are on a CD-ROM or DVD disc, you may leave them on the disc, but provide this information to your students. To play one of these links, students will have to specify the location of the multimedia file.

NOTES:

- Use the *Test Preferences* and *Class Roster* options in the **Online** menu if you want to make any changes to the test parameters. These two options let you change any of the settings you selected using the Online Test Wizard.
- You must close the test before your students can access it with the Test Player.
- If you set up a class roster for a test/study guide, you cannot modify the test (e.g., edit a question, change the order) once any student has taken it unless you clear the results first.
- Provide your students with the Test Player setup program and a copy of the test/study guide if you want them to take it at home.

INSTALLING THE TEST PLAYER

Follow the instructions provided here to install the Test Player program for your students. You may copy the Test Player to a network (recommended), install it on individual computers, or provide it on a floppy disk for your students to take home.

Even if you have a network, you can install the Test Player on individual computers. Students will still be able to access tests/study guides you store on a local area network.

ExamView Test Player Installation

Windows

Step 1
Turn on your computer.

Step 2
Insert the *ExamView* disc into your CD-ROM drive. If you are using floppy disks, insert the *ExamView* Test Player installation disk into Drive A.

Step 3
Click the **Start** button on the *Taskbar* and choose the *Run* option.

Step 4
If you are using a CD-ROM, use the drive letter that corresponds to the CD-ROM drive on your computer (e.g., **d:\evplayer\setup** or **d:\evpro\evplayer\setup**).

If you are installing the software from a floppy disk, type **a:\setup** and press **Enter** to run the installation program.

Step 5
When prompted for a location to install the program, select a folder (e.g., **x:\programs\evplayer** for network installation or **c:\evplayer** on your local hard drive).

Step 6
For local area network (LAN) installations, complete the following steps at each workstation:

- Click the **Start** button and choose *Taskbar* from the **Settings** menu.
- Click the **Start Menu Programs** tab and click **Add.**
- Type the location and program name for the Test Player software, or use the **Browse** button to enter this information (e.g., **x:\programs\evplayer\evplayer.exe**).
- Proceed to the next screen and add a new folder (e.g., **ExamView Test Player**).
- Enter **ExamView Test Player** as the shortcut name and then click the **Finish** button.

Repeat Steps 1–5 if you plan to install the software at each computer instead of installing the program once on your network.

Macintosh

Step 1
Turn on your computer.

Step 2
Insert the *ExamView* installation disc into your CD-ROM drive. If you are using floppy disks, insert the *ExamView* Test Player installation disk into a disk drive.

Step 3
Open the installer window, if necessary.

Step 4
Double-click the installation icon to start the program.

Note: The installation program is configured to copy the Test Player to a new folder on your hard drive. You can, however, change this location. For example, you can select a location on your network server.

Step 5
When prompted for a location to install the program, select a folder on your local area network that is accessible to all students. If you are installing the software on a stand-alone computer, choose a location on the hard drive.

Step 6
At each workstation, enable file sharing and program linking if you installed the application on your network server.

For stand-alone computers, repeat Steps 1–5.

Installing the Test Player at Home

You can give your students the Test Player software to take home. Give your students the separate Test Player setup disk that is part of the floppy disks. You can also use the CD-ROM by copying all of the setup files in the ***evplayer*** folder onto a floppy disk. Students should follow Steps 1–5 on page 12 to install the software on their computer. When students take a test home, they should copy it into the same folder as the Test Player program.

TAKING AN ONLINE (STAND-ALONE/LAN-BASED) TEST

Make sure that you have properly installed the *ExamView* Test Player software and copied the test/study guide to a location easily accessible to your students. If you linked multimedia files to any of the questions, it is recommended that you copy those files to the same folder as the test/study guide. Provide the instructions below to your students.

If you created a test with a class roster, students must correctly enter their IDs to be able to take the test/study guide. Provide this information to your students, if necessary. **Note**: If you do not want to track student scores, you should set up a test to allow anyone to take it.

Step 1
Start the *ExamView* Test Player software.

Step 2
Enter your name and ID. (See Figure 6.)

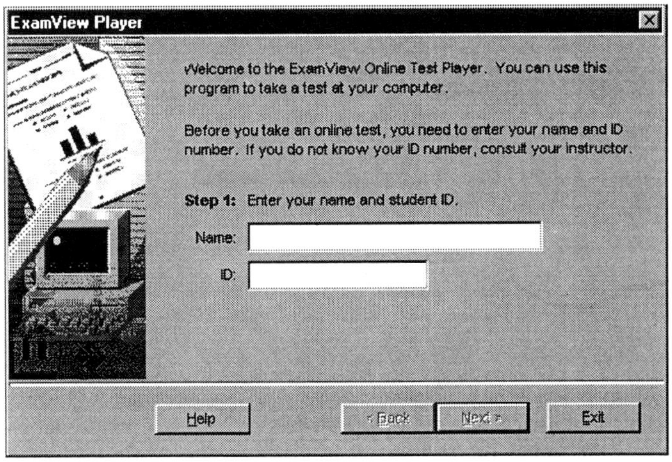

Figure 6 – Online Test/Study Guide Registration

Step 3
Select a test/study guide. (See Figure 7.)

If no tests (or study guides) appear in the list, click the **Folder** button to identify where the tests are located.

Step 4
(Optional) Enter a password, if prompted.

Step 5
Review the summary information and click **Start** when you are ready to begin.

Step 6
Answer all of the questions and click the **End** button when you finish.

Verify that you want to end the test. If you do not answer all of the questions in one session, you will ***not*** be able to resume the test at a later time.

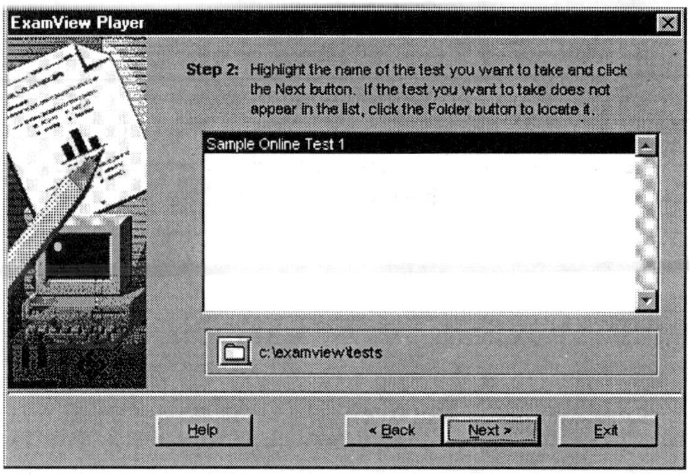

Figure 7 – Online Test/Study Guide Selection

Step 7
Review the test report.

Step 8
Click **New Test** to take another test or click **Exit** to quit the program.

VIEWING ONLINE (STAND-ALONE/LAN-BASED) RESULTS

If you set up a test with a class roster (instead of allowing anyone to access a test/study guide), the *ExamView* Test Player will automatically collect the results for each student. The program saves this information in the test/study guide file itself.

Step 1
Start the *ExamView* software and open the online test/study guide that your students have already taken.

Step 2
Choose *View Test Results* from the **Online** menu.

Step 3
Review the results, item-by-item analysis, and statistics reports.

Step 4
Choose *Export Test Results* if you want to export the scores to your favorite grade book program or spreadsheet application.

SECTION 4 — INTERNET TESTING

ExamView lets you easily create Internet tests and study guides. Build a test and then simply choose the *Publish Internet Test* option. You can choose to post tests to your own Web site or to publish tests directly to the *ExamView* Web site. (Visit us at www.examview.com to learn more about subscribing to the Internet test-hosting service.)

With the Internet test-hosting feature, you can publish a test or study guide directly to the *ExamView* Web site. Simply create a test and then follow the easy step-by-step instructions to publish it to the Internet. It's that simple! You can manage tests online, view reports, and download results. Students access your tests from one convenient location.

If you do not use the ExamView test-hosting service, you can manually post tests/study guides to your own Web site. If you create a test, your students' results are sent to you via e-mail automatically. You can also create a study guide that your students can use to review various topics at their own pace.

INTERNET TESTING FAQs

Review the FAQs (frequently asked questions) below for more information on the Internet test-hosting features available to *ExamView Pro 3.0* users.

What are the advantages to using the Internet test-hosting feature? (1) Publishing an Internet test to your own Web site and setting up links can be quite challenging. With the Internet test-hosting feature, the process is completely automated. In minutes, you can post a test to the Internet. (2) When you post tests/study guides to your own Web site, only a few options are available. Using the *ExamView* test-hosting service, you have many more options available, such as setting up a class roster and viewing detailed item analysis reports.

How do you register for the test-hosting service? Visit our Web site at www.examview.com to learn how to register. Before you can post tests/study guides, you must sign up to obtain a valid instructor ID and a password.

Is there an additional charge for the Internet test-hosting service? Yes, there is an additional yearly subscription charge to use this service. If you received the *ExamView* software from a publisher, you may be eligible for a discount or a free trial membership. (See our Web site for current prices and special promotions.)

Do you have to use the Internet test-hosting service? No, using the test-hosting service is not required. The *Publish Internet Test* feature includes an option to save an Internet test/study guide to a local hard drive. Then, you can manually post it to your own Web site.

Why aren't the same features available for tests posted to my own Web site? To offer the numerous Internet test-hosting features, we have developed many programs and databases that are stored on our servers. If you post to your own server or Web site, these programs are not available.

IMPORTANT: Your students must use a browser such as Netscape 4.0/Internet Explorer 4.0 (or a more recent version) that supports cascading style sheets level 1 (CSS1) and JavaScript. To post tests or study guides for delivery via the Internet, you must have your own access to an Internet server.

USING THE INTERNET TEST-HOSTING SERVICE

Using the *ExamView* Test Generator software, you can publish tests directly to the *ExamView* Web site if you have signed up for the test-hosting service. With a few simple steps, you can publish tests and study guides directly to the Internet. Refer to the following instructions to register for the Internet test-hosting service, create a test, publish a test to the Internet, take tests online, manage tests, and view student results.

Register for the Internet Test-Hosting Service

Step 1
Launch your Web browser and go to www.examview.com.

Step 2
Go to the **Instructor Center** to register for the test-hosting service. Follow the instructions provided at the Web site to sign up.

Record the instructor ID and password assigned to you. You will need this information to publish a test or study guide to the *ExamView* Web site. When you choose to publish a test, you will be prompted to enter this information.

Step 3
Quit the browser.

Publish a Test/Study Guide to the ExamView Web Site

Step 1
Start the *ExamView* software.

Step 2
Create a new test or open an existing test.

Select the questions you want to include on the test. You can include any of the 12 question types on a test, but only the objective questions are scored.

Step 3
Select the *Publish Internet Test* option from the **File** menu.

ExamView presents a window with various Internet testing options to help you prepare the online test. (See Figure 8.) **Note**: Click the **Help** button if you need more assistance.

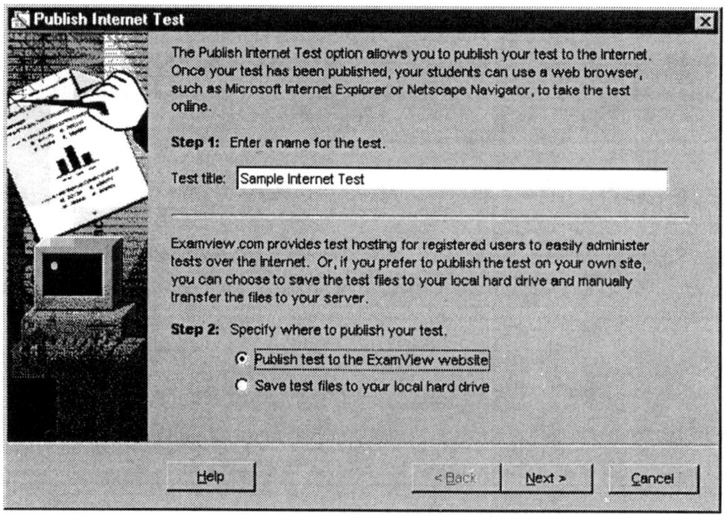

Figure 8 – Publish Internet Test Window

Step 4
Name the test.

Step 5
Select the option to publish your test to the *ExamView* Web site, and then click the **Next** button.

Step 6
Enter your instructor ID and password.

If you do not already have an instructor ID and password, click the **Register Now** button to launch your Web browser and go to the www.examview.com Web site. You cannot proceed until you have a valid instructor ID and password.

Step 7
Choose whether you want to publish a test or a study guide.

Step 8
Specify when students may access the test/study guide.

Step 9
Enter the expiration date.

Step 10
Specify who should have access to this test/study guide.

Anyone may take the test or study guide, or you may limit access to a particular group of students. If you specify a roster, students must enter an ID and password.

Step 11
Enter a student password and click **Next**.

Step 12
Review the summary information. Click the **Back** button if you need to make changes. (See Figure 9.)

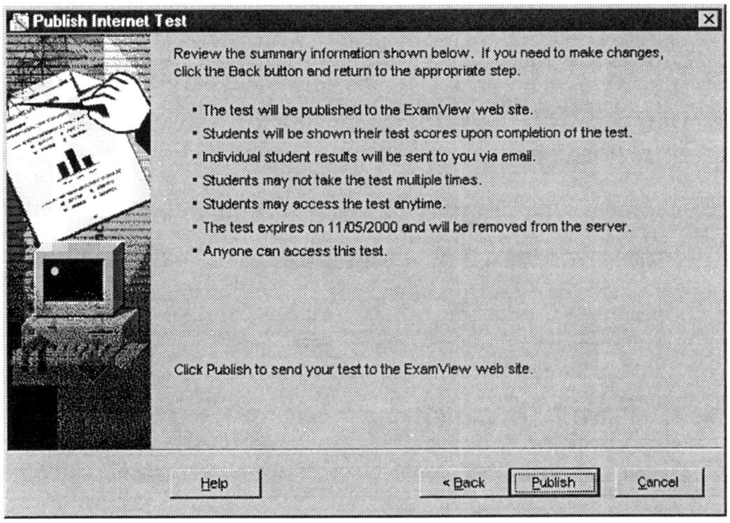

Figure 9 – Publish Internet Test Window (Summary)

Step 13

Click the **Publish** button when you are ready to post the test/study guide to the *ExamView* Web site.

The program automatically connects to the Internet and posts the test/study guide to the *ExamView* server. Access the instructor options on the *ExamView* Web site (www.examview.com) to preview a test, change selected parameters, or view results. If you need to edit or delete questions, you must change the test locally and then publish a new version. **Note:** An Internet connection is required to publish a test/study guide.

Step 14

Print a copy of the test/study guide for your records, create another test, or exit the software when you are finished.

Take a Test/Study Guide Online at www.evtestcenter.com

Once you publish a test/study guide to the *ExamView* server, anyone in the world can access it if you provide him or her with your instructor ID and the appropriate student password. (**IMPORTANT:** *Do **not** give students your instructor password, just your ID.*) Provide the instructions below to your students so that they can take the test or study guide.

To take a test:

Step 1

Start your Web browser.

Step 2

Go to the URL www.evtestcenter.com.

Step 3

Enter your instructor's ID code. (See Figure 10.)

Upon entering a valid instructor code, you will see a list of tests your instructor has published.

Step 4

Select a test.

Step 5

Enter your name (if requested), student ID, and student password.

Contact your instructor if you have not been assigned a student ID or you do not have a student password.

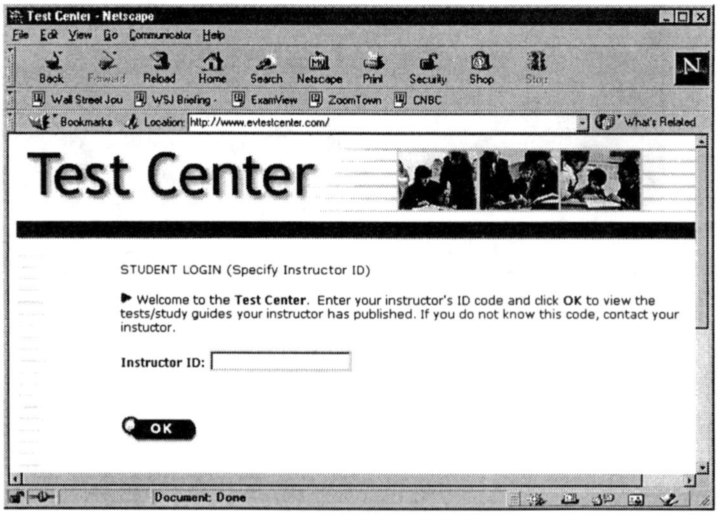

Figure 10 – Test Center Login (www.evtestcenter.com)

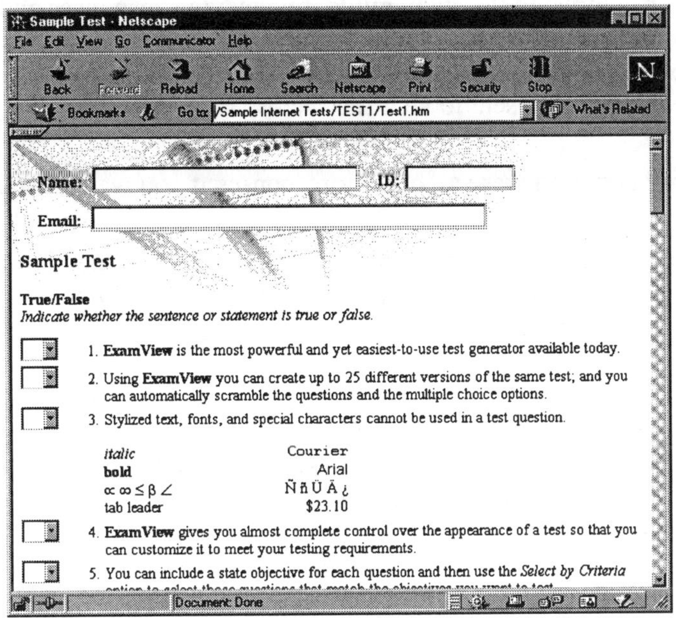

Figure 11 – Sample Internet Test

Step 6
Review the test and respond to all of the questions. (See the sample test in Figure 11.)

If you need help while working with a test, click the **Help** button shown at the bottom of the test. Click the browser's **Back** button to return to the test.

Step 7
When you have completed the test, review the entire test and then click the **Grade & Submit** button located at the bottom of the test.

Your results will be e-mailed to your instructor. Depending on the test settings, you may be notified of your results immediately.

To complete a study guide:

Step 1
Start your Web browser.

Step 2
Go to the URL www.evtestcenter.com.

Step 3
Enter your instructor's ID.

You will see a list of study guides and tests your instructor has published.

Step 4
Select a study guide.

Step 5
Enter your name (if requested), student ID, and student password.

Contact your instructor if you have not been assigned a student ID or you do not have a student password.

Step 6
Review the study guide and answer all of the questions.

If you need help while working with a study guide, click the **Help** button shown at the bottom of the screen. Click the browser's **Back** button to return to the study guide.

Step 7
When you have completed the study guide, review your responses and then click the **Check Your Work** button located at the bottom of the study guide.

Your work is scored and you will see whether you answered each question correctly or incorrectly. No results are sent to your instructor.

Step 8
Click the **Reset** button to erase all of your responses if you want to start over.

Note: You must use a browser such as Netscape 4.0/Internet Explorer 4.0 (or a more recent version) that supports cascading style sheets level 1 (CSS1) and JavaScript. An active Internet connection is also required.

Review Student Results and Manage Tests

When your students complete an Internet test, their results are automatically stored on the server so that you can easily access this information. If you chose to receive results via e-mail, you will also receive the following information for each student: (1) student name and ID, (2) raw score and percentage score for objective-based questions, and (3) responses for each question (objective and open-ended questions).

At the *ExamView* Web site, you may also change test-setup options, preview tests, download student results, and view your account information.

Step 1
Start your Web browser.

Step 2
Go to the URL www.examview.com and access the Instructor Center.

Step 3
Log in using your instructor ID and password to view the main menu options. (See Figure 12.)

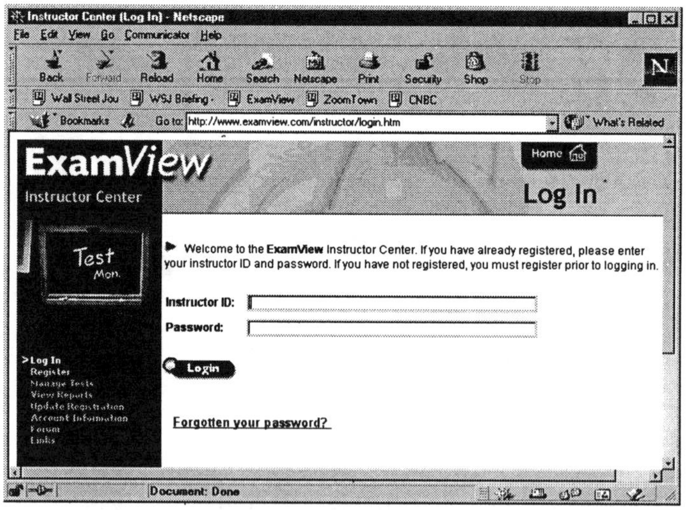

Figure 12 – *ExamView* Web Site (Instructor Center)

PUBLISHING TESTS TO YOUR OWN WEB SITE

If you choose not to sign up for the *ExamView* test-hosting service, you can still publish tests/study guides to your own Web site. You must save the test/study guide to your hard drive, upload the files to your Web site, and then provide access to your students. Refer to the following sections for step-by-step instructions.

Save an Internet Test/Study Guide to Your Hard Drive

Follow the steps shown below to create an Internet test/study guide and save it to your hard drive. Before you begin, make sure that you installed the *ExamView* Test Generator software.

Step 1
Start the *ExamView* software.

Step 2
Create a new test or open an existing test.

Select the questions you want to include on the test. You can include any of the 12 question types on a test, but only the objective questions will be graded.

Step 3
Select the *Publish Internet Test* option from the **File** menu.

ExamView presents a window with various Internet testing options to help you prepare the online test. (See Figure 13.) **Note**: Click the **Help** button if you need more assistance.

Step 4
Name the test.

Step 5
Select the option to save the test files to your local hard drive and then click the **Next** button.

Step 6
Choose whether you want to publish a test or a study guide.

Step 7
Review the summary information. Make changes, if necessary.

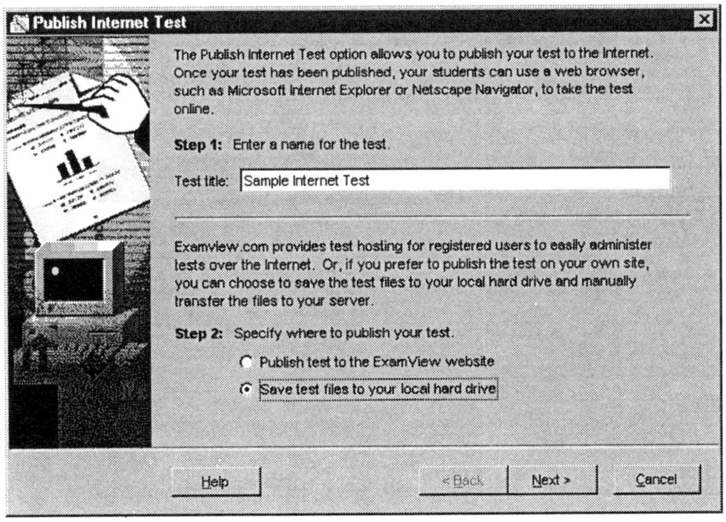

Figure 13 – Publish Internet Test Window

Step 8
Click the **Save** button to save the test/study guide files.

When you choose to save an Internet test to your local hard drive, *ExamView* creates an HTML file and an accompanying folder with all of the necessary image files. This makes it easier for you to post the files to a Web server. If, for example, you enter a path such as **c:\examview\tests\chapter1** (Windows) or **HD:ExamView:Tests:Chapter1** (Macintosh), the software will create a file called **chapter1.htm** and a new folder called **chapter1_files** with all of the required picture files. (See the illustration below.)

Step 9
Post the test/study guide to a server to make it available to your students. (See the next section for instructions for posting a test to a server.)

Step 10
Once you post a test, you should verify that students can access it. You may also want to try the *Grade & Submit* feature for tests to make sure that the results are e-mailed to the correct address.

Note: When you create a test, *ExamView* encrypts the answer information so that a student cannot see the answers in the HTML page source. While this does help to prevent cheating, there is no foolproof method in an unsupervised environment.

Post a Test to Your Own Internet/Intranet Server

Once you save a test/study guide formatted for the Internet, you must post all of the related files to a location on a server that your students can access. You can post the files to a local area network, Intranet server, or an Internet server. You ***must*** have an Internet connection for students to be able to submit test results. (This is not required for a study guide.)

Step 1
Start an FTP program or other utility that allows you to copy files from your hard drive to an Internet/Intranet server.

Step 2
Log in to your server.

Step 3
Create a new folder on your server to hold the test/study guide files.

Step 4
Copy the HTML file and the accompanying folder to a location on your server that your students can access.

When you choose to save an Internet test to your hard drive, *ExamView* creates an HTML file and an accompanying folder with all of the necessary image files. This makes it easier for you to post the files to a Web server.

IMPORTANT: By default, all of the file names are lowercase. Do not change the case since these files are referenced in the HTML document. You ***must*** copy the HTML file and the accompanying folder as is. Do not copy the HTML file into the corresponding folder. (See the illustration below.)

Step 5
Log off the server, if necessary.

Step 6
Record the URL for the test/study guide HTML document or set up a link to the test.

Note: The specific steps will vary depending on the hardware and software configuration of your server. If you are not familiar with the required steps, contact your network administrator for assistance.

Take a Test or Study Guide Using the Internet

Once you post a test on a server, anyone in the world can access the test if you provide him or her with the Web (URL) address. Follow the instructions provided below to take a test or study guide.

Note: You must use a browser such as Netscape 4.0/Internet Explorer 4.0 (or a more recent version) that supports cascading style sheets level 1 (CSS1) and JavaScript. An active Internet connection is required to submit test results.

To take a test via the Internet:

Step 1
Start your Web browser.

Step 2
Type the Web address (URL) and test name (e.g., **www.school.edu/economics/test1.htm**), or enter an address for a page with a link to the test. (See the sample test in Figure 14 on page 22.)

If the test is located on a local area network, use the option to open a page in the browser to display the test.

Step 3
Enter your name, student ID, and e-mail address (optional).

Step 4
Answer all of the questions.

If you need help while working with a test, click the **Help** button shown at the bottom of the test. Click the browser's **Back** button to return to the test.

Step 5
When you complete the test, review your responses and then click the **Grade & Submit** button located at the bottom of the screen.

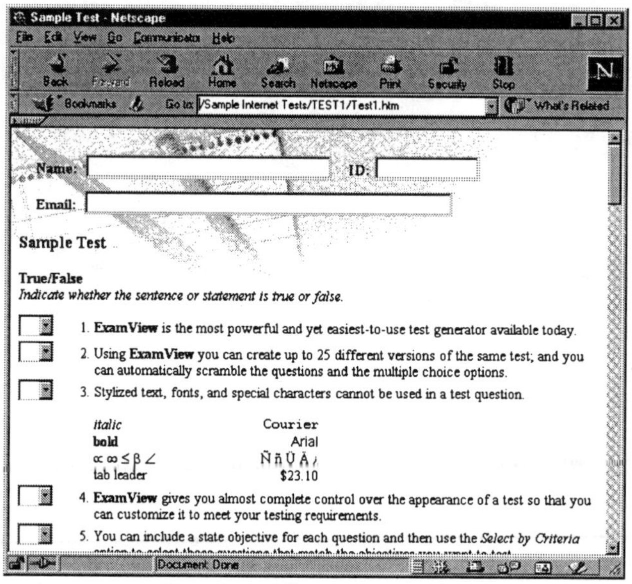

Figure 14 – Sample Internet Test

To complete a study guide via the Internet:

Step 1
Start your Web browser.

Step 2
Type the Web address (URL) and study guide name (e.g., **www.school.edu/history/study.htm**), or enter an address for a page with a link to the study guide.

Step 3
Enter your name.

Step 4
Answer all of the questions.

Step 5
When you complete the study guide, review the entire test and then click the **Check Your Work** button located at the bottom of the study guide.

Your work is scored, and you will see whether you answered each question correctly or incorrectly. No results are sent to your instructor.

Step 6
Click the **Reset** button to erase all of your responses if you want to start over.

Receive Student Results via E-mail

When your students complete an Internet test, the browser sends the students' test results and all of their responses directly to you via e-mail. The e-mail will include the following information:

- student name and ID
- raw score and percentage score for objective questions
- responses for each question (objective and open-ended questions)

Note: **You will not receive any student results for Internet study guides.**

CHAPTER 1—GEOGRAPHY AND HISTORY

MULTIPLE CHOICE

1. The middle layer of the earth, made of solid, hot rock, is the
   a. mantle.
   b. crust.
   c. core.
   d. tectonic plate.

   ANS: C DIF: E

2. The five themes of geography help explain
   a. where a place is on the earth.
   b. what a place is like and why.
   c. what a place is like.
   d. how people and places are linked together.

   ANS: B DIF: C

3. Which of the following is NOT a kind of major landform?
   a. Mountains
   b. Plateaus
   c. Glaciers
   d. Plains

   ANS: C DIF: E

4. Which of these statements about legends is true?
   a. Legends are always about the creation of the universe.
   b. Legends may be based on stories of real people and events.
   c. Legends were all written down at first.
   d. Legends are never based on facts or real events.

   ANS: B DIF: E

5. About what percent of the surface of the earth is made up of land?
   a. 50 percent
   b. 70 percent
   c. 30 percent
   d. 10 percent

   ANS: C DIF: A

6. "What is the place like?" is the question answered by which theme of geography?
   a. Regions
   b. Location
   c. Place
   d. Human/environmental interaction

   ANS: C DIF: C

7. Heat and pressure from the earth's core cause the crust to
   a. split into several pieces.
   b. move smoothly like a shell.
   c. move slowly in sections called plates.
   d. rise up under the mantle.

   ANS: C DIF: C

8. Which of these commonly occurs at the edges of tectonic plates?
   a. Earthquakes and volcanoes
   b. Glaciers
   c. Floods and water erosion
   d. Monsoons

   ANS: A DIF: C

9. The earliest people usually built their villages
   a. near the summits of mountains.
   b. in river valleys.
   c. in the center of the plains.
   d. in desert oases.

   ANS: B DIF: E

10. The part of the earth where the sun's rays strike most directly is the area called the
    a. polar zone.
    b. climate zone.
    c. tropical zone.
    d. temperate zone.

    ANS: C DIF: A

11. One example of a nonrenewable resource is
    a. sunlight.
    b. coal.
    c. water.
    d. trees.

    ANS: B DIF: A

12. Which geographic factor had the greatest effect on the growth of modern industry?
    a. Climate
    b. Landforms
    c. Natural resources
    d. Waterways

    ANS: C DIF: A

MATCHING

Match each item with the correct statement below.

a. movement
b. landforms
c. river system
d. legend
e. elevation
f. absolute location
g. tectonic plates
h. artifacts

1. Exact position of a place on the earth's surface
2. Sections of the earth's crust that move slowly
3. Things that were made by people
4. Natural features of the earth's land surface
5. River plus all the streams that flow into it
6. Folktale that helps explain the past
7. Height above sea level
8. Geographic theme that tells how all people and places are linked together

1. ANS: F DIF: A
2. ANS: G DIF: A
3. ANS: H DIF: A
4. ANS: B DIF: A
5. ANS: C DIF: A

6. ANS: D DIF: A
7. ANS: E DIF: A
8. ANS: A DIF: A

SHORT ANSWER

1. Why is preserving the earth's natural resources more important to people today than it was to early people?

   ANS:
   Answers will vary, but could include: because modern people have the knowledge to recognize what would happen if resources were used up.

   DIF: C

2. How are tectonic plates responsible for mountains, volcanoes, and earthquakes?

   ANS:
   Tectonic plates move toward or away from each other. When tectonic plates collide, sometimes the earth's crust is pushed up, making mountains or causing earthquakes. Volcanoes occur when melted rock from inside the earth flows upward through an opening between tectonic plates.

   DIF: A

3. What movements of the sun affect the climate of a place?

   ANS:
   rotation and revolution

   DIF: E

4. What contributions to world history did the Leakey family make?

   ANS:
   Louis Leakey proved that the human race was older than previously thought; Mary Leakey found evidence of prehumans; Richard Leakey found the most complete remains of an early human being so far.

   DIF: C

5. Using the map below, explain why most of the world's population lives between latitude 60° north and latitude 60° south.

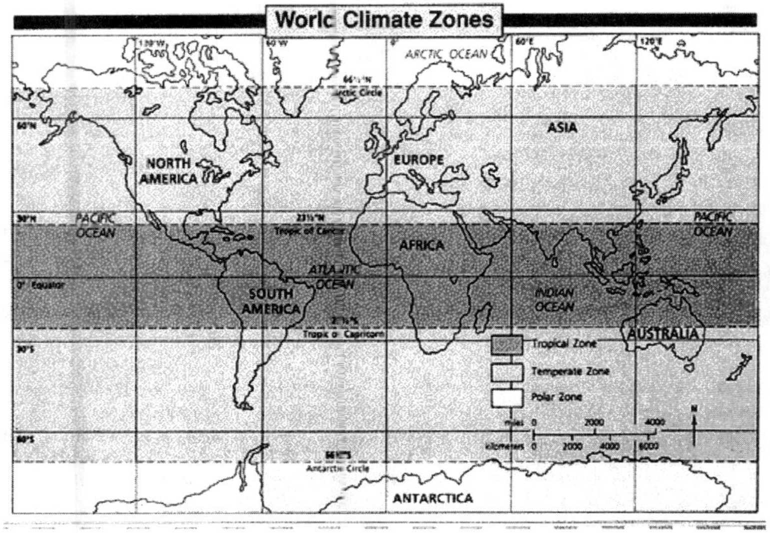

   ANS:
   These are the temperate zones where climate is most comfortable for human beings. Above and below the 60° north and 60° south latitudes, the climate is too cold for most people to live comfortably.

   DIF: A

SECTION QUIZ 1-1—FIVE THEMES OF GEOGRAPHY

MULTIPLE CHOICE

1. The movement of goods and people is known as
   a. communication.
   b. relative location.
   c. transportation.
   d. absolute location.

   ANS: C DIF: A

2. Which of the following is NOT a main theme of geography?
   a. place
   b. movement
   c. region
   d. culture

   ANS: D DIF: E

3. An example of a functional region is
   a. a common language.
   b. communication.
   c. a city.
   d. a culture.

   ANS: C DIF: C

4. Human/environmental interaction deals with
   a. how people communicate.
   b. how people use products made in other countries.
   c. how people adapt to or change their environment.
   d. how people form a common language.

   ANS: C DIF: A

5. No two places on earth have the same
   a. language.
   b. transportation.
   c. absolute location.
   d. cultural tradition.

   ANS: C DIF: A

MATCHING

Match each item with the correct statement below.

a. absolute location
b. movement
c. relative location
d. communication
e. regions

1. the exact location of a place
2. links people and places together
3. location in relation to other places
4. movement of ideas and information
5. used by geographers to organize the world

1. ANS: A DIF: A
2. ANS: B DIF: A
3. ANS: C DIF: A
4. ANS: D DIF: A
5. ANS: E DIF: A

SHORT ANSWER

1. How are absolute and relative location different?

   ANS:
   Absolute location is the exact location of a place on the earth's surface; relative location is the location of a place in relation to other places.

   DIF: A

2. What are two ways in which people respond to their environment?

   ANS:
   by adapting to it or by modifying it

   DIF: A

3. How does communication relate to the theme of movement?

   ANS:
   Communication is the movement of ideas and information from person to person and culture to culture.

   DIF: A

4. How has movement affected world history?

   ANS:
   People from one place carried their ideas and cultures with them to new places. Ideas and beliefs traveled from one culture to another, often changing both cultures.

   DIF: A

SECTION QUIZ 1-2—LAND, WATER, AND CLIMATE

MULTIPLE CHOICE

1. The pattern of a place's weather over many years is its
   a. climate.
   b. latitude.
   c. geography.
   d. temperate zone.

   ANS: A DIF: E

2. The tropical zone is
   a. between the Tropic of Cancer and the Arctic Circle.
   b. north of the Arctic Circle and south of the Antarctic Circle.
   c. between the Tropic of Cancer and the Tropic of Capricorn.
   d. between the Tropic of Capricorn and the Antarctic Circle.

   ANS: C DIF: C

3. The longest river system in the world is
   a. the Mediterranean.
   b. the Mississippi.
   c. the Nile.
   d. the Ohio.

   ANS: C DIF: C

4. Wind, water, and ice are the forces behind
   a. tectonic plates.
   b. erosion.
   c. continental drift.
   d. orbit.

   ANS: B DIF: C

5. The earth's mantle is made up mostly of
   a. rock, sand, and soil.
   b. loess.
   c. solid rock.
   d. melted rock.

   ANS: C DIF: E

MATCHING

Match each item with the correct statement below.

a. landform
b. continental drift
c. core
d. latitude
e. projection

1. natural feature of the earth's land surface
2. the center of the earth
3. the movement of tectonic plates
4. distance north or south of the equator
5. mapmaker's way of showing earth on a flat surface

1. ANS: A DIF: A
2. ANS: C DIF: A
3. ANS: B DIF: A
4. ANS: D DIF: A
5. ANS: E DIF: A

SHORT ANSWER

1. How do heat and pressure change the earth's surface?

   ANS:
   Heat and pressure cause movement inside the earth, which results in changes on the earth's surface such as mountains, volcanoes, and earthquakes.

   DIF: C

2. What are the three main forces of erosion?

   ANS:
   wind, water, and ice

   DIF: E

3. What are the earth's largest waterways?

   ANS:
   the four oceans: Atlantic, Pacific, Indian and Arctic

   DIF: E

4. What natural features and forces affect climate?

   ANS:
   the earth's tilt in relation to the sun; bodies of water; wind; altitude

   DIF: A

5. How does climate affect history?

   ANS:
   Climate determines where people choose to live, and also affects their clothing, housing, and how they make a living.

   DIF: C

SECTION QUIZ 1-3—NATURAL RESOURCES

MULTIPLE CHOICE

1. Which of the following is NOT a mineral?
   a. iron
   b. copper
   c. gold
   d. water

   ANS: D DIF: E

2. During the 1200s, Marco Polo traveled to
   a. Italy.
   b. Nigeria.
   c. China.
   d. Australia.

   ANS: C DIF: E

3. The most important natural resources are
   a. air, water, soil, and sunlight.
   b. fossil fuels.
   c. oil, water, coal, and air.
   d. copper, gold, and natural gas.

   ANS: A DIF: C

4. Fossil fuels are used to
   a. heat homes and power machines.
   b. keep soil from blowing away.
   c. make tools, weapons, and jewelry.
   d. develop new sources of energy.

   ANS: A DIF: A

5. Which of the following is NOT a natural resource?
   a. gold
   b. plastic
   c. oil
   d. coal

   ANS: B DIF: A

6. Some natural resources are not essential for life but are still important because
   a. they make other resources easier to use.
   b. people use them to make money.
   c. they can be burned to create warmth and electricity.
   d. they allow people to make their lives better and more comfortable.

   ANS: D DIF: C

7. Two ways that countries try to make better use of natural resources are by
   a. planting fewer trees and using better farming methods.
   b. passing anti-pollution laws and developing new energy sources.
   c. using coal for heat rather than gas and oil.
   d. reading history and science books for answers.

   ANS: B DIF: A

8. All through history, natural resources have affected
   a. where people settled.
   b. how tall people grew.
   c. whether or not people shared resources.
   d. how people managed their soil and water.

   ANS: A DIF: A

MATCHING

Match each item with the correct statement below.

a. minerals
b. natural resources
c. nonrenewable resources
d. renewable resources
e. fossil fuels

1. all materials found in nature
2. coal, oil, natural gas
3. cannot be replaced as they are used
4. nonliving substances under earth's surface
5. can be replaced as they are used

1. ANS: B DIF: A
2. ANS: E DIF: A
3. ANS: C DIF: A
4. ANS: A DIF: A
5. ANS: D DIF: A

SECTION QUIZ 1-4—LEGENDS

MULTIPLE CHOICE

1. People developed writing
   a. more than 50,000 years ago.
   b. more than 15,000 years ago.
   c. more than 5,000 years ago.
   d. less than 1,000 years ago.

   ANS: C DIF: C

2. In the Chinese legend in this section,
   a. the sun was a huge egg.
   b. the earth was a huge egg.
   c. the first man was called Man Chu.
   d. the first man was called P'an Gu.

   ANS: D DIF: E

3. In the African legend,
   a. the moon attacked the sun.
   b. the moon was once brighter than the sun.
   c. the sun and the moon were friends.
   d. God ignored the sun and the moon.

   ANS: B DIF: E

4. The Rumanian legend explains
   a. how mountains and valleys were made.
   b. the eating habits of moles.
   c. why bees fly.
   d. why the earth is round.

   ANS: A DIF: E

5. The legends in this section tell about
   a. the placement of stars.
   b. the origin of human beings.
   c. the development of writing.
   d. the creation of the world.

   ANS: D DIF: E

COMPLETION

1. Some legends are about the ____________________ of great men and women.

   ANS: deeds DIF: A

2. Other legends explain ____________________ elements, such as the color of leaves or the position of stars.

   ANS: natural DIF: A

3. Many legends explain the existence of ____________________ features, such as rivers or mountains, near the areas where people live.

   ANS: geographic DIF: A

MATCHING

Match each item with the correct statement below.

a. archaeologists
b. sun
c. legends
d. anthropologists
e. mole

1. they study remains of past human life
2. stories that were spoken or sung
3. character in the African legend
4. character in the Rumanian legend
5. they study origins of past human life

1. ANS: A DIF: A
2. ANS: C DIF: A
3. ANS: B DIF: A
4. ANS: E DIF: A
5. ANS: D DIF: A

SECTION QUIZ 1-5—ARCHAEOLOGY

MULTIPLE CHOICE

1. Archaeology began
   a. about 100 years ago.
   b. about 500 years ago.
   c. about 1,000 years ago.
   d. about 2 million years ago.

   ANS: B DIF: C

2. Italian farmers discovered
   a. the Rosetta Stone.
   b. Olduvai Gorge.
   c. Laetoli.
   d. Herculaneum.

   ANS: D DIF: C

3. To date an archaeological find, scientists first used
   a. trees.
   b. artifacts.
   c. the Rosetta Stone.
   d. footprints.

   ANS: A DIF: E

4. Louis Leakey excavated at
   a. Herculaneum.
   b. Olduvai Gorge.
   c. Pompeii.
   d. Atlantis.

   ANS: B DIF: E

5. The Rosetta Stone was found in
   a. Egypt.
   b. Tanzania.
   c. Olduvai Gorge.
   d. Lake Turkana.

   ANS: A DIF: E

MATCHING

Match each item with the correct statement below.

a. archaeology
b. ages
c. excavate
d. decipher
e. artifacts

1. things made by people
2. study of remains of past human life
3. dig into the earth
4. historical periods
5. explain the meaning of

1. ANS: E DIF: A
2. ANS: A DIF: A
3. ANS: C DIF: A
4. ANS: B DIF: A
5. ANS: D DIF: A

SHORT ANSWER

1. Why is it often difficult to make archeological discoveries?

   ANS:
   There may be few artifacts of a civilization; artifacts may be broken into many small pieces; or only parts of artifacts may exist.

   DIF: C

2. Why were archaeologists able to divide the Stone Age into three periods?

   ANS:
   because the people of the different ages used different materials for tools and weapons

   DIF: C

CHAPTER 2—PREHISTORIC PEOPLE

MULTIPLE CHOICE

1. To historians today, the most important difference between the Paleolithic and the Neolithic ages was
   a. how people got their food.
   b. the way people made tools.
   c. the kind of art people made.
   d. the material used for tools.

   ANS: A DIF: C

2. The first people to bury their dead were
   a. Cro-Magnons.
   b. Neanderthals.
   c. *Homo habilis.*
   d. Neolithic people.

   ANS: B DIF: A

3. The period of time after people first appeared but before they developed writing is known as
   a. civilization.
   b. history.
   c. prehistory.
   d. the Paleolithic Age.

   ANS: C DIF: E

4. Which of these abilities did Paleolithic people lack?
   a. Making fire
   b. Using language
   c. Making clothing
   d. Working with metal

   ANS: D DIF: E

5. The first humans probably lived in
   a. Africa.
   b. Northern Europe.
   c. the Neander Valley, Germany.
   d. America.

   ANS: A DIF: E

6. The first people on earth are known as
   a. Cro-Magnons.
   b. *Homo sapiens.*
   c. *Homo habilis.*
   d. Neanderthals.

   ANS: C DIF: A

7. What does the term "Neolithic Revolution" mean?
   a. The rapid change in hunting methods using spears and pitfalls
   b. The quick spread of prehistoric people throughout the world
   c. The change from hunting and gathering food to farming
   d. The development of a new form of Neolithic government

   ANS: C DIF: A

8. Which development of early people made it possible for them to settle in one place and develop villages?
   a. Food production
   b. Increased food supplies
   c. Burying their dead
   d. Making tools

   ANS: A DIF: E

9. Which development of early people made it possible for them to work together and share ideas?
   a. Hunting and gathering
   b. Fire
   c. Language
   d. Campsites

   ANS: C DIF: E

10. The post-and-lintel was an important step forward in
    a. working with metals.
    b. developing agriculture.
    c. hunting large animals.
    d. constructing buildings.

    ANS: D DIF: C

MATCHING

Match each effect with the correct cause below.

a. they could help each other stay alive
b. their lives depended on the food they grew on the land
c. people developed language and writing
d. crops to keep both people and animals alive came from the earth
e. it is easier to chew and digest
f. land was uncovered when water froze during the Ice Age

1. The period of time called *history* developed because _____.
2. Paleolithic people could migrate from Africa to Asia and Europe because _____.
3. People lived in groups so that _____.
4. Cooked food gave early people more time because _____.
5. People protected their land and passed it on to their children because _____.
6. The Earth Mother was the most important goddess because _____.

1. ANS: C DIF: A
2. ANS: F DIF: A
3. ANS: A DIF: A
4. ANS: E DIF: A
5. ANS: B DIF: A
6. ANS: D DIF: A

SHORT ANSWER

1. Choose one important discovery or development made by prehistoric people and explain how life today would be different without it.

   ANS:
   Answers will vary, but could include: the development of language; without it we could not communicate.

   DIF: A

2. Look at the map below. Use cardinal and intermediate directions to describe how people from Africa and Asia reached North America.

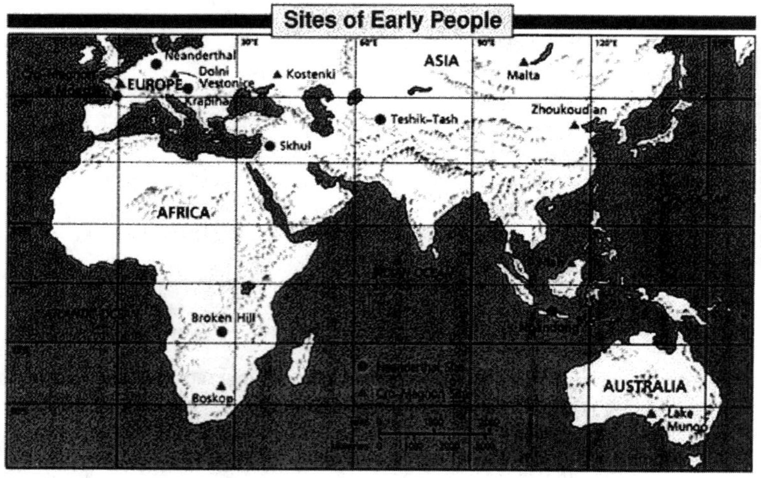

   ANS:
   People from Africa—traveled north to the Mediterranean Sea, then went northeast around the Mediterranean; continued northeast across Asia to the Bering Strait; traveled east across the Bering Strait into North America, then began to spread southward
   People from Asia—probably went north and/or northeast to the Bering Strait; traveled east across the Bering Strait into North America; then spread southward

   DIF: C

SECTION QUIZ 2-1—THE PALEOLITHIC AGE

MULTIPLE CHOICE

1. Many scientists believe people once lived only
   a. at the North and South poles.
   b. in southern and eastern Africa.
   c. in Europe and Asia.
   d. at Olduvai Gorge.

   ANS: B DIF: E

2. Paleolithic people lived
   a. no more than 18 years.
   b. no more than 20 or 25 years.
   c. about 50 years.
   d. about 65 years.

   ANS: B DIF: C

3. The first people on earth are known as
   a. *Homo sapiens.*
   b. *Homo habilis.*
   c. Cro-Magnons.
   d. *Homo erectus.*

   ANS: B DIF: E

4. *Homo habilis* means
   a. man who walks upright.
   b. skillful man.
   c. man who thinks.
   d. toolmaker.

   ANS: B DIF: C

5. The two kinds of *Homo sapiens* are
   a. *Homo habilis* and *Homo erectus.*
   b. *Homo habilis* and Neanderthal.
   c. Paleolithic and Cro-Magnon.
   d. Cro-Magnon and Neanderthal.

   ANS: D DIF: C

6. As the ocean waters froze about 900,000 years ago,
   a. the weather got warmer.
   b. land bridges between the continents were uncovered.
   c. glaciers eroded most of the continents.
   d. the New Stone Age began.

   ANS: B DIF: A

7. Prehistoric people stayed at a campsite until
   a. the food supply in the area was used up.
   b. each band grew to 40 or 50 members.
   c. members of the band reached the age of 25.
   d. they had eaten all the meat killed during a hunt.

   ANS: A DIF: A

8. Discovering ways to make clothing meant that people
   a. found a use for animal fat.
   b. had learned how to kill large animals.
   c. could live in more places.
   d. were ready to develop language.

   ANS: C DIF: A

9. In addition to making tools, clothing, and fire, another important achievement of early people was
   a. learning to hold their tents down with rocks.
   b. locating caves to protect them from storms or large animals.
   c. painting on cave walls.
   d. developing language so that they could share ideas, beliefs, and learning.

   ANS: D DIF: A

MATCHING

Match each item with the correct statement below.

a. prehistory
b. *Homo sapiens*
c. Paleolithic
d. migrate
e. band

1. Old Stone Age
2. began when people first appeared
3. small group
4. to make one's way
5. man who thinks"

1. ANS: C DIF: A
2. ANS: A DIF: A
3. ANS: E DIF: A
4. ANS: D DIF: A
5. ANS: B DIF: A

SECTION QUIZ 2-2—THE NEOLITHIC AGE

MULTIPLE CHOICE

1. Experts call the beginning of farming
   a. the Neolithic Revolution.
   b. specialization.
   c. the Agricultural Revolution.
   d. the Occupational Revolution.

   ANS: A DIF: A

2. People changed from food gatherers to food producers
   a. about 500 A.D.
   b. about 200 B.C.
   c. about 2000 B.C.
   d. about 8000 B.C.

   ANS: D DIF: C

3. The earliest known villages have been found in
   a. southwestern Asia.
   b. the area that is now South America.
   c. Mexico.
   d. the area that is now the United States.

   ANS: A DIF: E

4. Specialization was the result of
   a. population explosion.
   b. increased food supply.
   c. village government.
   d. the development of religion.

   ANS: B DIF: C

5. Jericho, one of the oldest known villages, is in
   a. present-day Turkey.
   b. present-day Syria.
   c. present-day Israel.
   d. southwestern Africa.

   ANS: C DIF: A

COMPLETION

1. People settled villages where they found good, rich ____________________ and a plentiful ____________________ supply.

   ANS: soil; water DIF: A

2. With posts and lintels, people could construct a building with a ____________________, or even build one room above another.

   ANS: roof DIF: A

3. Even though Neolithic people learned how to shape ____________________, they didn't use it much because it was scarce.

   ANS: metals DIF: A

4. Neolithic people worshiped gods and goddesses instead of the forces of ____________________.

   ANS: nature DIF: A

MATCHING

Match each item with the correct statement below.

a. population
b. Neolithic
c. domesticated
d. specialization
e. cardinal directions

1. development of occupations
2. New Stone Age
3. tamed
4. north, south, east, west
5. number of people

1. ANS: D DIF: A
2. ANS: B DIF: A
3. ANS: C DIF: A
4. ANS: E DIF: A
5. ANS: A DIF: A

CHAPTER 3—MESOPOTAMIA

MULTIPLE CHOICE

1. The land called Mesopotamia in ancient times is today part of
   a. Arabia.
   b. Turkey.
   c. Iraq.
   d. Persia.

   ANS: C DIF: A

2. The Sumerians settled in Mesopotamia in about
   a. 1800 B.C.
   b. 3500 B.C.
   c. 2500 B.C.
   d. 4000 B.C.

   ANS: B DIF: C

3. The Sumerians took an important step in changing their physical environment by
   a. using clay to make bricks for building.
   b. controlling the floods on the rivers.
   c. crossing the sea to trade with other countries.
   d. cutting down the forests that covered Mesopotamia.

   ANS: B DIF: A

4. At the center of each Sumerian city-state was
   a. a walled courtyard with bronze gates.
   b. a temple which was the home of the city's chief god.
   c. a shrine for all the priest-kings of Sumer.
   d. the marketplace where traders came.

   ANS: B DIF: E

5. In Sumerian society, the middle class included
   a. farmers.
   b. unskilled workers.
   c. priests and merchants.
   d. artisans and shopkeepers.

   ANS: D DIF: E

6. What eventually happened to the city-states of Sumer?
   a. Judges replaced military leaders as heads of government.
   b. Sargon I, a king from northern Mesopotamia, conquered them.
   c. The city-states of Sumer conquered Babylonia and Akkad.
   d. They chose Hammurabi to make laws for them.

   ANS: B DIF: A

7. As a ruler, Hammurabi is best remembered for
   a. creating a written code of laws.
   b. conquering Sumer and building the first empire.
   c. building the first ziggurat.
   d. inventing the cuneiform style of writing.

   ANS: A DIF: E

8. When Sargon I united the conquered city-states, he created the world's first
   a. ziggurat.
   b. code of laws.
   c. government.
   d. empire.

   ANS: D DIF: A

9. The oldest written records known come from the culture of
   a. Sumer.
   b. Babylonia.
   c. Akkad.
   d. the Amorites.

   ANS: A DIF: E

10. Which of the following inventions is NOT a contribution of Mesopotamia?
    a. Wheel
    b. Stone buildings
    c. Plow
    d. Sailboats

    ANS: B DIF: E

MATCHING

Match each item with the correct statement below.

a. Gilgamesh
b. cuneiform
c. Babylon
d. code
e. ziggurat
f. city-state
g. Euphrates
h. Ur
i. scribe
j. artisan

1. Wedge-shaped Sumerian writing system
2. Leading city-state of Sumer
3. Chief city of Hammurabi's empire
4. Legendary hero of Sumerian culture
5. Person who is skilled in a craft
6. A Sumerian city and its surrounding land
7. Organized system of laws
8. Person who is skilled in writing
9. One of the rivers bounding Mesopotamia
10. Sumerian temple with many levels

1. ANS: B DIF: A
2. ANS: H DIF: A
3. ANS: C DIF: A
4. ANS: A DIF: A
5. ANS: J DIF: A
6. ANS: F DIF: A
7. ANS: D DIF: A
8. ANS: I DIF: A
9. ANS: G DIF: A
10. ANS: E DIF: A

SHORT ANSWER

1. Choose several aspects of the Mesopotamian civilization that you think have had the greatest impact on modern civilization. List them in order of their importance and explain your judgment.

   ANS:
   Answers will vary, but could include: code of laws, writing, number system, the wheel, plow, sailboat.

   DIF: A

2. Besides a good water supply, what else did the Sumer area offer settlers?

   ANS:
   mountain barriers that protected them from invasion; fertile soil

   DIF: A

3. Why did the Sumerians build their houses of mud-and-reed bricks?

   ANS:
   no building stone, no wood supply

   DIF: A

4. What two districts made up a Sumerian city-state?

   ANS:
   the city itself and the farmland around it

   DIF: E

5. What classes of citizens lived in a Sumerian city-state?

   ANS:
   priests, royalty, rich, artisans

   DIF: E

6. Why did the Sumerian religion worship thousands of gods?

   ANS:
   The Sumerians believed that all the forces of nature were alive and could not be controlled; therefore, such forces must be gods.

   DIF: A

7. How did Sumerians feel about their city-states? How did these feelings affect the relations among the city-states?

   ANS:
   They were very proud; they often went to war to prove which city-state was stronger.

   DIF: C

8. How did Hammurabi create his code of laws?

   ANS:
   He used what he thought were the best laws from each city-state.

   DIF: A

9. Look at the map below. What geographical feature is present everywhere except in the Tigris-Euphrates area? Why would the absence of this feature make it easier for Sargon I and Hammurabi to unite the city-states?

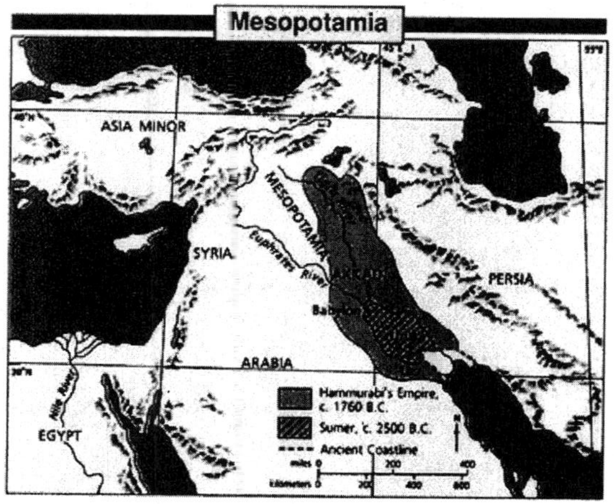

   ANS:
   Mountains; they would not have to take their troops through mountain country or plan an invasion of an area that was protected by mountains.

   DIF: A

SECTION QUIZ 3-1—THE RISE OF SUMER

MULTIPLE CHOICE

1. The earliest known civilization is
   a. cuneiform.
   b. ziggurat.
   c. Sumerian.
   d. Mesopotamian.

   ANS: C DIF: E

2. Scribes were
   a. farmers.
   b. priests.
   c. students.
   d. writers.

   ANS: D DIF: E

3. The first person known to pass laws was
   a. Urukagina.
   b. Gilgamesh.
   c. Ningirsu.
   d. Enkidu.

   ANS: A DIF: C

4. In all, Sumerian gods numbered
   a. 100.
   b. 1,500.
   c. 3,000.
   d. 5,000.

   ANS: C DIF: A

5. Sumerians built houses out of
   a. levees.
   b. stone.
   c. timber.
   d. mud bricks.

   ANS: D DIF: A

COMPLETION

1. So that they could plan and work together more easily, people organized ____________________.

   ANS: governments DIF: A

2. The government passed ____________________ so that people knew what the government expected.

   ANS: laws DIF: E

3. City-states often went to war over ____________________ lines.

   ANS: boundary DIF: A

4. Each walled Sumerian city-state was protected by bronze ____________________ that were closed at night.

   ANS: gates DIF: E

5. Because the Sumerians could not ____________________ the forces of nature, they viewed them as gods and goddesses.

   ANS: explain DIF: A

6. To keep track of their business dealings, Sumerians invented ____________________.

   ANS: writing DIF: A

MATCHING

Match each item with the correct statement below.

a. artisan
b. cuneiform
c. ziggurat
d. Gilgamesh
e. city-state

1. Sumerian temple
2. Sumerian writing
3. famous priest-king
4. a city and the surrounding farmland
5. skilled worker

1. ANS: C DIF: A
2. ANS: B DIF: A
3. ANS: D DIF: A
4. ANS: E DIF: A
5. ANS: A DIF: A

SECTION QUIZ 3-2—LATER MESOPOTAMIAN EMPIRES

MULTIPLE CHOICE

1. The man who became king of Sumer and Akkad was
   a. Hammurabi.
   b. Sargon I.
   c. Gilgamesh.
   d. Babylon.

   ANS: B DIF: C

2. Hammurabi was the king of
   a. Babylon.
   b. Sumer and Akkad.
   c. Mesopotamia.
   d. the Tigris-Euphrates Valley.

   ANS: A DIF: A

3. Hammurabi ruled for
   a. 20 years.
   b. less than 15 years.
   c. more than 40 years.
   d. 57 years.

   ANS: C DIF: C

4. The power of Sumer began to fade
   a. about 2400 B.C.
   b. about 3000 B.C.
   c. in 500 A.D.
   d. in the early 1200s.

   ANS: A DIF: E

5. Under Sargon I, the Sumerian language was used only
   a. in the marketplace.
   b. in the home.
   c. for religious purposes.
   d. by the king.

   ANS: C DIF: E

MATCHING

Match each item with the correct statement below.

a. reform
b. culture
c. empire
d. surplus
e. reign

1. group of states under one ruler
2. extra
3. period of power
4. improvement
5. way of life

1. ANS: C DIF: A
2. ANS: D DIF: A
3. ANS: E DIF: A
4. ANS: A DIF: A
5. ANS: B DIF: A

SHORT ANSWER

1. How did Hammurabi's change in religion affect the people of his kingdom?

   ANS:
   It united his people, because then they all worshiped the same god.

   DIF: A

2. How were the reigns of Sargon I and Hammurabi alike?

   ANS:
   Both united the separate city-states of Mesopotamia.

   DIF: A

SECTION QUIZ 3-3—CONTRIBUTIONS

MULTIPLE CHOICE

1. Sumerians developed the earliest known
   a. church.
   b. civilization.
   c. painting.
   d. religious festivals.

   ANS: B DIF: E

2. Which of the following was NOT invented by Sumerians?
   a. the wheel
   b. the sailboat
   c. the tractor
   d. the water clock

   ANS: C DIF: E

3. Modern transportation evolved from what invention?
   a. the wheel
   b. the sailboat
   c. the plow
   d. the tractor

   ANS: A DIF: A

4. Sumerian ideas and inventions
   a. frightened other peoples.
   b. were copied by other peoples.
   c. were ignored by other peoples.
   d. died along with Hammurabi.

   ANS: B DIF: A

5. The people of Mesopotamia developed a number system
   a. based on the number 6.
   b. based on the number 60.
   c. using drops of water.
   d. using a series of dots.

   ANS: B DIF: C

MATCHING

Match each item with the correct statement below.

a. Sumerians
b. laws
c. Mesopotamia
d. calendar
e. plow

1. inventors of the wheel
2. the "cradle of civilization"

3. farm implement invented by Sumerians
4. marked the times for religious festivals
5. Sumerians wrote the first of these

1. ANS: A	DIF: A
2. ANS: C	DIF: A
3. ANS: E	DIF: A
4. ANS: D	DIF: A
5. ANS: B	DIF: A

SHORT ANSWER

1. How did the Sumerians and Babylonians influence civilizations around them?

   ANS:
   Because they were the earliest civilizations, other civilizations around them copied many of their ideas, inventions, and customs.

   DIF: A

2. Why were the inventions of the wheel and the plow important?

   ANS:
   The wheel improved transportation; the plow helped farmers grow more food with less work.

   DIF: A

CHAPTER 4—EGYPT

MULTIPLE CHOICE

1. The rich delta area where the Nile flows into the Mediterranean Sea was originally known as
   a. Mesopotamia.
   b. Land of Punt.
   c. Upper Egypt.
   d. Lower Egypt.

   ANS: D DIF: A

2. Which of the following was NOT a benefit the Egyptians gained from the Nile River?
   a. Traders' ships could travel far into the center of Africa.
   b. The river's yearly floods left rich soil on the riverbanks.
   c. Cataracts on the river stopped invaders from traveling upriver.
   d. River water was used for irrigation in the dry season.

   ANS: A DIF: C

3. Most Egyptians of the Old Kingdom lived
   a. in large cities.
   b. on their large estates.
   c. in villages on large estates.
   d. on their own small farms.

   ANS: C DIF: E

4. Which of these Egyptians probably did NOT live in a city?
   a. A goldsmith for the temple
   b. A government tax collector
   c. A boat builder
   d. All of the above.

   ANS: C DIF: A

5. Egyptians thought that the pharaoh was responsible for
   a. building granaries to store food for all the people.
   b. repairing the irrigation system.
   c. performing religious rituals correctly.
   d. all of the above.

   ANS: D DIF: A

6. The pyramids were built during the Old Kingdom, when
   a. the priests of Amon-Re were gaining great power.
   b. the pharaohs had power over all of Egyptian life.
   c. Hyksos invaders ruled Egypt.
   d. the pharaoh and priests were quarreling over religion.

   ANS: B DIF: A

7. The Hyksos were able to conquer Egypt because of
   a. their bronze and iron weapons and horse-drawn chariots.
   b. a shortage of grain in Egypt.
   c. floods along the Nile.
   d. their sharp stone spears.

   ANS: A DIF: E

8. The period after Ahmose drove out the Hyksos is known as
   a. the Middle Kingdom.
   b. the New Kingdom.
   c. the Old Kingdom.
   d. the Assyrian Empire.

   ANS: B DIF: E

9. Some lasting contributions of the Egyptians were in
   a. cuneiform writing.
   b. working with iron.
   c. mathematics and medicine.
   d. government and lawmaking.

   ANS: C DIF: E

10. About how much time passed between the beginning of the Old Kingdom and the final Assyrian conquest of Egypt?
   a. 500 years
   b. 1,000 years
   c. 1,500 years
   d. 2,000 years

   ANS: D DIF: C

MATCHING

Match each item with the correct statement below.

a. Isis
b. Narmer
c. Tutankhamen
d. Thutmose III
e. Amon-Re
f. Ahmose
g. Aton
h. Akhenaton
i. Hatshepsut
j. Osiris

1. Single god worshiped in religion favored by Amenhotep IV
2. God of the harvest and of eternal life
3. Ruler who united Upper and Lower Egypt
4. Egyptian hero who defeated the Hyksos invaders
5. Name taken by the pharaoh who tried to establish a new religion
6. Goddess who, with her husband, ruled over the land of the dead
7. Warrior-pharaoh who made Egypt an empire by extending Egyptian control into Syria
8. Pharaoh who encouraged trade during her reign in the New Kingdom period
9. Young pharaoh who succeeded Akhenaton
10. Most powerful god worshiped during the New Kingdom period

1. ANS: G DIF: A
2. ANS: J DIF: A
3. ANS: B DIF: A
4. ANS: F DIF: A
5. ANS: H DIF: A
6. ANS: A DIF: A
7. ANS: D DIF: A
8. ANS: I DIF: A
9. ANS: C DIF: A
10. ANS: E DIF: A

SHORT ANSWER

1. Why do you think the Egyptian civilization lasted longer than those in Mesopotamia or other earlier civilizations?

   ANS:
   Answers will vary, but could include: because the Egyptian civilization was more unified and did not fight within itself.

   DIF: A

2. How long did the ancient Egyptian empire last?

   ANS:
   more than 2,000 years

   DIF: E

3. What were some reasons why the Egyptian empire lasted as long as it did?

   ANS:
   It was united by religion, language, and culture; protected for a long time by geographical features; and able to support a large population because of the Nile's yearly deposits of fertile soil.

   DIF: C

4. What two groups generally struggled for power during Egyptian history?

   ANS:
   pharaohs and priests

   DIF: E

5. What group had very little power in Egypt during its history?

   ANS:
   average citizens

   DIF: E

6. How are Egyptian tomb paintings and Cro-Magnon cave paintings alike?

   ANS:
   Both left information about early ways of life.

   DIF: A

SECTION QUIZ 4-1—THE NILE

MULTIPLE CHOICE

1. To water their crops the Egyptians
   a. dug irrigation canals.
   b. waited for the Nile to flood.
   c. used cataracts.
   d. carried buckets of river water to the fields.

   ANS: A DIF: A

2. The last 600 miles (960 kilometers) of the Nile
   a. flow through Australia.
   b. flow through Greece.
   c. flow through Southeast Asia.
   d. flow through Egypt.

   ANS: D DIF: E

3. The Nile River flows into
   a. the Pacific Ocean.
   b. the Mediterranean Sea.
   c. the Indian Ocean.
   d. the Red Sea.

   ANS: B DIF: E

4. The Nile River is about
   a. 9,000 miles long.
   b. 21,000 miles long.
   c. 4,100 miles long.
   d. 450 miles long.

   ANS: C DIF: C

5. The Egyptians raised
   a. rice, soybeans, and rye.
   b. peaches, apples, rice, and beans.
   c. flax, wheat, barley, and grapes.
   d. peanuts, olives, figs, and potatoes.

   ANS: C DIF: A

MATCHING

Match each item with the correct statement below.
a. cataract
b. delta
c. basin
d. irrigation canal
e. shadoof

1. bowl-shaped area
2. used for draining water to fields
3. waterfall
4. fan-shaped area of fertile land
5. machine for lifting water

1. ANS: C DIF: A
2. ANS: D DIF: A
3. ANS: A DIF: A
4. ANS: B DIF: A
5. ANS: E DIF: A

SHORT ANSWER

1. How was the Nile delta like the Mesopotamian region?

   ANS:
   Both have rivers that flooded yearly, leaving a rich soil deposit.

   DIF: C

2. What three things protected the Egyptians from invasion?

   ANS:
   desert, seas, and the cataracts of the Nile

   DIF: A

SECTION QUIZ 4-2—THE OLD KINGDOM

MULTIPLE CHOICE

1. Which of the following was NOT another name for Narmer?
   a. "Wearer of Both Crowns"
   b. Menes
   c. Memphis
   d. "Lord of Two Lands"

   ANS: C DIF: C

2. Narmer conquered Lower Egypt in
   a. about 2000 B.C.
   b. about 3100 B.C.
   c. 5000 B.C.
   d. 500 A.D.

   ANS: B DIF: A

3. The pyramids were designed to
   a. protect the bodies of the pharaohs.
   b. fit many hundreds of people.
   c. serve as churches.
   d. serve as prisons.

   ANS: A DIF: E

4. The Egyptian river god was
   a. Osiris.
   b. Re.
   c. Narmer.
   d. Hapi.

   ANS: D DIF: E

5. To learn magic spells the Egyptians
   a. studied the *Book of the Pharaohs*.
   b. studied the movements of the sun.
   c. studied the *Book of the Dead*.
   d. studied the moon and stars.

   ANS: C DIF: E

MATCHING

Match each item with the correct statement below.

a. Memphis
b. pharaoh
c. granaries
d. pyramid
e. Narmer (Menes)

1. "Lord of Upper and Lower Egypt"
2. Egyptian city
3. Egyptian tomb
4. buildings for storing grain
5. means "great house"

1. ANS: E DIF: A
2. ANS: A DIF: A
3. ANS: D DIF: A
4. ANS: C DIF: A
5. ANS: B DIF: A

SHORT ANSWER

1. Where does much of the information about Egyptian life come from?

   ANS:
   tomb paintings

   DIF: A

2. What did Egyptians believe about the effect of having a strong ruler?

   ANS:
   Their country would be strong and unified.

   DIF: A

3. What were some of the duties that a pharaoh performed?

ANS:
The pharaoh was a ruler and a priest, and considered to be a god. He ordered dams built and repaired, chose all government officials, oversaw trade with other countries, and carried out religious rituals.

DIF: C

SECTION QUIZ 4-3—THE MIDDLE KINGDOM

MULTIPLE CHOICE

1. Government officials took control of Egypt
   a. in 1550 B.C.
   b. in 1786 B.C.
   c. about 2100 B.C.
   d. about 500 B.C.

   ANS: C DIF: C

2. In the Middle Kingdom, pharaohs
   a. lost some of their power.
   b. gained more power.
   c. were buried in pyramids.
   d. were executed.

   ANS: A DIF: A

3. The Hyksos fought the Egyptians with weapons of
   a. copper and stone.
   b. lead and steel.
   c. bronze and iron.
   d. stone and silver.

   ANS: C DIF: E

4. The Hyksos ruled Egypt for
   a. 50 years.
   b. 150 years.
   c. 1,500 years.
   d. 2,500 years.

   ANS: B DIF: E

5. Ahmose was
   a. a soldier in the pharaoh's army.
   b. a Hyksos warrior.
   c. a priest-king.
   d. an Egyptian prince.

   ANS: D DIF: A

MATCHING

Match each item with the correct statement below.

a. Ahmose
b. pharaohs
c. chariot
d. Middle Kingdom
e. Hyksos

1. a people from western Asia

2. period ending in 1786 B.C.
3. drove the Hyksos out of Egypt
4. method the Hyksos used to cross the desert
5. had less power in the Middle Kingdom

1. ANS: E DIF: A
2. ANS: D DIF: A
3. ANS: A DIF: A
4. ANS: C DIF: A
5. ANS: B DIF: A

SHORT ANSWER

1. How was treatment of the pharaohs different in the Middle Kingdom and the Old Kingdom?

   ANS:
   Pharoahs of the Middle Kingdom had less power than those of the Old Kingdom.

   DIF: A

2. How did the Egyptians change their dealings with other countries during the Middle Kingdom?

   ANS:
   Egyptians began to trade with civilizations beyond the Nile Valley.

   DIF: A

3. Why didn't the desert protect the Egyptians from the Hyksos?

   ANS:
   The Hyksos developed horse-drawn chariots and weapons made of bronze and iron.

   DIF: C

SECTION QUIZ 4-4—THE NEW KINGDOM

MULTIPLE CHOICE

1. The new god worshiped in the New Kingdom was
   a. Hatshepsut.
   b. Punt.
   c. Amon.
   d. Amon-Re.

   ANS: D DIF: A

2. Akhenaton set up a religion to worship
   a. Amon-Re.
   b. Aton.
   c. Re.
   d. Amon.

   ANS: A DIF: A

3. Egypt's empire was gone by
   a. 1150 B.C.
   b. 671 B.C.
   c. 150 B.C.
   d. 12 B.C.

   ANS: A   DIF: E

4. In 671 B.C., Egypt was taken over by
   a. the "Spirit of Aton."
   b. Tutankhamen.
   c. the Sumerians.
   d. the Assyrians.

   ANS: B   DIF: E

5. During the New Kingdom, temples were
   a. used as courts of law.
   b. used to buy pharaohs.
   c. industrial centers.
   d. military training centers.

   ANS: C   DIF: A

MATCHING

Match each item with the correct statement below.
a. Thutmose III
b. hieroglyphs
c. incense
d. Amenhotep IV
e. Hatshepsut

1. picture symbols
2. female pharaoh
3. burned for its pleasant smell
4. extended Egyptian control to Syria
5. changed his name to Akhenaton

1. ANS: B   DIF: A
2. ANS: E   DIF: A
3. ANS: C   DIF: A
4. ANS: A   DIF: A
5. ANS: D   DIF: A

SHORT ANSWER

1. How did Egypt change during the New Kingdom period?

   ANS:
   Egypt became richer and its cities grew larger.

   DIF: A

2. How did Hatshepsut change the economy of Egypt?

   ANS:
   She increased Egypt's trade and riches by allowing traders to travel farther to more areas for trade goods.

   DIF: A

3. What functions besides religious ceremonies took place in and around the temples of the New Kingdom?

   ANS:
   business, production of goods and art, money collected and stored, and training of scribes

   DIF: A

4. What did Egyptian scribes do?

   ANS:
   wrote religious works, kept records of laws, recorded payments made to the pharaoh, copied fairy tales, wrote prescriptions

   DIF: A

5. How did Amenhotep IV contribute to the weakening of Egypt?

   ANS:
   He was one of the pharaohs who struggled with the priests for power.

   DIF: A

SECTION QUIZ 4-5—CONTRIBUTIONS

MULTIPLE CHOICE

1. Papyrus was from
   a. reeds.
   b. trees.
   c. mud.
   d. wheat.

   ANS: A   DIF: E

2. How many special feast days were on the Egyptian calendar?
   a. 5
   b. 15
   c. 25
   d. 100

   ANS: A   DIF: E

3. Egyptians were the first
   a. specialists in medicine.
   b. writers of music.
   c. farmers.
   d. artisans.

   ANS: A DIF: E

4. Egyptians invented a number system based on
   a. the number 10.
   b. the number 60.
   c. geometry.
   d. algebra.

   ANS: A DIF: A

5. Each season of the Egyptian calendar had
   a. 78 days.
   b. 100 days.
   c. 120 days.
   d. 150 days.

   ANS: C DIF: C

MATCHING

Match each item with the correct statement below.

a. survey
b. boat
c. castor oil
d. geometry
e. papyrus

1. type of paper
2. to measure land
3. indigestion remedy
4. item built of papyrus
5. mathematics used in surveying

1. ANS: E DIF: A
2. ANS: A DIF: A
3. ANS: C DIF: A
4. ANS: B DIF: A
5. ANS: D DIF: A

SHORT ANSWER

1. What else did Egyptians use papyrus for besides paper?

   ANS:
   baskets and sandals, house columns, rafts, and riverboats

   DIF: C

2. How was the Egyptian calendar different from ours?

   ANS:
   It had three seasons instead of four, and included five special feast days for the gods.

   DIF: E

CHAPTER 5—EASTERN RIVER VALLEYS

MULTIPLE CHOICE

1. The oldest civilization in present-day India grew up along the
   a. Harappan River.
   b. Nile River.
   c. Indus River.
   d. Yellow River.

   ANS: C DIF: A

2. Buildings in the Harappan civilization were made from
   a. bricks baked in an oven.
   b. stone cut from cliffs.
   c. bricks dried in the sun.
   d. wood from the forests.

   ANS: A DIF: A

3. Among ancient civilizations, the cities of Harappa and Mohenjo-daro are unusual because
   a. they were built in a river valley.
   b. both cities had granaries where food was stored.
   c. the streets were laid out in a square grid pattern.
   d. buildings were built of brick rather than wood or stone.

   ANS: C DIF: C

4. Nearly all our information about the Harappan civilization comes from
   a. artifacts and jewelry found in the tombs of kings.
   b. toys, tools, and other artifacts found in ruined cities.
   c. a library of clay tablets with records written in cuneiform.
   d. written records kept by the Aryan invaders.

   ANS: B DIF: A

5. How was the earliest civilization in China unlike the other early civilizations?
   a. It had no contact with other early civilizations.
   b. It was located on a river that flooded each year.
   c. Most of the people in ancient China were farmers.
   d. It had no written language.

   ANS: A DIF: E

6. The center of an early Chinese city was usually
   a. a palace and a temple.
   b. a building to store grain.
   c. a fortress or citadel.
   d. a public garden.

   ANS: A DIF: E

7. How did kings in ancient China use oracle bones?
   a. To show respect for their ancestors.
   b. To ask advice from their ancestors.
   c. To please the spirits in mountains and rivers.
   d. To ask advice from the nobles of the kingdom.

   ANS: B DIF: E

8. A skilled weaver of silk in Shang times would probably live
   a. on a farm in the country.
   b. in a cave or mud hut.
   c. in a house near the palace.
   d. in a house on the edge of the city.

   ANS: D DIF: A

9. Some historians believe that the Shang civilization became weakened by
   a. rivalry between the king and wealthy nobles.
   b. the nobles' lack of loyalty to the king.
   c. the great differences between rich and poor people.
   d. the king's concern for poor people's welfare.

   ANS: C DIF: A

10. The outstanding works of art from the Shang period are
    a. carvings on bone.
    b. bronze sculptures and objects.
    c. gold jewelry and cups.
    d. paintings on papyrus.

    ANS: B DIF: A

11. The Eastern valley civilizations include the
    a. Nile and Tigris rivers.
    b. Tigris and Euphrates rivers.
    c. Euphrates and Huang Ho rivers.
    d. Indus and Huang Ho rivers.

    ANS: D DIF: E

12. The Eastern valley peoples were isolated from the rest of the world by
    a. mountains, deserts, and water.
    b. religious beliefs.
    c. a mysterious lack of written records.
    d. legends of danger beyond their valleys.

    ANS: A DIF: E

13. Historians believe that Harappan civilization was
    a. largely legendary.
    b. twice the size of either Sumer or Egyptian civilization.
    c. composed of just two cities.
    d. mainly made of baked clay bricks.

    ANS: C DIF: A

14. The Harrapan religion had
    a. many gods, most of whom were female.
    b. only one god, such as the Egyptian religion.
    c. beliefs about spirit and ancestor worship.
    d. a man-god named Yu.

    ANS: A DIF: A

15. Because the gap between rich and poor was so wide in the Shang culture,
    a. the Shang could not make fine bronze work.
    b. only farmers could produce silk.
    c. the Shang kings lost their power.
    d. neither class gave loyalty or support to the other.

ANS: D DIF: A

SHORT ANSWER

1. Why was the location of the eastern river valley people so important to the way their civilization developed?

ANS:
Answers will vary, but could include: because the river valley provided rich soil to produce crops like cotton and building materials like bricks.

DIF: A

2. Use the maps below to identify at least one of each of the following features that isolated the eastern river valleys:
a) high mountains
b) broad deserts
c) large bodies of water

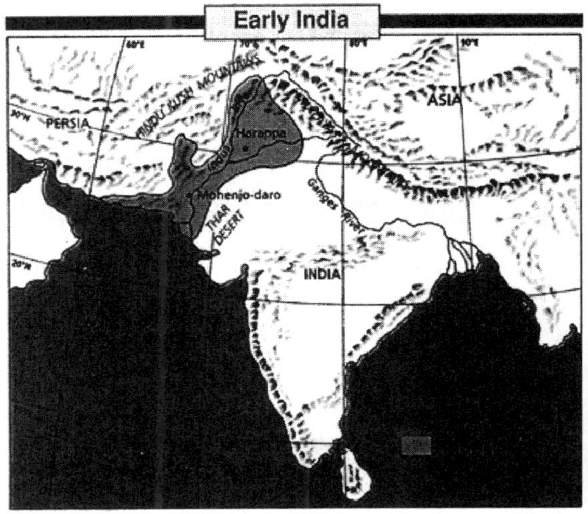

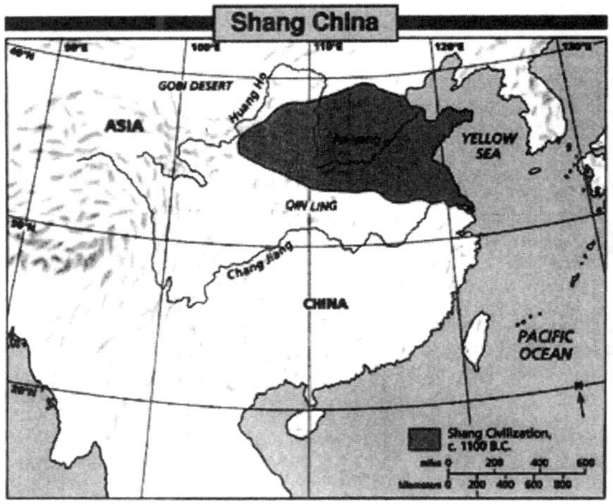

ANS:
a) high mountains: Hindu Kush; Himalayas
b) broad deserts: Thar Desert; Gobi Desert
c) large bodies of water: Arabian Sea; Bay of Bengal; Yellow Sea; Pacific Ocean

DIF: A

SECTION QUIZ 5-1—THE INDUS RIVER VALLEY

MULTIPLE CHOICE

1. The Harappans settled the Indus River valley around
   a. 600 B.C.
   b. 1200 B.C.
   c. 2500 B.C.
   d. 3500 B.C.

   ANS: C DIF: A

2. To build houses and public buildings, Harappans used
   a. fired bricks.
   b. papyrus.
   c. grids.
   d. timber.

   ANS: A DIF: E

3. The Indus River runs through the countries known today as
   a. China and Japan.
   b. Pakistan and India.
   c. Pakistan and Africa.
   d. Australia and India.

   ANS: B DIF: A

4. One reason for the decline of the Harappans was that
   a. they died of a series of plagues.
   b. they grew too much cotton.
   c. they used up their natural resources.
   d. the Indus River flooded.

   ANS: C DIF: C

5. Harappan civilization centered around
   a. Great Bath.
   b. Harappa and Mohenjo-daro.
   c. lapis lazuli.
   d. Pakistan and India.

   ANS: B DIF: A

MATCHING

Match each item with the correct statement below.

a. kiln
b. planned community
c. lapis lazuli
d. citadel
e. Harappan civilization

1. twice the size of Mesopotamia
2. fortress
3. blue stone
4. city built to a plan
5. oven

1. ANS: E DIF: A

2. ANS: D DIF: A
3. ANS: C DIF: A
4. ANS: B DIF: A
5. ANS: A DIF: A

SHORT ANSWER

1. How has much of the information about the ancient eastern peoples come to archaeologists and historians?

   ANS:
   through legends

   DIF: A

2. What crop did the Harappans introduce to civilization? How did they use it?

   ANS:
   cotton; wove it into cloth and dyed it bright colors

   DIF: C

SECTION QUIZ 5-2—THE HUANG HO VALLEY

MULTIPLE CHOICE

1. Which of the following was NOT done by Yu the Great?
   a. He drove serpents and dragons from Huang Ho.
   b. He drained the land so people could grow crops.
   c. He ruled most of northern China
   d. He overthrew the Shang.

   ANS: D DIF: C

2. Most Shang soldiers were
   a. nobles.
   b. poor peasants.
   c. ancestors.
   d. Zhou.

   ANS: B DIF: A

3. Nobles went into battle
   a. in horse-drawn chariots.
   b. on horseback.
   c. on foot.
   d. in chariots pulled by peasants.

   ANS: A DIF: E

4. The Shang civilization came to an end in
   a. 1122 B.C.
   b. 1225 B.C.
   c. 1450 B.C.
   d. 810 B.C.

   ANS: A DIF: A

5. The oldest known writing is found
   a. in Zhou temples.
   b. on Shang scrolls.
   c. carved into lapis lazuli.
   d. on oracle bones.

   ANS: C DIF: A

COMPLETION

1. The Huang Ho valley was like the Nile valley because each year their rivers' flood waters left fertile ____________________ behind.

   ANS: soil DIF: A

2. Early Chinese settlers used ____________________ as their chief building material.

   ANS: clay DIF: A

3. Only three classes of people could live in the cities of the Shang dynasty: the ____________________, the ____________________, and ____________________ workers.

   ANS: rich; learned; skilled DIF: C

4. Shang government was tied closely to ____________________ so that the kings could receive power and wisdom from the spirits and their ancestors.

   ANS: religion DIF: A

MATCHING

Match each item with the correct statement below.

a. spirit
b. noble
c. oracle bones
d. dynasty
e. Zhou

1. person of high rank in a kingdom
2. used by the Shang in important decisions
3. ruling family
4. conquerors of the Shang
5. supernatural being

1. ANS: B DIF: A
2. ANS: C DIF: A
3. ANS: D DIF: A
4. ANS: E DIF: A
5. ANS: A DIF: A

CHAPTER 6—THE PHOENICIANS AND THE HEBREWS

MULTIPLE CHOICE

1. In ancient times, the piece of land between Egypt and Mesopotamia was known as
   a. Lebanon.
   b. Canaan.
   c. Saba.
   d. Phoenicia.

   ANS: B DIF: C

2. The group of early Phoenicians who were traders and shipbuilders were called
   a. Canaanites.
   b. Hebrews.
   c. Philistines.
   d. Mediterraneans.

   ANS: C DIF: A

3. Government in Phoenicia was organized as
   a. independent city-states.
   b. city-states under one king.
   c. part of a large empire.
   d. two warring kingdoms.

   ANS: A DIF: A

4. The Phoenicians' writing system was carried to other parts of the Mediterranean by
   a. armies who conquered North Africa.
   b. wandering teachers who wrote and spoke about religion.
   c. traders and merchants who traveled by sea.
   d. soldiers who had fought to conquer the Hebrews.

   ANS: C DIF: E

5. According to the Bible, what did Yahweh promise Abraham in return for the Hebrews' accepting one god?
   a. Freedom from enslavement in Egypt
   b. The land of Canaan for themselves and their descendants
   c. Land and herds of sheep in Egypt
   d. The Ten Commandments

   ANS: B DIF: A

6. The term "exodus" refers to
   a. the Hebrews' escape from Egypt led by Moses.
   b. the time the Hebrews spent in Babylonia.
   c. a meeting to study Jewish religious writings.
   d. Abraham's journey from Ur to Canaan.

   ANS: A DIF: E

7. The warrior-king who united the 12 tribes after the Hebrews returned from Egypt was
   a. Solomon.
   b. Abraham.
   c. Judah.
   d. Saul.

   ANS: D DIF: C

8. The Hebrews' religious ideas were unusual at the time because they believed that
   a. gods and goddesses were everywhere in nature.
   b. there was only one God, who was just and fair.
   c. their gods would protect them from enemies.
   d. they should build temples for worship.

   ANS: B DIF: A

9. The Hebrew kingdom split into the kingdoms of Judah and Israel soon after
   a. the Jews were taken to Babylonia.
   b. the destruction of the Temple.
   c. the death of King Solomon.
   d. Moses led the Hebrews out of Egypt.

   ANS: C DIF: A

10. Where did the Jews begin the custom of meeting in groups on the Sabbath to study religion with a rabbi?
    a. Jerusalem
    b. Babylonia
    c. Egypt
    d. Carthage

    ANS: B DIF: C

MATCHING

Match each item with the correct statement below.

a. Dido
b. Judah
c. Carthage
d. Torah
e. David
f. Joshua
g. Tyre
h. Abraham
i. Solomon
j. Moses

1. Hebrew leader who received the Ten Commandments
2. Leading Phoenician seaport and city-state
3. Hebrew king, a poet, musician, and warrior
4. Five books of Jewish laws and history
5. Legendary founder of the city of Carthage
6. Hebrew kingdom in southern Canaan
7. North African colony established by Phoenicians
8. King who had the Temple built in Jerusalem
9. Military leader who brought the Hebrews into Canaan
10. Leader whose descendants were promised the land of Canaan

1. ANS: J DIF: A
2. ANS: G DIF: A
3. ANS: E DIF: A
4. ANS: D DIF: A
5. ANS: A DIF: A
6. ANS: B DIF: A
7. ANS: C DIF: A

8. ANS: I DIF: A
9. ANS: F DIF: A
10. ANS: H DIF: A

SHORT ANSWER

1. How might modern life be different if alphabets had never been invented and used?

   ANS:
   Answers will vary, but could include: we would not write our languages or would do so crudely with pictures, therefore limiting our ability to communicate across space and time.

   DIF: A

2. The ancient land of Canaan lay between what two lands?

   ANS:
   Egypt and Mesopotamia

   DIF: A

3. The Phoenicians and the Hebrews shared what two interests?

   ANS:
   trade and learning

   DIF: A

4. Which geographic theme explains why the Phoenicians became traders?

   ANS:
   human/environmental interaction

   DIF: C

5. From whom did the Phoenicians learn metal working?

   ANS:
   the Egyptians and Mesopotamians

   DIF: A

6. What did the Hebrews do after settling in Canaan once again?

   ANS:
   farmed and raised herd animals such as sheep and goats

   DIF: A

7. How did the Hebrews adapt to their environment?

   ANS:
   by collecting and saving water during the rainy season for use during the dry season

   DIF: A

8. Hebrews from the southern kingdom of Judah came to be called Jews while living where?

   ANS:
   in Babylonia

   DIF: A

SECTION QUIZ 6-1—THE PHOENICIANS

MULTIPLE CHOICE

1. The two groups that made up the Phoenicians were
   a. the Sumerians and the Philistines.
   b. the Mesopotamians and the Canaanites.
   c. the Egyptians and the Mesopotamians.
   d. the Philistines and the Canaanites.

   ANS: D DIF: A

2. The word "Phoenician" means
   a. a type of shellfish.
   b. he who hears all.
   c. of purple merchants.
   d. born of the Phoenix.

   ANS: C DIF: E

3. The Phoenicians' most important gift was
   a. the idea of the alphabet.
   b. hieroglyphs.
   c. the concept of tin-mining.
   d. the urn.

   ANS: A DIF: E

4. Carthage is located in
   a. present-day Turkey.
   b. present-day Tunisia.
   c. Egypt.
   d. present-day Phoenicia.

   ANS: B DIF: A

5. The Canaanite writing system used
   a. 8 major symbols.
   b. 22 symbols.
   c. 22 words.
   d. a series of dots.

   ANS: B DIF: C

MATCHING

Match each item with the correct statement below.

a. holy of holies
b. treaties
c. colonies
d. urns
e. Carthage

1. agreements between countries
2. sacred chamber
3. ornamental vases
4. famous Phoenician city
5. permanent settlements

1. ANS: B DIF: A
2. ANS: A DIF: A
3. ANS: D DIF: A
4. ANS: E DIF: A
5. ANS: C DIF: A

SHORT ANSWER

1. In addition to trade goods, what else did Phoenician traders introduce to the places where they traveled?

   ANS:
   Middle Eastern culture; an alphabet

   DIF: A

2. In return for not charging shipping fees, what did the Phoenicians usually get from treaties?

   ANS:
   their independence

   DIF: C

3. What kept the Phoenician city-states from uniting?

   ANS:
   mountains

   DIF: A

4. What was the Phoenicians' most important contribution?

   ANS:
   the idea of using an alphabet

   DIF: A

SECTION QUIZ 6-2—THE HEBREWS

MULTIPLE CHOICE

1. Most early Hebrews
   a. were nomadic.
   b. lived in cities.
   c. were farmers.
   d. worshiped ar-Razi.

   ANS: A DIF: C

2. According to the Bible, Abraham
   a. wrote the Torah.
   b. made an agreement with Yahweh.
   c. made an agreement with Moses.
   d. had six sons.

   ANS: B DIF: E

3. The word "covenant" means
   a. a day of rest.
   b. a god or idol.
   c. an agreement.
   d. wandering.

   ANS: C DIF: E

4. One of the first people to study smallpox was
   a. Moses.
   b. ar-Razi.
   c. Abraham.
   d. Yahweh.

   ANS: B DIF: A

5. Many of the psalms in the Bible were written by
   a. ar-Razi.
   b. David.
   c. Moses.
   d. Jacob.

   ANS: B DIF: A

MATCHING

Match each item with the correct statement below.

a. prophet
b. judge
c. descendant
d. psalm
e. Sabbath

1. a person claiming messages from God
2. offspring
3. temporary leader
4. day of rest
5. sacred song

1. ANS: A DIF: A
2. ANS: C DIF: A
3. ANS: B DIF: A

4. ANS: E DIF: A
5. ANS: D DIF: A

CHAPTER 7—MILITARY EMPIRES

MULTIPLE CHOICE

1. The cultures of the Assyrians and the Chaldeans took some elements from the ancient empire of
   a. the pharaohs of Egypt.
   b. Hammurabi of Babylonia.
   c. King Solomon.
   d. Darius.

   ANS: B DIF: A

2. The Assyrians gained a reputation as
   a. excellent administrators and traders.
   b. cruel warriors and strict rulers.
   c. scientists and astronomers.
   d. good soldiers and fair rulers.

   ANS: B DIF: C

3. Which people captured the Assyrian capital of Nineveh in 612 B.C.?
   a. Hittites
   b. Phoenicians
   c. Chaldeans
   d. Persians

   ANS: C DIF: E

4. The most famous leader of the Chaldeans was
   a. Nebuchadrezzar.
   b. Hammurabi.
   c. Ashurbanipal.
   d. Cyrus.

   ANS: A DIF: E

5. The secret of smelting iron ore to make superior weapons was developed about 1400 B.C. by the
   a. Assyrians.
   b. Chaldeans.
   c. Hittites.
   d. Babylonians.

   ANS: C DIF: E

6. The ancient city that was famous for its huge ziggurat and hanging gardens was
   a. Nineveh.
   b. Babylon.
   c. Persepolis.
   d. Marduk.

   ANS: B DIF: E

7. The Aryan people who settled Persia were originally
   a. Mesopotamians from the Tigris-Euphrates Valley.
   b. desert sheep herders from Egypt.
   c. merchants and traders from Phoenicia.
   d. cattle herders from Central Asia.

   ANS: D DIF: C

8. Within the Persian empire, the Immortals were
   a. the leading soldiers in the army.
   b. governors of the provinces in the empire.
   c. inspectors who traveled to distant provinces.
   d. merchants who used the silk route to China.

   ANS: A DIF: A

9. Which of these statements is true about the religion introduced in Persia by Zoroaster?
   a. It was a religion that had only one God.
   b. The gods in this religion were found in nature.
   c. People could choose between good and evil deeds.
   d. People built a ziggurat to honor the gods.

   ANS: C DIF: A

10. Under Persian rule, people in distant parts of the empire were
    a. forced to follow Persian laws and religion.
    b. forbidden to trade or travel.
    c. forced to serve in the Persian army.
    d. allowed to trade and keep their own cultures.

    ANS: D DIF: A

COMPLETION

1. As theAssyrians, Chaldeans, and Persians conquered other lands, they spread their ____________________.

   ANS: ideas and customs DIF: A

2. Assyrians ruled through ____________________.

   ANS: fear and cruelty DIF: A

3. The spring procession of Marduk in Babylon took place so that the Chaldeans would have ____________________.

   ANS: good crops and peace DIF: A

4. The Persian Empire stretched between ____________________.

   ANS: India and Egypt DIF: A

5. Under Persian rule, conquered peoples kept their own ____________________.

   ANS: language, laws, and religion DIF: A

6. To govern the provinces, the Persian king appointed a ____________________.

   ANS: general, secretary, and governor DIF: A

MATCHING

Match each item with the correct statement below.

a. Aramaic
b. smelting
c. Aryan
d. Ahura Mazda
e. caravans
f. ziggurat
g. Ahriman
h. Marduk
i. astronomers
j. provinces

1. Groups of traveling merchants
2. Process of working iron ore
3. Chief god of Babylonia
4. Zoroastrian god of darkness and evil
5. Language used for trade in the Middle East
6. Political districts of a larger government
7. Scholars who study the stars and planets
8. Multi-level Babylonian temple
9. Zoroastrian god of goodness and light
10. Central Asian people who settled Persia

1. ANS: E DIF: A
2. ANS: B DIF: A
3. ANS: H DIF: A
4. ANS: G DIF: A
5. ANS: A DIF: A
6. ANS: J DIF: A
7. ANS: I DIF: A
8. ANS: F DIF: A
9. ANS: D DIF: A
10. ANS: C DIF: A

SHORT ANSWER

1. List what you think were the special strengths and the weaknesses of the Assyrians, the Chaldeans, and the Persians.

ANS:
Answers will vary, but could include: ASSYRIANS' STRENGTH: powerful army; WEAKNESS: empire too large to manage; CHALDEANS' STRENGTH: scientific knowledge; WEAKNESS: could not control conquered peoples; PERSIANS' STRENGTH: fair rulers who encouraged trade; WEAKNESS: attitude toward traders.

DIF: C

2. Look at the map below. What bodies of water did the Persians control? What advantages would control of the seas give the Persians?

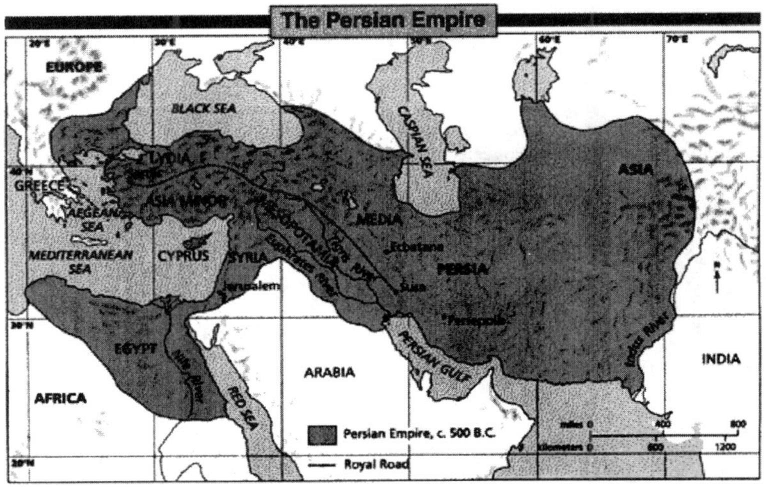

ANS:
Mediterranean Sea, Caspian Sea, Black Sea, Red Sea, Persian Gulf; they would probably control most ports, so they would control trade; they might also be better able to patrol seas to keep enemies from landing and attacking Persian cities and peoples.

DIF: C

SECTION QUIZ 7-1—THE ASSYRIANS

MULTIPLE CHOICE

1. Assyrian power was partly due to
   a. overthrowing the Chaldeans.
   b. iron weapons.
   c. huge palaces.
   d. swift horses.

   ANS: B DIF: A

2. The Assyrians used the same writing system as the
   a. Egyptians.
   b. Chinese.
   c. Persians.
   d. Babylonians.

   ANS: D DIF: C

3. Overall, the Assyrians were
   a. farmers.
   b. merchants.
   c. warriors.
   d. artisans.

   ANS: C DIF: E

4. One of the world's first libraries was started by
   a. the Chaldeans.
   b. Ashurbanipal.
   c. Nineveh.
   d. the Hittites.

   ANS: B DIF: C

5. Nineveh was captured by
   a. the Hebrews.
   b. Ashurbanipal.
   c. the Assyrians.
   d. the Chaldeans.

   ANS: D DIF: E

MATCHING

Match each item with the correct statement below.

a. province
b. Assyria
c. Nineveh
d. smelting
e. Ashurbanipal

1. a political district
2. process developed by the Hittites
3. Assyrian capital city
4. Tigris River valley country
5. great Assyrian king

1. ANS: A DIF: A
2. ANS: D DIF: A
3. ANS: C DIF: A
4. ANS: B DIF: A
5. ANS: E DIF: A

SHORT ANSWER

1. In what area of the ancient world was Assyria?

   ANS:
   Mesopotamia

   DIF: C

2. What natural geographic barriers did Assyria lack?

   ANS:
   mountains, deserts, and any geographical formation that would have protected them from invasion

   DIF: A

3. Why were early Assyrians "summertime" soldiers?

   ANS:
   During the fall and winter, they farmed.

   DIF: C

4. Why did some people simply surrender to the Assyrians rather than fight?

   ANS:
   They were frightened of the stories they had heard about the cruelty of the Assyrians.

   DIF: A

5. How did the Assyrians connect and control their provinces?

   ANS:
   with a system of roads

   DIF: E

SECTION QUIZ 7-2—THE CHALDEANS

MULTIPLE CHOICE

1. The Chaldeans called themselves
   a. Serbs.
   b. Babylonians.
   c. Palestinians.
   d. caravans.

   ANS: B DIF: C

2. The Chaldeans were descendants of
   a. Moses.
   b. the people of Marduk's empire.
   c. the people of Hammurabi's empire.
   d. Assyrian warriors.

   ANS: C DIF: C

3. Babylonian astronomers built one of the first
   a. sundials.
   b. temples.
   c. empires.
   d. caravans.

   ANS: A DIF: E

4. The approaches to Babylon were
   a. guarded by swordsmen.
   b. impossible to tunnel under.
   c. guarded by archers.
   d. surrounded by "hanging gardens."

   ANS: C DIF: E

5. For his wife, Nebuchadnezzar built
   a. a sundial.
   b. caravans.
   c. the "hanging gardens."
   d. a gold statue of Marduk.

   ANS: C DIF: E

MATCHING

Match each item with the correct statement below.
a. Marduk
b. caravan
c. astronomer
d. Ishtar Gate
e. Nebuchadnezzar

1. one who studies heavenly bodies
2. Chaldean god
3. Chaldean king
4. entrance to Babylon
5. group of traveling merchants

1. ANS: C DIF: A
2. ANS: A DIF: A
3. ANS: E DIF: A
4. ANS: D DIF: A
5. ANS: B DIF: A

SHORT ANSWER

1. Who were the ancestors of most Chaldeans?

   ANS:
   descendants of the Babylonians under Hammurabi

   DIF: A

2. What were some ways that the Chaldeans used their riches to make Babylon a great center of learning and culture?

   ANS:
   developed a postal system; established a police force; built beautiful temples and huge brick walls

   DIF: A

3. What did Nebuchadnezzar build for his wife?

   ANS:
   the Hanging Gardens

   DIF: E

4. What did Nebuchadnezzar build to please his subjects?

   ANS:
   a street paved with limestone and marble

   DIF: A

5. Besides warfare, what other national occupation made the Babylonian empire rich?

   ANS:
   trade from all over the ancient world

   DIF: A

SECTION QUIZ 7-3—THE PERSIANS

MULTIPLE CHOICE

1. Persian officials spoke
   a. Hebrew.
   b. Ahura Mazda.
   c. Aramaic.
   d. Assyrian.

   ANS: C DIF: C

2. Which of the following was NOT a feature of Persian houses?
   a. one room in poor homes
   b. pointed roof
   c. porch faced the sun
   d. wooden floor

   ANS: D DIF: E

3. The homes of noble Persian families had
   a. different sets of rooms for men and women.
   b. treasuries.
   c. granaries.
   d. more than 20 rooms.

   ANS: A DIF: A

4. The two gods Zoroaster told the Persians about were
   a. Aryan and Darius.
   b. Medes and Cyrus.
   c. Darius and Cyrus.
   d. Ahriman and Ahura Mazda.

   ANS: D DIF: A

5. The first coins were made in
   a. Iran.
   b. Lydia.
   c. Persepolis.
   d. Egypt.

   ANS: B   DIF: A

MATCHING

Match each item with the correct statement below.

a. Persepolis
b. litter
c. Iran
d. Darius
e. Zoroaster

1. "the land of the Aryans"
2. Persian king
3. carriage
4. Persian capital city
5. religious leader

1. ANS: C   DIF: A
2. ANS: D   DIF: A
3. ANS: B   DIF: A
4. ANS: A   DIF: A
5. ANS: E   DIF: A

SHORT ANSWER

1. What was the occupation of the early Persians?

   ANS:
   cattle herders

   DIF: E

2. What two things did the Persians require from the people they conquered?

   ANS:
   paying taxes and producing goods for trade

   DIF: A

3. What three things did the Persian officials do in the provinces?

   ANS:
   collected taxes, settled local quarrels, and protected people from bandits

   DIF: A

4. How did the Persian king keep his officials honest?

   ANS:
   Each official reported to the king separately.

   DIF: A

CHAPTER 8—AFRICA AND THE AMERICAS

MULTIPLE CHOICE

1. About 750 B.C., the kings of Kush conquered land and established a dynasty to rule
   a. Mali.
   b. Assyria.
   c. Egypt.
   d. Aksum.

   ANS: C DIF: E

2. A most valuable skill the Kushites learned from the Assyrians was
   a. building pyramids.
   b. smelting iron ore.
   c. irrigating land.
   d. trading in salt.

   ANS: B DIF: A

3. The ancient kingdom of Aksum was unusual because
   a. its merchants traded with Arabia.
   b. Greek traders settled there.
   c. its people learned how to smelt iron ore.
   d. its king converted to Christianity.

   ANS: D DIF: A

4. By conquering Ghana, King Sundiata Keita established the trading kingdom of
   a. Mali.
   b. Maya.
   c. Mansa Musa.
   d. Kilwa.

   ANS: A DIF: E

5. The caravan trade in gold and salt was the basis for the wealth of the kingdom of
   a. Ghana.
   b. Kush.
   c. Zimbabwe.
   d. Olmec.

   ANS: A DIF: E

6. The culture known as Swahili is a blend of which two other cultures?
   a. Egyptian and Greek
   b. Indian and African
   c. Arabic and African
   d. Greek and Arabic

   ANS: C DIF: A

7. Mesoamerican cultures took their hieroglyphic writing systems and ways of measuring time from the culture of
   a. the Egyptians.
   b. the Incas.
   c. the Olmecs.
   d. the Spanish.

   ANS: C DIF: A

8. Which of these is the best description of the Mayas?
   a. Strict rulers who conquered a vast mountain empire
   b. Traders at the crossroads between Africa and Asia
   c. Warlike conquerors and skilled builders of cities
   d. Prosperous traders who were peaceful and religious

   ANS: D DIF: C

9. The Aztecs practiced human sacrifice because they believed
   a. sacrifice was the proper punishment for criminals.
   b. conquered people deserved to be killed.
   c. the sun god required sacrifices in order to rise.
   d. the jaguar god would not send rain without sacrifices.

   ANS: C DIF: C

10. Under Inca rule, the people of the Andes Mountains had to
    a. use only the Inca roads for travel and trade.
    b. accept the Inca religion and language.
    c. use the hieroglyphic writing system of the Inca.
    d. play the religious ritual of a ball game.

    ANS: B DIF: C

11. Sundiata Kieta, the king of Mali, divided his kingdom into provinces ruled by generals. This kind of government was
    most like that of
    a. King Solomon of the Hebrews.
    b. the Phoenician city-states.
    c. the huge Assyrian empire.
    d. the warrior pharaohs of Egypt's New Kingdom.

    ANS: C DIF: A

12. Africa's Middle Kingdoms came under attack from
    a. Egyptians in eastern Africa.
    b. Arabs in northern Africa.
    c. Shona in southern Africa.
    d. Phoenician traders from the Mediterranean.

    ANS: B DIF: A

13. East African trading centers brought goods to Africa from
    a. Neolithic and Paleolithic villages.
    b. the Americas.
    c. India and China.
    d. Aksum and Kush.

    ANS: C DIF: A

14. The stone cities of the Olmec were
    a. religious centers.
    b. huge markets.
    c. made of sun-dried bricks.
    d. based on Mayan temples.

    ANS: A DIF: E

15. Like the Olmec, the Maya lived
    a. on an island with paved roads.
    b. on top of high mountains.
    c. in farming villages around religious cities.
    d. in the Andes mountains.

    ANS: C   DIF: A

16. Of the three great Mesoamerican civilizations, the most warlike appears to be the
    a. Olmec.
    b. Aztec.
    c. Maya.
    d. Inca.

    ANS: B   DIF: A

17. Both the Inca and the Aztec were conquered by
    a. Mayans.
    b. Olmecs.
    c. Middle Kingdoms.
    d. Spaniards.

    ANS: D   DIF: E

MATCHING

Match each item with the correct statement below.

a. Shona
b. Songhai
c. Mali
d. Kush
e. Olmec
f. Tenochtitlan
g. Aztec
h. Bantu
i. Inca
j. Kilwa

1. Trading kingdom on the Nile south of Egypt
2. People who settled in ancient Zimbabwe
3. The "mother culture" of Mesoamerica
4. Last and largest of West African trading kingdoms
5. People who ruled an empire in the Andes
6. Language spoken by many African peoples
7. East African city-state, home of Swahili culture
8. Warlike people who ruled Mexico until the early 1500s
9. Wealthy trading kingdom ruled by Mansa Musa
10. Capital city of the Aztec Empire

1. ANS: D   DIF: A
2. ANS: A   DIF: A
3. ANS: E   DIF: A
4. ANS: B   DIF: A
5. ANS: I   DIF: A
6. ANS: H   DIF: A
7. ANS: J   DIF: A
8. ANS: G   DIF: A
9. ANS: C   DIF: A
10. ANS: F   DIF: A

SHORT ANSWER

1. How were the early civilizations of Africa and the Americas similar? How were they different?

    ANS:
    Answers will vary, but could include: SIMILARITIES: empires developed that included trading, religions, languages, roads DIFFERENCES: people in Africa before Americas.

    DIF: A

SECTION QUIZ 8-1—ANCIENT AFRICAN KINGDOMS

MULTIPLE CHOICE

1. The Kushites were
    a. nomadic cattle herders.
    b. nomadic shepherds.
    c. city-dwelling merchants.
    d. savannah-dwelling artisans.

    ANS: A   DIF: A

2. Kush was part of Egypt for
    a. 100 years.
    b. 500 years.
    c. 1,000 years.
    d. 2,500 years.

    ANS: B   DIF: E

3. Around 540 B.C. the Kushites moved their capital to
    a. Napata.
    b. Meroe.
    c. a savannah.
    d. Aksum.

    ANS: B   DIF: A

4. Aksumite armies
    a. burned Meroe down.
    b. built great temples in Meroe.
    c. conquered all of present-day Egypt.
    d. conquered all of present-day Africa.

    ANS: A   DIF: E

5. What people most likely brought Christianity to Aksum?
    a. the Egyptians
    b. the Kushites
    c. the Greeks
    d. the Hittites

    ANS: C   DIF: C

MATCHING

Match each item with the correct statement below.

a. savannah
b. interior
c. slag
d. terrace
e. Kush

1. grassy plain
2. smelting waste
3. raised level of land
4. early African civilization
5. inland area

1. ANS: A DIF: A
2. ANS: C DIF: A
3. ANS: D DIF: A
4. ANS: E DIF: A
5. ANS: B DIF: A

SHORT ANSWER

1. Why were the Kush able to win independence from Egypt?

   ANS:
   Egypt's power declined, and it became weak.

   DIF: A

2. What did the Kush use iron-smelting for?

   ANS:
   making stronger tools and weapons

   DIF: A

3. How did the Kush use their iron knives and spears?

   ANS:
   as trade goods

   DIF: E

4. How were Kush and Aksum alike?

   ANS:
   Both were trading nations.

   DIF: A

5. What happened to the Aksumites?

   ANS:
   Arab armies drove them to the inner regions of their territory, where they lived in isolation for about 1,000 years.

   DIF: C

SECTION QUIZ 8-2—THE MIDDLE KINGDOMS

MULTIPLE CHOICE

1. In 1042 A.D., Arabs from North Africa
   a. started a war with Europe.
   b. started a war with Ghana.
   c. converted to Christianity.
   d. converted to Judaism.

   ANS: B DIF: C

2. Sundiata Keita was king of
   a. Morocco.
   b. the Songhai.
   c. Mali.
   d. the Sahara.

   ANS: C DIF: C

3. Timbuktu became
   a. a center of learning.
   b. the capital of Morocco.
   c. a holy city.
   d. a military outpost.

   ANS: A DIF: E

4. The powerful kingdom of Songhai lasted
   a. until the beginning of the nineteenth century.
   b. only 10 years.
   c. only 40 years.
   d. only 100 years.

   ANS: D DIF: A

5. In 1324 A.D., Mansa Musa began a pilgrimage to
   a. Ghana.
   b. Mali.
   c. Egypt.
   d. Arabia.

   ANS: D DIF: A

MATCHING

Match each item with the correct statement below.

a. pilgrimage
b. Sundiata Keita
c. refugee
d. King Moses I
e. silent barter

1. person who flees for safety
2. trading technique
3. Hungering Lion"
4. another name for Mansa Musa
5. religious journey

1. ANS: C DIF: A
2. ANS: E DIF: A
3. ANS: B DIF: A
4. ANS: D DIF: A
5. ANS: A DIF: A

SHORT ANSWER

1. What were the three Middle Kingdoms of Africa?

   ANS:
   Ghana, Mali, and Songhai

   DIF: A

2. How did the Middle Kingdoms support themselves?

   ANS:
   through trade

   DIF: E

3. How did iron-smelting "travel" from East to West Africa?

   ANS:
   It was brought by refugees from Kush.

   DIF: A

4. How did Songhai extend its territory?

   ANS:
   by conquering other lands

   DIF: A

SECTION QUIZ 8-3—EAST AFRICAN CIVILIZATIONS

MULTIPLE CHOICE

1. The people of Zimbabwe viewed their chief as a
   a. high priest.
   b. god-king.
   c. beast-king.
   d. man-god.

   ANS: B DIF: E

2. When a Zimbabwe priest grew old, he
   a. killed himself.
   b. left the country.
   c. gave the throne to his son.
   d. moved to Kilwa.

   ANS: A DIF: E

3. The people of Zimbabwe traded
   a. sheep, goats, and cattle.
   b. gold, copper, and ivory.
   c. ebony, diamonds, and silk.
   d. olives, flax, and grapes.

   ANS: B DIF: A

4. The Swahili language is a combination of
   a. Arabic and Chinese.
   b. Kilwa and Zimbabwe.
   c. Persian and Indian.
   d. Bantu and Arabic.

   ANS: D DIF: A

5. The people of Zimbabwe approached their leader
   a. coughing.
   b. with bowed heads.
   c. crawling on their stomachs.
   d. dressed in fine cotton and silk.

   ANS: C DIF: C

MATCHING

Match each item with the correct statement below.

a. Swahili
b. Kilwa
c. Bantu
d. population explosion
e. trade

1. sudden population growth
2. Zimbabwe language
3. East African city-state
4. mix of African and Arabic cultures
5. reason for Zimbabwe's power

1. ANS: D DIF: A
2. ANS: C DIF: A
3. ANS: B DIF: A

4. ANS: A DIF: A
5. ANS: E DIF: A

SHORT ANSWER

1. Why did many Shona look for new homes?

   ANS:
   because their original home could not support all the people who lived there

   DIF: A

2. Where was one place that the East African Shona settled?

   ANS:
   Zimbabwe

   DIF: E

3. How did Zimbabwe remain strong?

   ANS:
   through trade

   DIF: E

4. From what part of Africa did Zimbabwe and Kilwa get goods?

   ANS:
   from the interior regions of Africa

   DIF: A

SECTION QUIZ 8-4—PATH TO THE AMERICAS

MULTIPLE CHOICE

1. Twenty-five thousand years ago people came to the Americas
   a. by sea only.
   b. only when hunting.
   c. over a land bridge.
   d. to bury their dead.

   ANS: C DIF: A

2. The Ice Age ended about
   a. 2000 B.C.
   b. 4000 B.C.
   c. 5000 B.C.
   d. 7000 B.C.

   ANS: D DIF: A

3. By 6000 B.C., the main occupation in the Tehuacan Valley was
   a. hunting.
   b. fishing.
   c. farming.
   d. weaving.

   ANS: D DIF: C

4. After the Ice Age,
   a. large game all but disappeared from the Americas.
   b. people could hunt larger game.
   c. people gave up farming.
   d. people worshiped the sun.

   ANS: A DIF: E

5. Between 3000 B.C. and 1000 B.C.,
   a. indoor plumbing was invented.
   b. people built irrigation systems.
   c. the Americas were under water.
   d. maize was no longer grown for food.

   ANS: B DIF: E

MATCHING

Match each item with the correct statement below.
a. Tehuacan Valley
b. maize
c. glacier
d. Ice Age
e. Bering Strait

1. south of present-day Mexico City
2. corn
3. ended about 7000 B.C.
4. covers the land bridge to the Americas
5. huge chunk of ice

1. ANS: A DIF: A
2. ANS: B DIF: A
3. ANS: D DIF: A
4. ANS: E DIF: A
5. ANS: C DIF: A

SHORT ANSWER

1. Why did people come to the Americas?

   ANS:
   in search of food; following grass-grazing animals

   DIF: A

2. How did the climate and land of the Americas change when the last Ice Age ended?

ANS:
The climate became hotter and drier, and deserts replaced grasslands.

DIF: C

3. How did people in farming communities provide enough food for increasing populations?

ANS:
They grew maize (corn).

DIF: A

SECTION QUIZ 8-5—MESOAMERICA

MULTIPLE CHOICE

1. Olmec cities were
   a. densely populated.
   b. mainly used as trade centers.
   c. mainly used as religious centers.
   d. the home of mainly slaves.

   ANS: C DIF: A

2. Tenochtitlan was
   a. built on an island.
   b. a great Olmec stone city.
   c. the largest aqueduct in the world.
   d. the largest causeway in the world.

   ANS: A DIF: E

3. The Mayas were
   a. mostly criminals.
   b. great traders.
   c. the first to use a calendar.
   d. great hunters.

   ANS: B DIF: A

4. The Mayas disappeared
   a. when the Olmecs took their land.
   b. when the Bering Strait covered their land bridge.
   c. about 900 A.D.
   d. about 1200 A.D.

   ANS: C DIF: E

5. During the reign of Montezuma II,
   a. the Spaniards made peace with the Aztecs.
   b. the Spaniards conquered the Olmecs.
   c. the Aztec culture centered on guns and horses.
   d. the Aztec Empire reached its height.

   ANS: D DIF: A

MATCHING

Match each item with the correct statement below.

a. Montezuma
b. Olmec
c. Mesoamerica
d. Tenochtitlan
e. causeways

1. Middle America
2. Mesoamerican "mother culture"
3. capital of Aztec Empire
4. paved roads
5. Aztec ruler

1. ANS: C DIF: A
2. ANS: B DIF: A
3. ANS: D DIF: A
4. ANS: E DIF: A
5. ANS: A DIF: A

SHORT ANSWER

1. Between what two continents is Mesoamerica located?

   ANS:
   North and South America

   DIF: A

2. Why was the Olmec civilization called the mother culture?

   ANS:
   because the Olmec civilization greatly influenced other peoples and cultures in the Mesoamerican region

   DIF: A

3. How did the Mayans punish lawbreakers?

   ANS:
   by selling them into slavery

   DIF: A

4. How did the Aztec treat the peoples they conquered?

ANS:
They made them pay tributes.

DIF: A

SECTION QUIZ 8-6—THE INCAS

MULTIPLE CHOICE

1. Pachacuti was
   a. the founder of the Aztec people.
   b. the founder of the Inca people.
   c. a South American explorer.
   d. a counting device.

   ANS: B DIF: C

2. By the 1500s, how many Incas were there?
   a. 2,500
   b. 4 million
   c. 12 million
   d. 20 million

   ANS: C DIF: E

3. Which of the following was NOT true of the Incas?
   a. They had a system of stone-paved roads.
   b. They raised alpacas and llamas.
   c. They lived near the Nile River.
   d. They built suspension bridges.

   ANS: C DIF: E

4. In the early 1500s, the Inca Empire
   a. devised a written language.
   b. was destroyed by the Spanish.
   c. used an official language known as Pachacuti.
   d. raised cattle and horses near the Andes.

   ANS: B DIF: A

5. Under Pachacuti, the Incas
   a. became great warriors.
   b. worshiped the Inca sun god.
   c. spoke the official language, Incan.
   d. conquered the Spanish.

   ANS: B DIF: A

MATCHING

Match each item with the correct statement below.

a. Quechua
b. alpacas
c. Andes
d. Pachacuti
e. quipus

1. official Inca language

2. South American mountain range
3. animals raised by the Incas
4. Inca ruler
5. counting devices

1. ANS: A DIF: A
2. ANS: C DIF: A
3. ANS: B DIF: A
4. ANS: D DIF: A
5. ANS: E DIF: A

SHORT ANSWER

1. Why were the Inca able to grow crops?

   ANS:
   because the valleys below the Andes Mountains had fertile soil

   DIF: A

2. How did the Inca people pay their taxes?

   ANS:
   They paid through their labor.

   DIF: E

3. How did the Inca display their wealth?

   ANS:
   by the way their ruler lived

   DIF: A

CHAPTER 9—BEGINNINGS

MULTIPLE CHOICE

1. Which of these is the best description of the land where the Minoans lived?
   a. Grasslands in southern Russia
   b. A forested island in the Mediterranean
   c. Plains and hilltops of southern Greece
   d. Rugged, rocky islands off the Greek peninsula

   ANS: B DIF: C

2. To protect their cities, the Minoans depended on
   a. sturdy walls and towers.
   b. hilltop fortresses.
   c. trained fighting bulls.
   d. the sea and their ships.

   ANS: D DIF: E

3. The Minoans' word for their sacred double-ax symbol was
   a. parchment.
   b. labyrinth.
   c. fresco.
   d. megaron.

   ANS: B DIF: A

4. The Minoans became well known in other countries through
   a. trading by sea.
   b. pirate raids on the coasts.
   c. conquering other peoples.
   d. migrating to Asia Minor.

   ANS: A DIF: A

5. The most important god in the religion of the Minoans was
   a. the Minotaur.
   b. a sacred bull.
   c. the priest-king.
   d. the Great Goddess.

   ANS: D DIF: A

6. The Mycenaeans borrowed many ideas from the Minoans, but did not copy their ways of
   a. shipbuilding and navigation.
   b. working with metal.
   c. olive growing.
   d. building cities.

   ANS: D DIF: C

7. Homer's poem the *Iliad* tells the story of a war between
   a. Mycenaeans and Trojans.
   b. opposing groups of Greeks.
   c. Greeks and Dorians.
   d. Minoans and Mycenaeans.

   ANS: A DIF: A

8. In Mycenae, the term "megaron" referred to
   a. a person who worked on another's estate.
   b. a kind of pirate ship.
   c. the central room of a fortress-palace.
   d. the large wooden statue of a horse.

   ANS: C DIF: C

9. About when was the "Dark Age" in the Aegean world?
   a. 2800-2000 B.C.
   b. 2000-1400 B.C.
   c. 1200s B.C.
   d. 1100-800 B.C.

   ANS: D DIF: C

10. The "Dark Age" resulted from civil wars and
    a. invasion by the Dorians.
    b. piracy by the Mycenaeans.
    c. war with the Trojans.
    d. war with Ionia.

    ANS: A DIF: A

MATCHING

Match each item with the correct statement below.

a. Aegean
b. Knossos
c. Asia Minor
d. Dorians
e. Crete
f. Minoans
g. Ionia
h. Minotaur
i. Theseus
j. Homer

1. Large peninsula at the eastern end of the Mediterranean
2. One of the largest cities of Crete
3. People who created an early civilization on Crete
4. People who conquered the Mycenaeans
5. Sea between Greece and Asia Minor
6. Legendary hero who killed the Minotaur
7. Area of Asia Minor settled by Greeks
8. Mediterranean island, home of an early civilization
9. Poet who told of Greek and Trojan heroes
10. Legendary monster who lived in Crete

1. ANS: C DIF: A
2. ANS: B DIF: A
3. ANS: F DIF: A
4. ANS: D DIF: A
5. ANS: A DIF: A
6. ANS: I DIF: A
7. ANS: G DIF: A
8. ANS: E DIF: A
9. ANS: J DIF: A
10. ANS: H DIF: A

Match each cause with the effect it produced.

a. they were able to adopt many Minoan customs and practices.
b. the Aegean world lost its skills and knowledge during a "Dark Age."
c. they lived in the houses nearest the palace of the king.
d. they were able to raid nearby lands.
e. the Minoans learned the skills of carpentry and shipbuilding.

11. Because Crete was heavily forested, _____
12. Because sea captains, merchants, and shipbuilders were important to Minoan trade, _____
13. Because the Mycenaeans traded with the Minoans, _____
14. Because the Mycenaeans learned shipbuilding and navigation, _____
15. Because of civil wars and invasion by the Dorians, _____

11. ANS: E DIF: A
12. ANS: C DIF: A
13. ANS: A DIF: A
14. ANS: D DIF: A
15. ANS: B DIF: A

SHORT ANSWER

1. Homer's long story-poems, the *Iliad* and the *Odyssey*, are still read. Why do you think people through the ages have continued to enjoy them?

   ANS:
   Answers will vary, but could include: because they are exciting stories about heroes who have many adventures.

   DIF: A

SECTION QUIZ 9-1—THE MINOANS

MULTIPLE CHOICE

1. The Minotaur had
   a. the head of a man.
   b. the body of a man.
   c. a large wooden beam.
   d. many frescoes.

   ANS: B DIF: E

2. The Minoans were also known as
   a. priest-kings.
   b. Cretans.
   c. Minotaurs.
   d. Theseus.

   ANS: B DIF: E

3. The largest city in Crete was
   a. Athens.
   b. Mycenaeans.
   c. Theseus.
   d. Knossos.

   ANS: D DIF: A

4. The Minoan palace at Knossos was
   a. called "House of the Double Ax."
   b. full of merchants and ship captains.
   c. at the top of Mount Juktas.
   d. ruled by the Minotaur.

   ANS: A DIF: A

5. Frescoes are
   a. half man and half bull.
   b. watercolor paintings on plaster.
   c. sacred places to worship.
   d. networks of paths through a palace.

   ANS: B DIF: E

COMPLETION

1. The Minoans developed smaller, faster ____________________, which helped them become a great seafaring country.

   ANS: ships DIF: E

2. We know how the Minoans looked and what they wore from ____________________ that decorated their palaces.

   ANS: frescoes DIF: A

3. Minoan cities had no ____________________ because they expected protection from their navy and from the ____________________.

   ANS: walls; sea DIF: A

4. Many historians think that the sport of bull leaping was also a ____________________ ceremony.

   ANS: religions DIF: E

MATCHING

Match each item with the correct statement below.

a. shrine
b. Crete
c. bull leaping
d. labyrinth
e. parchment

1. birthplace of Minoan civilization
2. form of bullfighting

3. sacred place of worship
4. network of paths
5. thin animal skin

1. ANS: B DIF: A
2. ANS: C DIF: A
3. ANS: A DIF: A
4. ANS: D DIF: A
5. ANS: E DIF: A

SECTION QUIZ 9-2—THE MYCENAEANS

MULTIPLE CHOICE

1. The Mycenaeans came from
   a. Troy.
   b. southern Russia.
   c. Crete.
   d. Greenwich, England.

   ANS: B DIF: E

2. The Mycenaeans made
   a. gold figures.
   b. peanut butter.
   c. olive oil.
   d. paper money.

   ANS: C DIF: E

3. Homer was a
   a. Greek poet.
   b. Greek king.
   c. Trojan warrior.
   d. friend of Odysseus.

   ANS: A DIF: E

4. After the civil wars and the Dorian invasion,
   a. Paris took Helen to Troy.
   b. the Aegean world entered a "Dark Age."
   c. the Mycenaeans killed the king of Troy.
   d. the people of Troy revolted.

   ANS: B DIF: C

5. Meridians
   a. run from the North Pole to the South Pole.
   b. were square rooms with fireplaces.
   c. came from southern Russia.
   d. were Greek settlements.

   ANS: A DIF: A

COMPLETION

1. The Mycenaeans preferred war to ____________________.

   ANS: trade DIF: E

2. The Mycenaeans warred with ____________________ to break that country's control of the ____________________ to the Black Sea.

   ANS: Troy; trade routes DIF: A

3. During the "Dark Age," no ____________________ were written.

   ANS: records DIF: A

4. After the "Dark Age," the Aegean people settled in small, independent ____________________ that each had its own leader.

   ANS: communities DIF: E

MATCHING

Match each item with the correct statement below.

a. Trojan War
b. tenants
c. meridians
d. megaron
e. civil war

1. people who live on another's land
2. lines of longitude
3. chief feature of fortress palaces
4. war between groups of citizens
5. war fought over Helen of Troy

1. ANS: B DIF: A
2. ANS: C DIF: A
3. ANS: D DIF: A
4. ANS: E DIF: A
5. ANS: A DIF: A

CHAPTER 10—THE CITY-STATES

MULTIPLE CHOICE

1. In ancient Greece, cities tended to develop
   a. at the top of an acropolis.
   b. on the edge of the polis.
   c. around the agora.
   d. in the farms and orchards.

   ANS: C DIF: A

2. Those who were considered citizens of a Greek city-state included
   a. all adult men and women born in that city-state.
   b. all adult males, Greek and foreign-born.
   c. free adult men born in Greece.
   d. Greek and foreign male workers, free or enslaved.

   ANS: C DIF: A

3. The central interest of the city-state of Sparta was
   a. military strength.
   b. religion and the arts.
   c. trade and prosperity.
   d. democratic government.

   ANS: A DIF: E

4. Sparta's army and government were run by
   a. merchants and artisans.
   b. helots and perioeci.
   c. priests.
   d. aristocrats.

   ANS: D DIF: A

5. One important result of the reforms made in Athens by Solon was that
   a. more Athenians could take part in government.
   b. a strong military government kept order in the city-state.
   c. punishments for crimes were extremely harsh.
   d. rules for Athenian citizenship were made stricter.

   ANS: A DIF: C

6. After Cleisthenes made changes in the government, Athens was run by
   a. leaders of the army and navy.
   b. an elected Council of 500.
   c. a Council of 500 chosen by lot.
   d. a volunteer Assembly.

   ANS: C DIF: C

7. The battle of Marathon was an important victory for
   a. Athens over Sparta.
   b. the Persians over Athens.
   c. Athens over the Persians.
   d. Sparta over Athens.

   ANS: C DIF: A

8. What was the Delian League?
   a. An alliance of city-states against Persia, led by Athens
   b. The alliance of Athens and Sparta against King Xerxes
   c. The opponents of Athens in the Peloponnesian War
   d. The city-states that revolted against Spartan rule

   ANS: A DIF: A

9. The leader who made Athens a center of art, philosophy, and architecture was
   a. Pericles.
   b. Darius.
   c. Draco.
   d. Cleisthenes.

   ANS: A DIF: E

10. The last city-state to take over the leadership of an independent Greece was
    a. Sparta.
    b. Thebes.
    c. Athens.
    d. Delos.

    ANS: B DIF: A

COMPLETION

1. The polis was the ____________________ center of Greek life because each polis was made up of homes and businesses.

   ANS: geographic DIF: A

2. The polis was the ____________________ center of Greek life because each polis had its own government and laws.

   ANS: political DIF: A

3. The ancient Greeks believed that being a good person meant being a good ____________________.

   ANS: citizen DIF: E

4. A citizen of Sparta had to be born an ____________________.

   ANS: aristocrat DIF: A

5. Any Athenian citizen could serve on the governing ____________________of Five Hundred.

   ANS: Council DIF: A

6. The ____________________ extended their empire by conquering the Greek city-states of Ionia.

   ANS: Persians DIF: A

MATCHING

Match each item with the correct statement below.

a. helots	f. perioeci
b. aristocrat	g. oligarchy
c. polis	h. constitution
d. agora	i. acropolis
e. democratic	j. Assembly

1. An open square or marketplace
2. Government controlled by a small group
3. Enslaved farm workers of Sparta
4. Nobles who held political power in Sparta
5. Rules and ideas by which a community is governed
6. Geographic and political center of Greek life
7. Favoring the equality of all people
8. Merchants and artisans of Sparta
9. Group that passed laws and decided questions of war and peace
10. Fortified hill at the center of a city-state

1. ANS: D DIF: A
2. ANS: G DIF: A
3. ANS: A DIF: A
4. ANS: B DIF: A
5. ANS: H DIF: A
6. ANS: C DIF: A
7. ANS: E DIF: A
8. ANS: F DIF: A
9. ANS: J DIF: A
10. ANS: I DIF: A

SHORT ANSWER

1. The modern English adjective "Spartan" comes from the name of the Greek city-state, Sparta. How does that help you figure out what the phrase "a Spartan existence" probably means?

   ANS:
   Answers will vary, but could include: a main part of Spartans' life was self-discipline and living with only bare essentials; thus "a Spartan existence" usually means one with no luxuries or frills.

   DIF: A

2. Use the map below to help explain why the war between Athens and Sparta was called the Peloponnesian War.

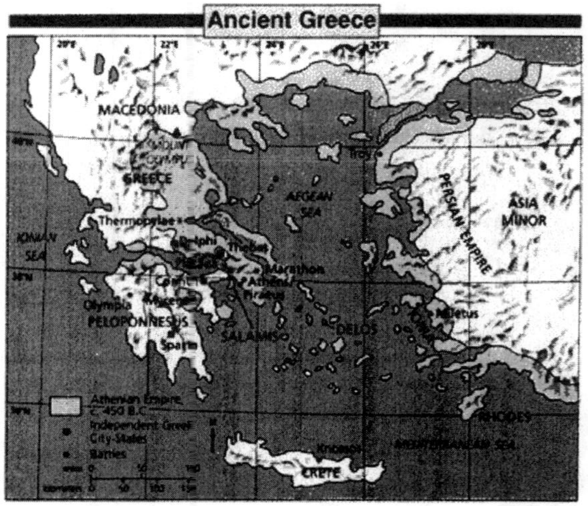

ANS:
Both Athens and Sparta are located in the region named Peloponnesus.

DIF: E

SECTION QUIZ 10-1—THE POLIS

MULTIPLE CHOICE

1. A polis was made up of
   a. open-air marketplaces and temples.
   b. government and laws.
   c. Sparta and Athens.
   d. villages, fields, and orchards.

   ANS: D DIF: C

2. At the top of the acropolis was
   a. an agora.
   b. a polis.
   c. an amphitheater.
   d. a temple.

   ANS: D DIF: A

3. The average Greek city-state contained
   a. about 60 temples.
   b. between 5,000 and 10,000 citizens.
   c. four agoras.
   d. massive armies and navies.

   ANS: B DIF: E

4. Only citizens of the city-state could
   a. travel on the roads.
   b. vote and own property.
   c. sell goods in the marketplace.
   d. worship at the temple.

   ANS: B   DIF: E

5. The agora was located
   a. in Sparta.
   b. in Athens.
   c. at the foot of the acropolis.
   d. at the top of the acropolis.

   ANS: C   DIF: E

MATCHING

Match each item with the correct statement below.

a. agora
b. acropolis
c. Athens
d. Sparta
e. polis

1. city-state
2. fortified hill
3. open-air marketplace
4. had the strongest army in Greece
5. had the strongest navy in Greece

1. ANS: E   DIF: A
2. ANS: B   DIF: A
3. ANS: A   DIF: A
4. ANS: D   DIF: A
5. ANS: C   DIF: A

SHORT ANSWER

1. What classes of citizens settled nearest the marketplace of a Greek city-state?

   ANS:
   artisans, traders, and members of the upper class

   DIF: A

2. Who were the only people in ancient Greece who could be Greek citizens?

   ANS:
   men born in a Greek city-state

   DIF: A

3. What was the most important thing to Greek citizens?

   ANS:
   the good of the polis

   DIF: A

SECTION QUIZ 10-2—SPARTA

MULTIPLE CHOICE

1. Sparta was located in a region of Greece known as
   a. the Chaldeans.
   b. the Peloponnesus.
   c. the elevation of ancient Greece.
   d. the helots.

   ANS: B   DIF: A

2. Spartan citizens were always
   a. helots.
   b. ephors.
   c. aristocrats.
   d. perioeci.

   ANS: C   DIF: A

3. Unhealthy Spartan newborns were
   a. left to die.
   b. given to the perioeci.
   c. given to the ephors.
   d. sold into enslavement.

   ANS: A   DIF: E

4. The life of a Spartan male centered on
   a. business and trade.
   b. farming and trade.
   c. the arts.
   d. physical fitness and military training.

   ANS: D   DIF: E

5. Spartan women
   a. spent most of their time on household tasks.
   b. went out only to attend religious festivals.
   c. did not mix with men.
   d. enjoyed wrestling and racing.

   ANS: D   DIF: E

MATCHING

Match each item with the correct statement below.

a. ephors
b. helots
c. aristocrats
d. perioeci
e. Council of Elders

1. nobles
2. enslaved people
3. merchants and artisans
4. Spartan managers
5. served as Sparta's high court

1. ANS: C DIF: A
2. ANS: B DIF: A
3. ANS: D DIF: A
4. ANS: A DIF: A
5. ANS: E DIF: A

SHORT ANSWER

1. Who held power in Sparta?

   ANS:
   aristocrats

   DIF: A

2. How did Spartan aristocrats control their workers?

   ANS:
   by force

   DIF: E

3. What was Sparta's only goal?

   ANS:
   to be the strongest military city-state

   DIF: E

SECTION QUIZ 10-3—ATHENS

MULTIPLE CHOICE

1. The first Athenian constitution was prepared by
   a. Solon.
   b. Draco.
   c. Peisistratus.
   d. Darius.

   ANS: A DIF: A

2. Another name for Siddhartha Gautama is
   a. Zeus.
   b. Nike.
   c. Darius.
   d. Buddha.

   ANS: D DIF: E

3. The Greek goddess of victory was
   a. Solon.
   b. Nike.
   c. Helen of Troy.
   d. Cleisthenes.

   ANS: B DIF: E

4. Xerxes was the
   a. son of Nike.
   b. son of Peisistratus.
   c. son of Darius.
   d. king of Athens.

   ANS: C DIF: E

5. Which of the following was NOT true of the defensive league?
   a. It was headquartered in Delos.
   b. It was also called the Delian League.
   c. It was formed from a group of city-states.
   d. It ruled Ionia.

   ANS: D DIF: A

MATCHING

Match each item with the correct statement below.

a. triremes
b. democratic
c. mercenaries
d. enlightenment
e. constitution

1. set of rules for governing
2. favoring equality for all
3. hired soldiers
4. understanding
5. ships with three levels of rowers

1. ANS: E DIF: A

2. ANS: B DIF: A
3. ANS: C DIF: A
4. ANS: D DIF: A
5. ANS: A DIF: A

SHORT ANSWER

1. What did the Athenian rulers hope to avoid by changing the government?

   ANS:
   a widespread uprising

   DIF: A

2. Why did people want to be citizens in Athens?

   ANS:
   for the right to serve on the Council of Five Hundred

   DIF: A

3. Why did the Persian king Darius attack Athens?

   ANS:
   Athens had helped the Ionians in a war against Darius.

   DIF: C

4. What city-states fought the Peloponnesian War?

   ANS:
   all the city-states on the Grecian and Peloponnesian peninsulas

   DIF: A

SECTION QUIZ 10-4—DECLINE OF THE CITY-STATES

MULTIPLE CHOICE

1. After the Peloponnesian War,
   a. bitterness developed between the classes.
   b. Philip II of Macedonia ruled Greece.
   c. Thebes ruled Greece.
   d. no one had any money.

   ANS: A DIF: A

2. The rule of Thebes
   a. was gentler than that of Sparta.
   b. was characterized by great wealth.
   c. was no better than that of Sparta.
   d. ended with the Peloponnesian War.

   ANS: C DIF: C

3. Thebes overthrew Sparta in
   a. 338 B.C.
   b. 404 B.C.
   c. 1500 A.D.
   d. 371 B.C.

   ANS: D DIF: E

4. Sparta and Thebes were both
   a. countries.
   b. classes.
   c. city-states.
   d. Greek gods.

   ANS: C DIF: A

5. The city-states of Greece were weakened by
   a. loss of community.
   b. Philip II of Macedonia.
   c. aristocrats.
   d. the rule of Pericles.

   ANS: A DIF: A

MATCHING

Match each item with the correct statement below.
a. Thebes
b. lower class
c. Peloponnesian War
d. Spartans
e. Philip II of Macedonia

1. conquered Greece in 338 B.C.
2. overthrew Spartan rule
3. fought between Sparta and Athens
4. ruled Greece until 371 B.C.
5. opposite of upper class

1. ANS: E DIF: A
2. ANS: A DIF: A
3. ANS: C DIF: A
4. ANS: D DIF: A
5. ANS: B DIF: A

SHORT ANSWER

1. How were the rulers of Sparta and Thebes alike?

   ANS:
   Both were harsh rulers.

   DIF: A

2. How did ancient Greece finally fall?

   ANS:
   Greek city-states became weak and were overthrown by Philip II of Macedonia.

   DIF: A

CHAPTER 11—CULTURAL CONTRIBUTIONS

MULTIPLE CHOICE

1. Which statement best describes religion in ancient Greece?
   a. Greeks thought the gods were cruel and demanded obedience.
   b. Priests and priestesses controlled the government.
   c. Greeks honored their gods by trying to do things well.
   d. The king headed the religion that all Greeks followed.

   ANS: C DIF: E

2. The ancient Olympic Games were held to honor
   a. the god Zeus.
   b. all the gods of Mount Olympus.
   c. the god Dionysus.
   d. the rulers of Greece.

   ANS: A DIF: E

3. The Olympic event that tested skill in running, discus-throwing, and three other sports was called the
   a. pancratium.
   b. pentathlon.
   c. Hippodrome.
   d. Olympiad.

   ANS: B DIF: E

4. Aeschylus created the first real play by
   a. writing stories for the chorus to chant.
   b. having two characters act out a story.
   c. having the chorus leader speak alone.
   d. writing parts that women could act.

   ANS: B DIF: A

5. Early Greek comedies generally poked fun at
   a. political figures.
   b. legendary heroes.
   c. gods and goddesses.
   d. ordinary citizens.

   ANS: A DIF: A

6. Sophocles and Euripides were famous as
   a. Olympic athletes.
   b. scientists.
   c. philosophers and teachers.
   d. writers of tragedies.

   ANS: D DIF: C

7. What we know about Socrates' philosophy comes from
   a. the speeches of characters in his plays.
   b. the ideas he makes fun of in his comedies.
   c. his speeches and discussions written down by Plato.
   d. the books he wrote for students at the Academy.

   ANS: C DIF: C

8. Plato's *Republic* is the first book written about
   a. the scientific method.
   b. medical science.
   c. Greek tragedy.
   d. political science.

   ANS: D DIF: A

9. Which Greek thinker believed that illnesses came from natural causes, not evil spirits?
   a. Thales of Miletus
   b. Aristophanes
   c. Hippocrates
   d. Socrates

   ANS: C DIF: A

10. Which Greek thinker used logical methods and observation to study the natural world?
    a. Aristotle
    b. Plato
    c. Euripides
    d. Socrates

    ANS: A DIF: A

11. The Greeks believed that the better their skills were,
    a. the better people they would be.
    b. the more olive wreaths they would win.
    c. the more they honored their gods.
    d. the more countries they could defeat in war.

    ANS: C DIF: A

12. A person who asked advice from the oracles
    a. traveled to Mount Olympus.
    b. often had to decide the true meaning of the advice.
    c. first asked his or her father's advice.
    d. offered sacrifice to the twelve gods.

    ANS: B DIF: C

13. Olympic winners were honored with
    a. parades, poems, and free meals.
    b. medals and new sports equipment.
    c. new Greek coins.
    d. a trip to a Greek colony.

    ANS: A DIF: A

14. The idea of a play came about when
    a. stories about gods and heroes were acted out.
    b. Greek theatres were built in the open air.
    c. all Greek citizens were required to attend.
    d. Greek actors began to wear costumes and masks.

    ANS: A DIF: A

15. *Philosophia* included study of the natural world and
   a. learning about different kinds of government.
   b. listening to Socrates.
   c. giving up private business.
   d. the search for truth.

   ANS: D DIF: A

16. The goal of Greek scientists was
   a. to make Greek life easier and better.
   b. to add to their store of knowledge.
   c. to figure out the gods' actions.
   d. to invent telescopes, microscopes, and scales.

   ANS: B DIF: A

MATCHING

Match each item with the correct statement below.

a. Socrates
b. Euripides
c. Hippocrates
d. Aeschylus
e. Thales
f. Herodotus
g. Aristophanes
h. Aristotle
i. Dionysus
j. Plato

1. Writer of comic plays
2. Athenian philosopher who was interested in the thinking process and encouraged self-knowledge
3. God whose festivals featured dance and drama
4. Earliest writer to create a two-character play
5. Scholar and teacher known as "the master of them that know" who was first to classify plants and animals
6. Scientist considered the "Father of Scientific Medicine"
7. Pupil of Socrates and founder of the Academy
8. Writer of tragedies about suffering caused by people doing bad things
9. Early scientist who encouraged observation
10. Writer of histories

1. ANS: G DIF: A
2. ANS: A DIF: A
3. ANS: I DIF: A
4. ANS: D DIF: A
5. ANS: H DIF: A
6. ANS: C DIF: A
7. ANS: J DIF: A
8. ANS: B DIF: A
9. ANS: E DIF: A
10. ANS: F DIF: A

SHORT ANSWER

1. How are the modern Olympic Games similar to the original ones? What are some differences?

   ANS:
   Answers will vary, but could include: SIMILARITIES: held every four years; people came from other countries to compete; DIFFERENCES: no longer in honor of Zeus; only men could compete.

   DIF: A

2. Study the map below. Describe where Mount Olympus is in relation to Athens. Use both cardinal and intermediate directions and latitude and longitude, as well as country and city names.

   ANS:
   Mount Olympus lies at latitude 41° N and longitude 22° E. It is northwest of Athens in Macedonia.

   DIF: A

SECTION QUIZ 11-1—RELIGIOUS PRACTICES

MULTIPLE CHOICE

1. The home of the Greek gods was
   a. Olympia.
   b. Mount Olympus.
   c. Asia Minor.
   d. the Hippodrome.

   ANS: B DIF: E

2. The first Greek plays were
   a. tragedies.
   b. comedies.
   c. melodramas.
   d. written by Aristophanes.

   ANS: A DIF: A

3. What came to be known as a play was created by
   a. Aristophanes.
   b. Zeus.
   c. Aeschylus.
   d. Euripides.

   ANS: C DIF: A

4. Greek comedies
   a. were also called soliloquies.
   b. had unhappy endings.
   c. had happy endings.
   d. were invented by Aristophanes.

   ANS: C DIF: A

5. Theater grew out of festivals honoring
   a. Zeus.
   b. Dionysus.
   c. Aeschylus.
   d. Euripides.

   ANS: B DIF: C

MATCHING

Match each item with the correct statement below.

a. prophecy
b. pancratium
c. oracles
d. pentathlon
e. Olympic Games

1. believed to speak to gods
2. festival to honor Zeus
3. fighting event
4. made up of five events
5. prediction of the future

1. ANS: C DIF: A
2. ANS: E DIF: A
3. ANS: B DIF: A

4. ANS: D DIF: A
5. ANS: A DIF: A

SHORT ANSWER

1. Who was in charge of religious ceremonies in ancient Greece?

   ANS:
   city-state officials

   DIF: A

2. What value let the Greeks approach their gods with dignity?

   ANS:
   self-respect

   DIF: A

3. What prize was awarded to Olympic winners?

   ANS:
   an olive-leaf wreath

   DIF: E

4. Who paid for the staging of Greek plays?

   ANS:
   wealthy citizens

   DIF: E

SECTION QUIZ 11-2—SCIENCE

MULTIPLE CHOICE

1. The "Father of Scientific Medicine" was
   a. Euripides.
   b. Hippocrates.
   c. Sophocles.
   d. Thales of Miletus.

   ANS: B DIF: E

2. One of Plato's brightest pupils was
   a. Sophocles.
   b. Hippocrates.
   c. Aristotle.
   d. Socrates.

   ANS: C DIF: A

3. Which of the following was NOT true of Socrates?
   a. He was a student of Plato.
   b. He was executed.
   c. He was interested in the thinking process.
   d. He left no writings after his death.

   ANS: A DIF: A

4. Plato set down his ideas about an ideal state in
   a. *The Dialogues.*
   b. *The Republic.*
   c. *The State.*
   d. *The Poetics.*

   ANS: B DIF: A

5. A method of reasoning using three related statements is
   a. a syllogism.
   b. a hypothesis.
   c. *The Dialogues.*
   d. the Hippocratic Oath.

   ANS: A DIF: C

MATCHING

Match each item with the correct statement below.
a. philosophia
b. hypothesis
c. scientific method
d. Socratic method
e. political science

1. "the study of the laws of nature"
2. possible explanation
3. form of questioning
4. the study of government
5. process used by scientists

1. ANS: A DIF: A
2. ANS: B DIF: A
3. ANS: D DIF: A
4. ANS: E DIF: A
5. ANS: C DIF: A

SHORT ANSWER

1. What quality caused the Greeks to question things and study the laws of nature?

   ANS:
   the ability to learn and reason; intellect

   DIF: C

2. Why did some Athenians dislike Socrates' method of self-examination?

   ANS:
   It pointed out their mistakes and shortcomings.

   DIF: A

3. Whom did Plato hope to train?

   ANS:
   government leaders

   DIF: E

4. How did Plato believe that people would discover truth?

   ANS:
   through a long, hard search

   DIF: A

5. How did Aristotle believe that people could learn about the natural world?

   ANS:
   by using one's senses

   DIF: A

CHAPTER 12—THE HELLENISTIC PERIOD

MULTIPLE CHOICE

1. The Greek city-states lost their independence in 338 B.C. when they were conquered by
   a. Ptolemy of Egypt.
   b. Xerxes of Persia.
   c. the king of Thebes.
   d. Philip II of Macedonia.

   ANS: D DIF: A

2. The kings of Macedonia differed from the ordinary people of their country in that
   a. they were bitter enemies of the Greeks.
   b. their ancestors were Persians.
   c. they were of Greek descent and admired Greek culture.
   d. they were descendants of the defenders of Troy.

   ANS: C DIF: C

3. Which of the following was NOT a tactic used by Philip to take over the Greek city-states?
   a. He developed strong battle formations for his soldiers.
   b. He made public speeches warning the people.
   c. He flattered Greek leaders and gave them gold.
   d. He married wives from countries whose help he wanted.

   ANS: B DIF: E

4. Chaeronea, where Philip defeated the Greek army, is located
   a. north of Greece.
   b. in central Greece.
   c. on the border of Persia.
   d. in the Aegean Sea.

   ANS: B DIF: A

5. The easternmost extent of Alexander's empire was
   a. the Nile River.
   b. the Euphrates River.
   c. the Indus River.
   d. the China River.

   ANS: C DIF: E

6. Alexander learned much about Greek culture, science, and philosophy from
   a. living as a hostage in Thebes.
   b. studying at the library in Alexandria.
   c. attending the Academy in Athens.
   d. having Aristotle as his teacher.

   ANS: D DIF: A

7. As a general, Alexander's first great victory was over
   a. the Persian Empire.
   b. the kingdom of Macedonia.
   c. the Greek city-states.
   d. the kings of India.

   ANS: A DIF: E

8. The cultural and intellectual center of Alexander's empire was
   a. Athens.
   b. Cairo, Egypt.
   c. Alexandria, Egypt.
   d. Babylonia.

   ANS: C DIF: A

9. One result of Alexander's conquests was
   a. an increase in Greek cultural influence.
   b. new power for the Greek city-states.
   c. a decline in trade in the Mediterranean.
   d. unity among the Greeks, Persians, and Macedonians.

   ANS: A DIF: A

10. By the first century B.C., the Greek city-states came under the control of
    a. the Ptolemies of Egypt.
    b. the Romans.
    c. the Persians.
    d. the Macedonians.

    ANS: B DIF: E

COMPLETION

1. Alexander was a greater general and leader than his father, ____________________ .

   ANS: Philip II DIF: A

2. Rulers spread Greek ____________________ through trade.

   ANS: culture DIF: E

3. ____________________ means "like the Greeks."

   ANS: Hellenistic DIF: A

4. The museum at Alexandria, Egypt, boasted the ancient world's largest collection of ____________________.

   ANS: books DIF: E

5. The Greek mathematician Euclid wrote about ____________________.

   ANS: geometry DIF: A

6. The areas of ____________________ that Alexander conquered returned to their original rulers after Alexander died.

   ANS: India DIF: E

7. The cities of Alexander's empire existed chiefly for ____________________.

   ANS: trade DIF: E

8. The laws, language, calendar, coins, business methods, customs, and ideas of the Hellenistic period were ____________________.

ANS: Greek DIF: E

MATCHING

Match each item with the correct statement below.

a. Ptolemies	f. hostage
b. Euclid	g. *barbaroi*
c. Hellenes	h. alliances
d. orator	i. Archimedes
e. factories	j. phalanx

1. Greek scientist who wrote a geometry book
2. Egyptian dynasty started by one of Alexander's generals
3. Places where quantities of goods are made
4. Person noted for skill in public speaking
5. Name given to the people of Greece and its colonies
6. Greek scientist who invented useful machines
7. Person held by an enemy to ensure a bargain is kept
8. Name used by the Greeks for all non-Greek peoples
9. Agreements or partnerships
10. Strong formation of soldiers in battle

1. ANS: B DIF: A
2. ANS: A DIF: A
3. ANS: E DIF: A
4. ANS: D DIF: A
5. ANS: C DIF: A
6. ANS: I DIF: A
7. ANS: F DIF: A
8. ANS: G DIF: A
9. ANS: H DIF: A
10. ANS: J DIF: A

SHORT ANSWER

1. Why do you think people called Alexander "the Great"? Would he have agreed with them? What makes you think so?

ANS:
Answers will vary, but could include: because he made such great contributions to his people and to history; he would have agreed, since he declared himself to be a god.

DIF: A

SECTION QUIZ 12-1—PHILIP II OF MACEDONIA

MULTIPLE CHOICE

1. Demosthenes was
   a. a soldier in Philip of Macedonia's army.
   b. an oracle.
   c. an orator.
   d. a hostage.

   ANS: C DIF: A

2. To Philip II of Macedonia, marriage was
   a. a way of conquering Greece.
   b. a way of forming political alliances.
   c. a romantic ceremony.
   d. destiny.

   ANS: B DIF: A

3. Which of the following was NOT a characteristic of the phalanx?
   a. overlapping shields
   b. charged as a group
   c. 16 rows of foot soldiers
   d. soldiers armed with bows and arrows

   ANS: D DIF: C

4. When Philip of Macedonia was killed,
   a. his wife took over the throne.
   b. his son took over the throne.
   c. Persia took over Greece.
   d. Greece had no ruler.

   ANS: B DIF: E

5. The term "Hellenistic" means
   a. like Helen of Troy.
   b. of the Christian faith.
   c. like the Greeks.
   d. womanly.

   ANS: C DIF: C

6. Macedonian kings were interested in Greek culture because
   a. they wanted all Macedonians to learn about Greek accomplishments.
   b. they wanted to better themselves.
   c. most were descendants of the Greeks.
   d. Greek banking methods were the best in the ancient world.

   ANS: C DIF: A

7. Although Philip admired Greek culture, he
   a. liked the Persian culture better.
   b. thought the Greek form of government had many weaknesses.
   c. believed his duty was to spread Macedonian culture.
   d. wanted to make changes in it.

   ANS: B DIF: A

MATCHING

Match each item with the correct statement below.

a. orator
b. alliance
c. phalanx
d. Philip II of Macedonia
e. hostage

1. person held by an enemy
2. infantry formation
3. partnership
4. public speaker
5. ruler of Greece in 338 B.C.

1. ANS: E DIF: A
2. ANS: C DIF: A
3. ANS: B DIF: A
4. ANS: A DIF: A
5. ANS: D DIF: A

SECTION QUIZ 12-2—ALEXANDER THE GREAT

MULTIPLE CHOICE

1. Alexander was a student of
   a. Aristotle.
   b. Euclid.
   c. Eratosthenes.
   d. Archimedes.

   ANS: A DIF: E

2. The most noted Alexandria was in
   a. Greece.
   b. Egypt.
   c. Spain.
   d. Ptolemy.

   ANS: B DIF: E

3. Hellenistic cities
   a. had more power than earlier city-states.
   b. contained great factories.
   c. were low in population.
   d. were governed by philosophers.

   ANS: B DIF: C

4. By 146 B.C., most Greek city-states were
   a. in ruins.
   b. overpopulated.
   c. under Roman control.
   d. owned by Persia.

   ANS: C DIF: A

5. Ptolemy established
   a. the Royal Tombs of Alexandria.
   b. great factories.
   c. the Seven Wonders of the World.
   d. a dynasty in Egypt.

   ANS: A DIF: C

MATCHING

Match each item with the correct statement below.

a. breakwater
b. *barbaroi*
c. emigrate
d. Alexander
e. factories

1. son of Philip II of Macedonia
2. barbarians
3. places where goods are made
4. barrier against waves
5. leave one place to settle another

1. ANS: D DIF: A
2. ANS: B DIF: A
3. ANS: E DIF: A
4. ANS: A DIF: A
5. ANS: C DIF: A

Match each cause with the effect it produced.

a. there were not enough people to fight them off.
b. leaders could not agree on a single ruler.
c. the Persians had a different language and different customs.
d. Alexander admired his teacher Aristotle, a scientist and philosopher.
e. his troops refused to go there.

6. Philosophers and scientists were part of Alexander's army because ____
7. Alexander could not extend his empire into India because ____
8. The Greeks objected to equality for Persians because ____
9. After Alexander's death, his empire broke apart because ____
10. Most of the Greek city-states fell to the Romans because ____

6. ANS: D DIF: A
7. ANS: E DIF: A
8. ANS: C DIF: A
9. ANS: B DIF: A
10. ANS: A DIF: A

CHAPTER 13—BEGINNINGS

MULTIPLE CHOICE

1. The first settlement at Rome was built
   a. on the Balkan Peninsula.
   b. on the Palatine hill.
   c. on the ruins of Troy.
   d. on the Capitoline hill.

   ANS: B DIF: A

2. According to historians, the founders of Rome were
   a. Trojans.
   b. Latins.
   c. Lydians.
   d. Etruscans.

   ANS: A DIF: A

3. Which is the best description of an Etruscan city?
   a. Wooden huts at the base of a hill
   b. Dome-shaped houses made of dirt
   c. Brick houses on a hilltop surrounded by a wall
   d. Stone houses around a central temple

   ANS: C DIF: E

4. Many historians believe the Etruscans came originally from
   a. southern Russia.
   b. Troy in Asia Minor.
   c. Lydia in Asia Minor.
   d. the island of Crete.

   ANS: C DIF: C

5. Which of the following was a characteristic of Etruscan society?
   a. Democratic ideals and no class differences
   b. Little regard for religion or religious rituals
   c. Relative equality and freedom for women
   d. Emphasis on farming rather than trading by sea

   ANS: C DIF: C

6. In Etruscan society, soothsayers were people who
   a. worked with metals.
   b. predicted the future.
   c. sailed pirate ships.
   d. led the army.

   ANS: B DIF: E

7. Lucius Tarquinius is important in Roman history as
   a. the hero who overthrew the Etruscans.
   b. a legendary king raised by a wolf.
   c. the first Etruscan ruler of Rome.
   d. builder of the first settlement on the Palatine hill.

   ANS: C DIF: C

8. The Roman custom of fights between gladiators came from
   a. an Etruscan funeral custom.
   b. a way of planning cities.
   c. a soothsayer's prediction.
   d. a welcome for heroes.

   ANS: A DIF: A

9. Where was the site of both the first temple in Rome and modern Rome's municipal government?
   a. Forum
   b. Mundus
   c. Palatine hill
   d. Capitoline hill

   ANS: D DIF: E

10. Which of the following aspects of Roman culture did NOT come from the Etruscans?
    a. Dome-shaped houses made of dirt
    b. The arch in building bridges
    c. Alphabet
    d. Belief in omens

    ANS: A DIF: A

MATCHING

Match each item with the correct statement below.

a. Latins
b. Aeneas
c. necropolis
d. mundus
e. forum
f. catacombs
g. Romulus
h. triumph
i. omens
j. fasces

1. Meeting point for the worlds of the living and the dead marked by a stone where two streets met
2. Underground tombs carved in rock
3. Bundle of rods bound around an ax symbolizing authority
4. Events interpreted as signs of the future
5. Trojan hero, legendary founder of the Roman people
6. Procession honoring a hero
7. First settlers of land near Rome
8. Cemetery area containing many tombs
9. Public square of a city where a palace, government buildings, and law courts were located
10. Founder and first king of the city of Rome

1. ANS: D DIF: A
2. ANS: F DIF: A
3. ANS: J DIF: A
4. ANS: I DIF: A
5. ANS: B DIF: A
6. ANS: H DIF: A
7. ANS: A DIF: A
8. ANS: C DIF: A
9. ANS: E DIF: A
10. ANS: G DIF: A

SHORT ANSWER

1. What qualities of the Etruscans and their way of life made them deserve to be called "Italy's first highly civilized people"?

   ANS:
   Answers will vary, but could include: their use of an alphabet; their successful trading, farming, mining, and army; and the foundations their civilization laid for the grandness of the later Roman Empire.

   DIF: A

2. Why is Rome often called "The City of the Seven Hills?"

   ANS:
   because it was built on seven hills

   DIF: E

3. What rivers flowed through Etruria?

   ANS:
   the Tiber and the Arno

   DIF: A

4. What people took over the Latin people and settlements?

   ANS:
   Etruscans

   DIF: A

5. Where do scholars think the Etruscans came from?

   ANS:
   the kingdom of Lydia in Asia Minor

   DIF: C

6. What relationship did the Etruscans have with their gods?

   ANS:
   Etruscans believed that humans were powerless before their gods and should want to please them.

   DIF: A

7. How did the Etruscans use the seven hills to protect their cities?

   ANS:
   They built cities on the hilltops, surrounded by thick walls.

   DIF: A

SECTION QUIZ 13-1—FOUNDING OF ROME

MULTIPLE CHOICE

1. Which of the following was NOT true of Romulus and Remus?
   a. They were left to die on a riverbank.
   b. They were found by a wolf.
   c. They were killed by wolves.
   d. They wanted the gods to choose between them.

   ANS: C DIF: E

2. Romulus and Remus were
   a. twins.
   b. wolves.
   c. princes.
   d. Palestinians.

   ANS: A DIF: E

3. Rome was given its name by
   a. Aeneas.
   b. Romulus.
   c. Remus.
   d. Mars.

   ANS: B DIF: E

4. In the legend, the she-wolf
   a. kills Romulus and Remus.
   b. kills Remus.
   c. is killed by a hunter.
   d. is killed by a shepherd.

   ANS: D DIF: E

5. The area where the Latins settled
   a. was on the Balkan Peninsula.
   b. had a cold, snowy climate.
   c. was on the Palatine.
   d. was in Egypt.

   ANS: C DIF: C

COMPLETION

1. Rome is named after ____________________, a legendary ____________________.

   ANS: Romulus; king DIF: A

2. Latin invaders settled on the Palatine, which had fertile ____________________, a pleasant ____________________, and dense ____________________.

ANS: soil; climate; forests DIF: A

3. The Latins built ____________________ roads to bring trade items inland from the ____________________.

ANS: gravel; coast DIF: A

MATCHING

Match each item with the correct statement below.

a. Mars
b. Aeneas
c. Remus
d. Romulus
e. Latins

1. was killed by his brother
2. king of Rome
3. Trojan prince
4. father of Romulus and Remus
5. group that settled on the Palatine

1. ANS: C DIF: A
2. ANS: D DIF: A
3. ANS: B DIF: A
4. ANS: A DIF: A
5. ANS: E DIF: A

SECTION QUIZ 13-2—THE ETRUSCANS

MULTIPLE CHOICE

1. Political maps show
   a. the great democracies of the world.
   b. the reign of Romulus.
   c. the rulers of the Shang.
   d. areas ruled by particular governments.

ANS: D DIF: A

2. In about 800 B.C., the Etruscans settled in
   a. Estonia.
   b. Etruria.
   c. Etruscia.
   d. Lydia.

ANS: B DIF: A

3. The Etruscans were called the
   a. first great warriors of Greece.
   b. boat people.
   c. people of the sea.
   d. best pirates in the world.

ANS: C DIF: C

4. The Etruscan army learned about batt e techniques from
   a. the Egyptians.
   b. the Greeks.
   c. Romulus.
   d. Zeus.

ANS: B DIF: C

5. One of the largest Etruscan cemeteries is
   a. outside the city of Lyre.
   b. in Lydia.
   c. outside the city of Caere.
   d. in Rome.

ANS: C DIF: E

MATCHING

Match each item with the correct statement below.

a. soothsayers
b. catacombs
c. omens
d. necropolis
e. social order

1. people who predict the future
2. how groups are classed
3. underground tombs
4. cemetery
5. signs of the future

1. ANS: A DIF: A
2. ANS: E DIF: A
3. ANS: B DIF: A
4. ANS: D DIF: A
5. ANS: C DIF: A

SHORT ANSWER

1. How did the Etruscans interact with their environment to make it livable?

ANS:
They dug tunnels and built dams to drain the marshes, and they built cities on tops of hills.

DIF: A

2. What two major occupations did the Etruscans engage in?

ANS:
trade and piracy

DIF: A

3. From what civilization did the Etruscans learn about warfare?

ANS:
Greek civilization

DIF: E

4. How was the life of Etruscan women different from the lives of Greek and Latin women?

ANS:
Etruscan women had more freedom, participated in public celebrations, and could own property.

DIF: A

5. How do scholars know so much about Etruscan life?

ANS:
through many artifacts, tombs, and cemeteries

DIF: A

SECTION QUIZ 13-3—ETRUSCANS AND ROMANS

MULTIPLE CHOICE

1. Lucius Tarquinius was
   a. the first Greek ruler of Rome.
   b. the first philosopher king.
   c. the first Etruscan ruler of Rome.
   d. a Latin king of Rome.

   ANS: C DIF: A

2. Gladiatorial games were
   a. held at funerals.
   b. held at weddings.
   c. played in the catacombs.
   d. usually played by young children.

   ANS: A DIF: C

3. The Romans believed mundus was
   a. a cemetery.
   b. a war among the gods.
   c. the intersection between the living and the dead.
   d. the sacred chamber of the gods.

   ANS: C DIF: E

4. Capitoline is
   a. one of the Seven Wonders of the World.
   b. one of the seven hills of Rome.
   c. the world's oldest cemetery.
   d. a parade-like welcome for a hero.

   ANS: B DIF: E

5. Roman city boundaries were decided by
   a. slaves.
   b. Lucius Tarquinius.
   c. soothsayers.
   d. the municipal council.

   ANS: C DIF: A

MATCHING

Match each item with the correct statement below.
a. Forum
b. triumph
c. gladiatorial games
d. fasces
e. municipal

1. fights of enslaved people
2. parade-like welcome
3. bundle of rods tied around an ax
4. Rome's public square
5. relating to a city

1. ANS: C DIF: A
2. ANS: B DIF: A
3. ANS: D DIF: A
4. ANS: A DIF: A
5. ANS: E DIF: A

SHORT ANSWER

1. What architectural advances did the Etruscans give the Romans?

   ANS:
   the arch and the sewer system

   DIF: A

2. What religious beliefs did the Romans adopt from the Etruscans?

ANS:
soothsayers, gods in human form

DIF: A

CHAPTER 14—THE ROMAN REPUBLIC

MULTIPLE CHOICE

1. In the early years of the Roman Republic, real political power belonged to
   a. the Senate.
   b. the patricians.
   c. the plebeians.
   d. tribunes.

   ANS: B DIF: C

2. The Twelve Tables of written laws were an important step because
   a. Rome had no laws before that time.
   b. they gave plebeians citizenship for the first time.
   c. they made laws public for all citizens to read.
   d. plebeians gained more rights that patricians.

   ANS: C DIF: A

3. After the Romans overthrew their Etruscan king, they created
   a. a republic.
   b. a dictator.
   c. legionaries.
   d. a corvus.

   ANS: A DIF: E

4. By about 275 B.C., the territory controlled by Rome included
   a. much of central Italy.
   b. Italy and North Africa.
   c. all of Italy and Greece.
   d. the whole Italian peninsula.

   ANS: D DIF: E

5. The Punic Wars were a long series of conflicts between
   a. Greece and Rome.
   b. Rome and Carthage.
   c. Generals Marius and Sulla.
   d. Romans and Etruscans.

   ANS: B DIF: E

6. Rome's victories in the Punic Wars brought it territory in
   a. Macedonia and Syria.
   b. Greece and its islands.
   c. Spain, North Africa, and Sicily.
   d. Etruria and northern Italy.

   ANS: C DIF: A

7. Which of these was NOT a cause of hardship for Roman farmers?
   a. Hannibal's siege of Rome
   b. Growth of latifundias
   c. Reforms by the Gracchi
   d. Enslaving war prisoners

   ANS: C DIF: A

8. The military hero who began paying professional soldiers to join the army was
   a. Julius Caesar.
   b. Gaius Marius.
   c. Gaius Gracchus.
   d. Hannibal Barca.

   ANS: B DIF: A

9. The group who planned to kill Julius Caesar included
   a. Romans angry about unemployment.
   b. former soldiers who wanted land.
   c. senators who feared he would become king.
   d. political rivals who wanted Pompey to be consul.

   ANS: C DIF: A

10. The civil war that followed the death of Caesar ended with
    a. a new Senate.
    b. victory for Mark Antony.
    c. a loss of Roman lands.
    d. victory for Octavian.

    ANS: D DIF: A

MATCHING

Match each item with the correct statement below.

a. consuls
b. legionaries
c. dictator
d. patricians
e. veto
f. triumvirate
g. publicans
h. tribunes
i. plebeians
j. latifundias

1. Members of Rome's old and wealthy families
2. Officials who protected citizens' rights
3. Tax collectors in the Roman provinces
4. Three-person group of rulers
5. Soldiers in the Roman army
6. Ordinary citizens of Rome
7. Administrative and military leaders of the Roman Republic
8. One ruler who has absolute power
9. Power to cancel another person's decision
10. Large farm estates near Rome

1. ANS: D DIF: A
2. ANS: H DIF: A
3. ANS: G DIF: A
4. ANS: F DIF: A
5. ANS: B DIF: A
6. ANS: I DIF: A
7. ANS: A DIF: A
8. ANS: C DIF: A
9. ANS: E DIF: A
10. ANS: J DIF: A

SHORT ANSWER

1. Compare the system of government in the United States to that of the Roman Republic. What are some similarities and differences?

   ANS:
   Answers will vary, but could include: SIMILARITIES: government officials represented the people; DIFFERENCES: two consuls headed Roman government; one president heads that of the United States.

   DIF: A

2. Look at the map below. Identify the continents, or parts of continents, and countries that were part of the Roman Republic at the time of Julius Caesar's death.

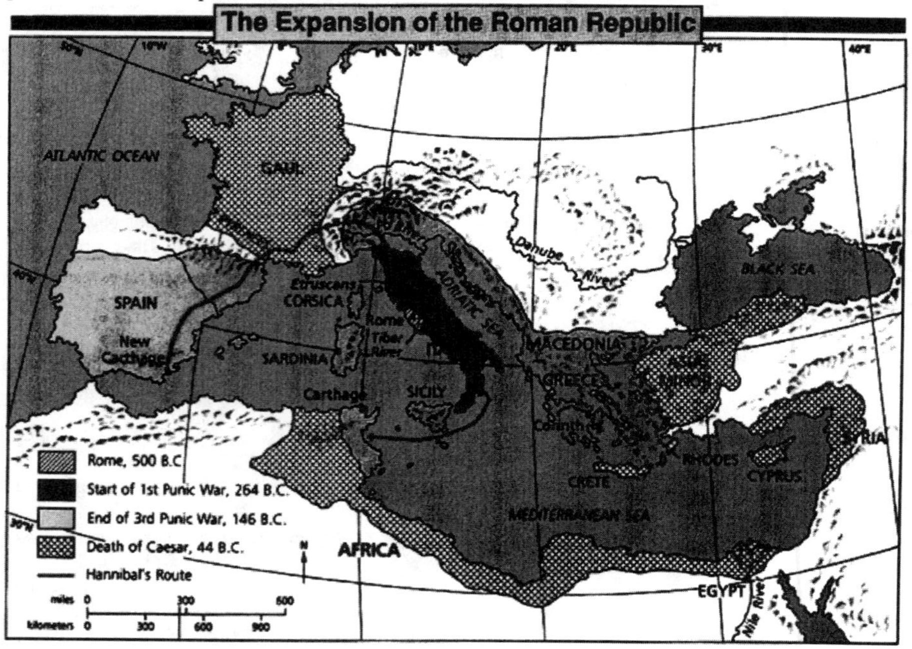

   ANS:
   Continents: Europe, Africa, Asia
   Countries: Spain, Gaul, Italy, Sardinia, Corsica, Sicily, Macedonia, Greece, Crete, Egypt, Cyprus, Rhodes, Syria

   DIF: C

SECTION QUIZ 14-1—THE GOVERNMENT

MULTIPLE CHOICE

1. The Roman Senate was made up of
   a. 300 men and women.
   b. 300 men.
   c. 300 women.
   d. 600 men.

   ANS: B DIF: A

2. Two consuls headed the
   a. Roman Republic.
   b. Senate.
   c. Twelve Tables.
   d. Tribune.

   ANS: A DIF: C

3. Roman laws were not written down until
   a. about 494 B.C.
   b. about 450 B.C.
   c. 250 B.C.
   d. 12 B.C.

   ANS: B DIF: C

4. The foundation for all future Roman law came from the
   a. Senate.
   b. plebeians.
   c. patricians.
   d. Twelve Tables.

   ANS: D DIF: E

5. Which of the following was NOT originally part of Roman government?
   a. tribunes
   b. judges
   c. plebeians
   d. assemblies

   ANS: C DIF: E

MATCHING

Match each item with the correct statement below.

a. plebeians
b. veto
c. patricians
d. tribunes
e. consuls

1. say no to
2. groups that ran the Roman Republic
3. Roman upper class
4. Roman lower class
5. government officials

1. ANS: B DIF: A
2. ANS: E DIF: A
3. ANS: C DIF: A

4. ANS: A DIF: A
5. ANS: D DIF: A

SHORT ANSWER

1. How often did Roman citizens elect consuls?

   ANS:
   every year

   DIF: A

2. What political business was discussed by the assemblies?

   ANS:
   They discussed dealings with other countries, proposal of laws, and approval of public contracts for building roads and temples.

   DIF: A

3. How did the law concerning debt change?

   ANS:
   No one could be sold into slavery because of debt.

   DIF: A

4. In what way did the plebeians finally gain equality with the patricians?

   ANS:
   Plebeians gained the right to hold public office.

   DIF: A

SECTION QUIZ 14-2—ROMAN EXPANSION

MULTIPLE CHOICE

1. Each Roman legion
   a. contained 5,000 soldiers.
   b. fought in groups of 500.
   c. depended on his own fighting ability.
   d. had his own double-edged sword.

   ANS: A DIF: A

2. Which of the following was NOT true of legionaries?
   a. They went on long marches.
   b. They used double-edged swords.
   c. They fought as a group, attacking from one direction.
   d. Each depended on his own fighting ability.

   ANS: D DIF: C

3. The Romans were
   a. harsh rulers.
   b. petty dictators.
   c. mild rulers.
   d. overthrown in 275 B.C.

   ANS: C DIF: E

4. Before going to sleep after a long march, legionaries
   a. built roads for supplies.
   b. practiced their formations.
   c. divided into groups of 60.
   d. built fortified camps.

   ANS: D DIF: C

5. By 290 B.C., Rome
   a. ruled most of the Mediterranean world.
   b. was the leading power in central Italy.
   c. had taken over Spain.
   d. was beginning to lose its power.

   ANS: B DIF: A

COMPLETION

1. Romans treated neighboring countries in two ways: they ____________________ them or made ____________________ with them.

   ANS: conquered; alliances DIF: A

2. Groups of soldiers in a Roman ____________________ could attack from different directions: either from the side, front, or back.

   ANS: legion DIF: A

3. Roman soldiers and supply trains could move quickly due to ____________________ made of lava blocks.

   ANS: roads DIF: A

4. Rome's mild treatment of conquered people often turned them from enemies to ____________________.

   ANS: loyal allies DIF: A

MATCHING

Match each item with the correct statement below.

a. legionaries
b. legions
c. double-edged
d. Rome
e. lava blocks

1. Roman military segment
2. soldiers in Roman army
3. type of iron sword
4. Roman road-building material
5. ruled the Mediterranean world

1. ANS: B DIF: A
2. ANS: A DIF: A
3. ANS: C DIF: A
4. ANS: E DIF: A
5. ANS: D DIF: A

SECTION QUIZ 14-3—THE PUNIC WARS

MULTIPLE CHOICE

1. The war that began in 264 B.C. was
   a. the First Punic War.
   b. the Second Punic War.
   c. the Third Punic War.
   d. Hannibal's War.

   ANS: A DIF: C

2. General Hannibal Barca fought in
   a. the First Punic War.
   b. the Second Punic War.
   c. the Third Punic War.
   d. the Fourth Punic War.

   ANS: B DIF: C

3. Hannibal's troops surprised the Romans by
   a. marching through Egypt into Rome.
   b. crossing the Alps into Italy.
   c. attacking only by sea.
   d. winning a battle at Zama.

   ANS: B DIF: A

4. Hannibal was from
   a. Zama.
   b. Corinth.
   c. Carthage.
   d. Rome.

   ANS: C DIF: E

5. Following the Second Punic War,
   a. there was peace for 50 years.
   b. Romans plowed salt into Carthaginian fields.
   c. Romans burned Corinth to the ground.
   d. Carthage destroyed Corinth.

   ANS: A DIF: A

MATCHING

Match each item with the correct statement below.

a. Carthage
b. Corinth
c. Hannibal
d. corvus
e. Gaul

1. Phoenician city
2. movable bridge
3. leader of the Carthaginian army
4. Greek city-state
5. present-day France

1. ANS: A DIF: A
2. ANS: D DIF: A
3. ANS: C DIF: A
4. ANS: B DIF: A
5. ANS: E DIF: A

SHORT ANSWER

1. Why did Rome go to war with Carthage?

   ANS:
   Rome felt threatened and also wanted Carthage's granaries.

   DIF: E

2. What Carthaginian equipment did the Romans copy?

   ANS:
   the equipment of Carthage's navy

   DIF: A

3. Why didn't Hannibal win the Second Punic War?

   ANS:
   He had no heavy equipment to batter down city walls.

   DIF: A

4. What country did Rome conquer to become a world leader?

ANS:
Greece

DIF: A

SECTION QUIZ 14-4—EFFECTS OF CONQUEST

MULTIPLE CHOICE

1. After the Punic Wars,
   a. small farms were replaced by large estates.
   b. Hannibal freed the enslaved.
   c. the Romans voted for lower taxes.
   d. most farmers prospered.

   ANS: A DIF: A

2. About 135 B.C.,
   a. Hannibal invaded Rome.
   b. the Second Punic War began.
   c. Rome was no longer politically stable.
   d. Rome was overthrown by Carthage.

   ANS: C DIF: C

3. When the Second Punic War ended,
   a. much Roman land was ruined.
   b. Carthage and Rome signed a peace agreement.
   c. Rome gave Corinth to Carthage.
   d. enslaved people revolted.

   ANS: A DIF: C

4. Latifundias
   a. fought in the Punic Wars.
   b. produced wheat.
   c. collected taxes from the conquered people.
   d. produced crops, cattle, and sheep.

   ANS: D DIF: A

5. Latifundias were owned by
   a. Roman patricians.
   b. Roman plebeians.
   c. Carthaginian soldiers.
   d. Syrian nobles.

   ANS: A DIF: E

MATCHING

Match each item with the correct statement below.
a. publicans
b. typhus
c. Second Punic War
d. mosaic
e. latifundias

1. large estates
2. tax collectors
3. life-threatening disease
4. floor decoration
5. caused Romans to burn farmland

1. ANS: E DIF: A
2. ANS: A DIF: A
3. ANS: B DIF: A
4. ANS: D DIF: A
5. ANS: C DIF: A

SHORT ANSWER

1. Why did the Romans introduce slavery?

   ANS:
   They were copying some customs of countries they conquered.

   DIF: A

2. How did poor sanitary conditions in Rome affect people's health?

   ANS:
   It caused the spread of many communicable diseases and a weakening of general health.

   DIF: C

3. How did many ex-farmers make money when they moved to Rome?

   ANS:
   as construction workers and by selling votes to politicians

   DIF: A

4. How did the rich feel about Rome's poor?

   ANS:
   They hated and feared the poor.

   DIF: A

SECTION QUIZ 14-5—ROMAN LEADERSHIP

MULTIPLE CHOICE

1. The first Roman reformer was
   a. Tiberius Gracchus.
   b. Gaius Gracchus.
   c. Gaius Marius.
   d. Marcus Antonius.

   ANS: A DIF: A

2. The First Triumvirate was made up of
   a. Octavian, Lepidus, and Marcus Antonius.
   b. Greece, Spain, and Rome.
   c. Crassus, Pompeius, and Caesar.
   d. the Gauls, the Egyptians, and the Romans.

   ANS: C DIF: A

3. Caesar was killed by
   a. plebeian rebels.
   b. latifundias.
   c. publicans.
   d. senators.

   ANS: D DIF: E

4. By 31 B.C., the sole leader of Rome was
   a. Caesar.
   b. Octavian.
   c. Mark Antony.
   d. Gnaeus Pompeius.

   ANS: B DIF: E

5. Which of the following was NOT true of Gnaeus Pompeius?
   a. He was known as Pompey.
   b. He believed in one-man rule.
   c. He was part of the First Triumvirate.
   d. He was murdered.

   ANS: B DIF: C

MATCHING

Match each item with the correct statement below.
a. Octavian
b. booty
c. the Ides of March
d. dictator
e. triumvirate

1. things taken from the enemy in war
2. absolute ruler
3. group of three with equal power
4. day on which Caesar was killed
5. Caesar's adopted son

1. ANS: B DIF: A
2. ANS: D DIF: A
3. ANS: E DIF: A
4. ANS: C DIF: A
5. ANS: A DIF: A

SHORT ANSWER

1. How were the Gracchi removed from office?

   ANS:
   through assassination

   DIF: A

2. Why was the war between the armies of Marius and Sulla a *civil* war?

   ANS:
   because two groups of citizens from the same country were fighting

   DIF: C

3. What kinds of support did Caesar have that helped him gain control of Rome?

   ANS:
   He had the support of the military and strong family alliances.

   DIF: A

CHAPTER 15—THE ROMAN EMPIRE

MULTIPLE CHOICE

1. The Roman emperor who was called the "Father of the Country" was
   a. Marcus Aurelius.
   b. Julius Caesar.
   c. Augustus.
   d. Constantine.

   ANS: C DIF: A

2. Augustus's main aim as emperor was
   a. conquering new territories to extend the empire.
   b. bringing new religious ideas to Rome.
   c. establishing the empire as stable and peaceful.
   d. dividing the empire to make his rule easier.

   ANS: C DIF: A

3. Under Augustus, the northern boundary of the empire was
   a. the Rhine and Danube rivers.
   b. the Tiber and Po rivers.
   c. the Alps.
   d. the English Channel.

   ANS: A DIF: C

4. The population count that Augustus ordered was called
   a. a *domus*.
   b. a census.
   c. an omen.
   d. a tariff.

   ANS: B DIF: E

5. What was the *Pax Romana*?
   a. The 41 years of Augustus's reign
   b. A system for choosing new emperors
   c. The standardization of Roman law
   d. A 200-year period of peace for Rome

   ANS: D DIF: E

6. As the empire expanded, Roman law changed because
   a. different laws were needed for each new territory.
   b. laws had to favor Romans over non-Romans.
   c. laws needed to be the same throughout the empire.
   d. there was a lack of skilled lawyers.

   ANS: C DIF: C

7. During the republic, Roman politicians sponsored public games in order to
   a. provide jobs for gladiators.
   b. educate the public.
   c. win people's votes.
   d. sell tickets at a profit.

   ANS: C DIF: E

8. Most city dwellers in Rome lived in
   a. small wooden huts.
   b. crowded apartments.
   c. a comfortable *domus*.
   d. the public baths.

   ANS: B DIF: A

9. From about 190 to 284 A.D., most Roman emperors were chosen by
   a. the Roman army.
   b. the adoption system.
   c. Germanic tribal chiefs.
   d. the citizens of Rome.

   ANS: A DIF: A

10. Which of these was NOT a cause of the fall of the empire?
    a. Economic problems
    b. Poor leadership
    c. Germanic invasions
    d. Unfair laws

    ANS: D DIF: C

11. Augustus cleverly appeared to
    a. change his name and the offices he held.
    b. fix the boundaries of Rome so that it was smaller.
    c. balance power between himself and the Senate.
    d. run the Roman government for 200 years.

    ANS: C DIF: A

12. Augustus preferred to improve the government instead of
    a. building libraries and theatres.
    b. conquering more territories.
    c. writing stricter laws.
    d. encouraging learning.

    ANS: B DIF: A

13. During his 41-year rule, Augustus
    a. let public officials keep tax money.
    b. ordered a population increase.
    c. brought peace, patriotism, and pride to Rome.
    d. appointed people to office because of their births.

    ANS: C DIF: A

14. For most Romans, life in the city of Rome was
    a. private and cheap.
    b. an improvement from that of the domus.
    c. oriented around politics and pleasure.
    d. crowded and expensive.

    ANS: D DIF: A

15. Diocletian's policy of rule by divine right meant that he
    a. ruled the eastern, or right, half of the Roman Empire.
    b. took away the people's right to choose leaders.
    c. made only good and right decisions for the Roman Empire.
    d. asked the Roman gods for the right to rule.

    ANS: D DIF: A

16. Wealthy Romans escaped Constantine's control by
    a. moving to their villas, which were like small cities.
    b. buying the right to ignore the emperor's rulings.
    c. letting their sons choose their own professions.
    d. serving in the Roman army.

    ANS: A DIF: A

17. Rome's frontiers in Greece and Gaul were attacked by
    a. Egyptians from the New Kingdom.
    b. Carthaginians under Hannibal.
    c. Germanic raiders from north and central Europe.
    d. Latins and Etruscans from Palatine.

    ANS: C DIF: A

MATCHING

Match each item with the correct statement below.

a. Marcus Aurelius	f. Adrianople
b. Commodus	g. Constantine I
c. Octavian	h. Constantinople
d. Alaric	i. Augustus
e. Diocletian	j. Circus Maximus

1. Real name of the Emperor Augustus
2. Emperor who established rule by divine right
3. Emperor who built a new capital for the Roman Empire
4. Emperor whose reign was "the holiest of times"
5. Name given to the first Roman emperor
6. City where Germans defeated the Roman army
7. City built as the new capital of the Roman Empire
8. Leader of Germanic tribes that invaded Rome
9. Emperor killed by his own bodyguards
10. Oval arena with a seating capacity of 200,000 people

1. ANS: C DIF: A
2. ANS: E DIF: A
3. ANS: G DIF: A
4. ANS: A DIF: A
5. ANS: I DIF: A
6. ANS: F DIF: A
7. ANS: H DIF: A

8. ANS: D DIF: A
9. ANS: B DIF: A
10. ANS: J DIF: A

SHORT ANSWER

1. Compare the gladiatorial games to professional sports in the United States. What similarities do you see?

    ANS:
    Answers will vary, but could include: audiences watched fighters who were managed by others.

    DIF: A

2. Use the table below to answer the following questions.
   a. When was Hadrian emperor?
   b. Which emperor conquered most of England?
   c. When did this emperor rule the Roman Empire?
   d. In addition to Vespasian and Titus, what other emperor strengthened the frontier regions?

EMPERORS DURING THE *PAX ROMANA*

Emperor	Reign	Accomplishments
Augustus	*27 B.C.–14 A.D.*	first emperor of Roman Empire reorganized government of Rome; brought peace to Rome
Tiberius	*14 A.D.–37 A.D.*	reformed taxes and improved financial state of government
Caligula	*37 A.D.–41 A.D.*	repaired roads and began construction of two aqueducts
Claudius	*41 A.D.–54 A.D.*	conquered most of England extended citizenship to many people outside Rome set up ministries to handle government administration
Nero	*54 A.D.–68 A.D.*	rebuilt Rome after the fire of 64 A.D. and gave it a city plan
Flavian Emperors **Vespasian** **Titus** **Domitian**	*69 A.D.–96 A.D.*	brought people from the provinces into the Senate secured frontier regions brought Rome new prosperity built the Coliseum
Five Good Emperors **Nerva** **Trajan** **Hadrian** **Antoninus Pius** Marcus Aurelius	*96 A.D.–180 A.D.*	built aqueducts, bridges, and harbors extended citizenship to more provinces cut dishonesty in business and government

ANS:
a. during the last years of the *Pax Romana*
b. Claudius
c. from 41 A.D. to 54 A.D.
d. Domitian

DIF: A

SECTION QUIZ 15-1—THE RULE OF AUGUSTUS

MULTIPLE CHOICE

1. Which of the following was NOT true of Augustus?
   a. He made the official religion important.
   b. He refused to be crowned emperor.
   c. He set up a Roman fire brigade.
   d. He was Caesar's father.

   ANS: D DIF: C

2. Pater Patriae means
   a. first citizen.
   b. revered one.
   c. Father of the Country.
   d. Emperor of Italy.

   ANS: C DIF: C

3. Augustus's real name was
   a. Octavian.
   b. Caesar.
   c. Marcus Antonius.
   d. Pater Patriae.

   ANS: A DIF: A

4. Augustus encouraged learning by
   a. reading to his people.
   b. making even the enslaved attend the university.
   c. building Rome's first library.
   d. making all teachers aristocrats.

   ANS: C DIF: E

5. In running his government, Augustus
   a. made the enslaved act as senators.
   b. chose people based on their talent.
   c. chose people based on their background.
   d. did not care about the common people.

   ANS: B DIF: E

MATCHING

Match each item with the correct statement below.

a. Augustus
b. freedom
c. emperor
d. princeps
e. census

1. absolute ruler of an empire
2. population count
3. former enslaved people

4. "first citizen"
5. ruled Rome for 41 years

1. ANS: C DIF: A
2. ANS: E DIF: A
3. ANS: B DIF: A
4. ANS: D DIF: A
5. ANS: A DIF: A

SHORT ANSWER

1. How did Augustus gain control of the armies?

   ANS:
   He had every soldier swear allegiance directly to him.

   DIF: A

2. How did Augustus gain control of the government's day-to-day business?

   ANS:
   He had his imperial household take charge of the daily business of government.

   DIF: A

3. Why did Augustus choose natural geographic features as boundaries for his empire?

   ANS:
   because they were easy to define and defend

   DIF: A

SECTION QUIZ 15-2—PAX ROMANA

MULTIPLE CHOICE

1. The *Pax Romana*
   a. lasted 100 years.
   b. lasted 200 years.
   c. was the result of the Punic Wars.
   d. is located on the Danube.

   ANS: B DIF: A

2. Roman law was standardized
   a. about 125 A.D.
   b. about 125 B.C.
   c. in 251 B.C.
   d. in a document known as *Pax Romana*.

   ANS: B DIF: A

3. Which of the following did NOT help trade during *Pax Romana*?
   a. There were high tariffs.
   b. There was a standardized money system.
   c. The Mediterranean was cleared of pirates.
   d. Goods and money moved freely along the trade routes.

   ANS: A DIF: C

4. Italy became a manufacturing center for
   a. silk.
   b. amber.
   c. pottery, bronze, and wool.
   d. brick, marble, and granite.

   ANS: C DIF: A

5. Roman legal principles formed the basis for
   a. Chinese laws.
   b. the Christian church.
   c. the Olympics.
   d. Judaism.

   ANS: B DIF: E

6. An important world-wide result of the *Pax Romana* was
   a. the mix of cultures.
   b. an increase in revolts.
   c. the halt of civilization.
   d. an increase in piracy.

   ANS: A DIF: A

7. Roman business and trade laws were changed so that
   a. Roman merchants got the best deal.
   b. non-Roman merchants got the best deal.
   c. Roman merchants could conquer new territories.
   d. Roman and non-Romans alike had the same rules.

   ANS: D DIF: C

8. Roman judges believed laws to be just when
   a. the government could enforce them.
   b. the innocent could not be proven guilty.
   c. they were reasonable and fair.
   d. special lawyers and writers helped develop them.

   ANS: C DIF: A

MATCHING

Match each item with the correct statement below.

a. tariffs
b. standardized
c. *Pax Romana*
d. olive oil
e. juris prudentes

1. taxes
2. special lawyers and legal writers
3. year peace
4. made the same way

5. Italian export item

1. ANS: A DIF: A
2. ANS: E DIF: A
3. ANS: C DIF: A
4. ANS: B DIF: A
5. ANS: D DIF: A

SECTION QUIZ 15-3—DAILY LIFE

MULTIPLE CHOICE

1. Which of the following was NOT a feature of a *domus*?
   a. marble walls
   b. windows with small panes of glass
   c. ground-floor shops
   d. colored stone walls

   ANS: C DIF: C

2. Roman boys and girls went to school together
   a. until they were 15.
   b. until they were 12.
   c. only if they came from wealthy families.
   d. if their parents were enslaved.

   ANS: B DIF: C

3. For girls, formal education stopped when they were
   a. 15 years old.
   b. 12 years old.
   c. 20 years old.
   d. 21 years old.

   ANS: A DIF: E

4. Chariot races were held at the
   a. Forum.
   b. Circus Maximus.
   c. Senate.
   d. Olympic Auditorium.

   ANS: B DIF: E

5. Gladiators were usually
   a. nobles and senators.
   b. plebeians and shopkeepers.
   c. the enslaved and poor people.
   d. Mesopotamian lions.

   ANS: C DIF: A

6. Which of the following was ***not*** a problem in Rome?
   a. inadequate housing
   b. air pollution
   c. high cost of living
   d. lack of entertainment

   ANS: D DIF: A

7. Which of the following was ***not*** true of the Roman family?
   a. The father was the head of the family.
   b. Wealthy boys trained for careers in politics or medicine.
   c. Roman women had no education after the age of 12.
   d. Marriages were arranged to increase wealth or status.

   ANS: C DIF: A

8. Which of the following was ***not*** true of leisure pastimes?
   a. Roman bathhouses often included gymnasiums and libraries.
   b. Romans loved betting on their favorite sports teams.
   c. The Roman government supported free public games.
   d. The public games often ran from dawn until dusk.

   ANS: B DIF: A

MATCHING

Match each item with the correct statement below.
a. Circus Maximus
b. rhetoric
c. gladiators
d. pigsticking
e. *domus*

1. fought in an arena
2. house
3. speech and writing
4. type of hunt
5. arena seating over 200,000

1. ANS: C DIF: A
2. ANS: E DIF: A
3. ANS: B DIF: A
4. ANS: D DIF: A
5. ANS: A DIF: A

SECTION QUIZ 15-4—FALL OF THE EMPIRE

MULTIPLE CHOICE

1. Marcus Aurelius's son Commodus was
   a. killed by Constantine I.
   b. killed by the Praetorian Guard.
   c. Rome's ruler for almost 50 years.
   d. a kind and devoted ruler.

   ANS: B DIF: C

2. Which of the following was NOT a reason for the fall of Rome?
   a. poor leadership
   b. economic problems
   c. the Twelve Tables
   d. foreign enemies

   ANS: C DIF: A

3. *The Tale of Genji* was written by
   a. Lady Kurasawa.
   b. Lord Kurasawa.
   c. Lady Murasaki.
   d. Prince Genji.

   ANS: C   DIF: E

4. In 330 A.D., the capital of the Roman Empire became
   a. Athens.
   b. Constantinople.
   c. Rome.
   d. Carthage.

   ANS: B   DIF: E

5. In 410 A.D., Rome was
   a. invaded by a Germanic chief.
   b. the capital of the Roman Empire.
   c. burned by the Senate.
   d. ruled by Octavian.

   ANS: A   DIF: A

MATCHING

Match each item with the correct statement below.

a. barter
b. Constantine I
c. Marcus Aurelius
d. inflation
e. rule by divine right

1. period of increasing prices
2. exchange goods without money
3. Diocletian's official policy
4. became Roman emperor in 312 A.D.
5. became Roman emperor in 161 A.D.

1. ANS: D   DIF: A
2. ANS: A   DIF: A
3. ANS: E   DIF: A
4. ANS: B   DIF: A
5. ANS: C   DIF: A

SHORT ANSWER

1. Why did taxes rise in Rome after the *Pax Romana* ended?

   ANS:
   The emperor needed more and more money to pay the Roman legions for their support.

   DIF: A

2. Why was gold going out of Rome?

   ANS:
   People were buying luxury items from other countries.

   DIF: C

3. Why were Rome's frontiers unprotected?

   ANS:
   Romans were busy fighting each other, and as a result they did not pay attention to their borders.

   DIF: A

4. Where did Constantine I relocate the Roman Empire's capital?

   ANS:
   to Constantinople in Asia Minor (modern-day Turkey)

   DIF: A

CHAPTER 16—CHRISTIANITY

MULTIPLE CHOICE

1. When Jesus began to preach, he traveled in
   a. Rome.
   b. Greece and Asia Minor.
   c. Palestine.
   d. Constantinople.

   ANS: C DIF: E

2. To help people understand his teachings, Jesus told them in the form of stories, called
   a. scriptures.
   b. parables.
   c. gospels.
   d. disciples.

   ANS: B DIF: A

3. The Jews hoped for the coming of a messiah who would
   a. start a new religion.
   b. help them leave Egypt.
   c. save them from Roman rule.
   d. convert the common people.

   ANS: C DIF: A

4. Jesus' followers believed that his death and resurrection showed that Christians would
   a. be forgiven their sins.
   b. convert other people.
   c. overthrow the Roman Empire.
   d. return to Earth after death.

   ANS: A DIF: A

5. The apostle Paul was the first to teach Christianity to
   a. Jews outside Palestine.
   b. Roman officials.
   c. non-Romans.
   d. non-Jews.

   ANS: D DIF: C

6. Which of these characteristics of the Roman Empire hurt, rather than helped, the spread of Christianity?
   a. Most Romans spoke either Latin or Greek.
   b. The emperor had to be publicly worshiped as a god.
   c. *Pax Romana* made travel safe throughout the empire.
   d. Poor and enslaved people welcomed Christianity.

   ANS: B DIF: C

7. The first Roman emperor to become a Christian was
   a. Constantine I.
   b. Diocletian.
   c. Augustus.
   d. Augustine.

   ANS: A DIF: E

8. The organization of the early Christian church was based on
   a. Greek democracies.
   b. Jerome's *Vulgate*.
   c. the Roman Empire.
   d. the kingdom of Carthage.

   ANS: C DIF: C

9. When the Christian church split in 1054, the leader accepted by Latin-speaking Christians was
   a. patriarch of Constantinople.
   b. archbishop of Rome.
   c. the apostle Paul.
   d. the emperor Theodosius.

   ANS: B DIF: E

10. A Christian scholar named Benedict is remembered for
    a. translating the Bible into Latin.
    b. advising Christians to become hermits.
    c. establishing rules for monks in monasteries.
    d. setting up the first Eastern Orthodox convent.

    ANS: C DIF: A

COMPLETION

1. Paul helped make Christianity a world religion by preaching to Jews and ____________________ alike.

   ANS: Gentiles DIF: A

2. Although Christianity first appealed to the poor and enslaved, the religion soon began to appeal to people from all ____________________.

   ANS: classes DIF: A

3. Early Christians organized the churches using the Roman ____________________ as a model.

   ANS: government DIF: C

4. ____________________ were people who lived and prayed in isolated areas.

   ANS: Hermits DIF: E

5. The Latin-speaking Christian churches became the ____________________ Church.

   ANS: Roman Catholic DIF: A

6. The Greek-speaking Christian churches became the ____________________ Church.

   ANS: Greek Orthodox DIF: A

MATCHING

Match each item with the correct statement below.

a. scriptures
b. patriarchs
c. gentiles
d. diocese
e. missionary
f. heresy
g. parish
h. abbot
i. apostles
j. convents

1. Religious communities for Christian women
2. Person who spreads religious beliefs to others
3. Term applied to anyone who is not Jewish
4. Sacred writings of any religion
5. The people chosen by Jesus to spread his teachings
6. Person who heads a monastery
7. Term for a local church in early Christianity
8. Doctrines that church authorities disapprove
9. Church division made up of several parishes
10. Five leading archbishops in the early Church

1. ANS: J DIF: A
2. ANS: E DIF: A
3. ANS: C DIF: A
4. ANS: A DIF: A
5. ANS: I DIF: A
6. ANS: H DIF: A
7. ANS: G DIF: A
8. ANS: F DIF: A
9. ANS: D DIF: A
10. ANS: B DIF: A

SHORT ANSWER

1. How are parables like legends and other old stories? How are they different?

ANS:
Answers will vary, but could include: SIMILARITIES: characters and situations often reflect real life; DIFFERENCES: parables are intended to teach lessons, which not all old stories did.

DIF: A

SECTION QUIZ 16-1—THE BEGINNINGS

MULTIPLE CHOICE

1. One famous parable concerns
   a. the Good Samaritan.
   b. the apostles.
   c. *Christos.*
   d. the Messiah's Song.

   ANS: A DIF: E

2. The holiday that marks the exodus of the Jews from Egypt is
   a. Christmas.
   b. Passover.
   c. Easter.
   d. the Crucifixion.

   ANS: B DIF: A

3. Which of the following was NOT true of Paul?
   a. He was blind from birth.
   b. He became a Christian.
   c. He taught Christianity to Jews and non-Jews.
   d. He was a missionary.

   ANS: A DIF: E

4. Another word for "gospel" is
   a. messiah.
   b. gentile.
   c. missionary.
   d. teachings.

   ANS: D DIF: A

5. "Resurrection" means
   a. being crucified.
   b. eating well.
   c. rising from the dead.
   d. doing missionary work.

   ANS: C DIF: A

MATCHING

Match each item with the correct statement below.

a. gentiles
b. scriptures
c. messiah
d. parables
e. missionaries

1. sacred writings
2. savior
3. non-Jews
4. spreaders of religious beliefs
5. stories

1. ANS: B DIF: A

2. ANS: C DIF: A
3. ANS: A DIF: A
4. ANS: E DIF: A
5. ANS: D DIF: A

SHORT ANSWER

1. What was the Romans' first reaction toward the new religion of Christianity?

   ANS:
   They did not pay much attention to it.

   DIF: A

2. What is a parable?

   ANS:
   a story about people or things that are familiar to the audience

   DIF: A

3. Why were the Jews unhappy with Roman rule?

   ANS:
   because of high taxes and the pressure Romans put on them to become citizens

   DIF: A

4. What kind of messiah did the Jews want?

   ANS:
   a political messiah

   DIF: A

5. For what crime was Jesus executed?

   ANS:
   treason

   DIF: A

SECTION QUIZ 16-2—CHRISTIANITY AND ROME

MULTIPLE CHOICE

1. Which of the following is NOT true of Constantine I?
   a. He had Christian churches built.
   b. He spent government money on Christian schools.
   c. He made Christianity the official religion.
   d. He won the throne of the Roman Empire in 312 A.D.

   ANS: C DIF: C

2. The Roman system of roads
   a. helped missionaries spread their word.
   b. was not used by missionaries.
   c. led only from one large city to another.
   d. was not open for Jews to travel.

   ANS: A DIF: A

3. Romans blamed Christians for
   a. plagues and famines.
   b. wars.
   c. the death of Constantine I.
   d. the poor system of roads.

   ANS: A DIF: E

4. Christianity was made illegal around
   a. 15 A.D.
   b. 64 A.D.
   c. 146 A.D.
   d. 640 A.D.

   ANS: B DIF: E

5. *In hoc signo vinces* means
   a. Here the battle will be won.
   b. In the name of the Father.
   c. In this sign thou shalt conquer.
   d. Thou shalt not kill.

   ANS: C DIF: C

MATCHING

Match each item with the correct statement below.
a. Edict of Milan
b. Constantine I
c. Emperor Theodosius
d. *in hoc signo vinces*
e. made Christianity illegal

1. gave religious freedom to all
2. made Christianity the official religion
3. saw flaming cross in the sky
4. victory message seen by Constantine I
5. Roman law

1. ANS: A DIF: A
2. ANS: C DIF: A
3. ANS: B DIF: A
4. ANS: D DIF: A
5. ANS: E DIF: A

SHORT ANSWER

1. How did Christians and Jews anger the Romans?

   ANS:
   They refused to recognize the Roman emperor as a god.

   DIF: A

2. What other things did Christians believe that angered Romans?

   ANS:
   They criticized Roman festivals and games, and they believed everyone would be equal in heaven.

   DIF: A

3. Why was Christianity popular with poor and enslaved people?

   ANS:
   They liked a religion that promised a happier life after death.

   DIF: A

4. What qualities of Christian missionaries did many Romans admire?

   ANS:
   the certainty of their beliefs; their courage

   DIF: A

SECTION QUIZ 16-3—THE CHURCH

MULTIPLE CHOICE

1. The New Testament is believed to have been written by
   a. Constantine I.
   b. Jerome and five archbishops.
   c. Augustine.
   d. Matthew, Mark, Luke, and John.

   ANS: D DIF: C

2. Which of the following was NOT a part of Benedictine Rule?
   a. religious services seven times a day
   b. simple clothes
   c. no marriage
   d. read *City of God* at each service

   ANS: D DIF: A

3. Nuns lived in quarters of their own called
   a. temples.
   b. monasteries.
   c. convents.
   d. parishes.

   ANS: C DIF: A

4. Augustine wrote
   a. the New Testament.
   b. the *Vulgate*.
   c. *City of God*.
   d. the Old Testament.

   ANS: C DIF: E

5. The Latin Churches as a group became known as the
   a. Christian Church of God.
   b. Roman Catholic Church.
   c. Eastern Orthodox Church.
   d. Fathers of the Church.

   ANS: B DIF: A

MATCHING

Match each item with the correct statement below.

a. abbot
b. parish
c. priest
d. diocese
e. patriarchs

1. church
2. church leader
3. group of several churches
4. the top five bishops
5. leader of a monastery

1. ANS: B DIF: A
2. ANS: C DIF: A
3. ANS: D DIF: A
4. ANS: E DIF: A
5. ANS: A DIF: A

SHORT ANSWER

1. What action did Christians take when they realized that Jesus' return to Earth might not happen soon?

   ANS:
   They organized their churches into a structure based on Roman government.

   DIF: A

2. What issue divided Christianity at this time?

   ANS:
   the question of whether the archbishop of Rome or the archbishop of Constantinople should be the leader of the church

   DIF: A

3. What was the goal of monks and nuns?

   ANS:
   to be protected from the evils of the world, but at the same time do good deeds and set a good example

   DIF: C

CHAPTER 17—THE GERMANS

MULTIPLE CHOICE

1. The Germans came into the Roman Empire looking for a warmer climate and
   a. to destroy Roman cities.
   b. to become Christians.
   c. new grazing lands.
   d. a new Latin alphabet.

   ANS: C DIF: A

2. Which of these best describes a Germanic settlement?
   a. Multistory apartment buildings with stores below
   b. Long thatched-roof houses with farmland around them
   c. Wooden houses crowded into narrow streets
   d. Brick houses around a central courtyard

   ANS: B DIF: C

3. In dealing with strangers, Germans behaved with
   a. great hospitality.
   b. cruelty and destruction.
   c. suspicion and hostility.
   d. fear and shyness.

   ANS: A DIF: A

4. In Germanic society, people gave their greatest loyalty to
   a. their clan.
   b. their farms.
   c. the gods.
   d. courts of law.

   ANS: A DIF: E

5. In Germanic society, the blood feud was
   a. a way of determining guilt or innocence by water.
   b. the memorizing of ancient laws.
   c. a pledge that a person was telling the truth.
   d. revenge sought by descendants of people who quarreled.

   ANS: D DIF: A

6. Germanic courts sometimes punished people by imposing a payment called
   a. an ordeal.
   b. a clan.
   c. the *wergeld.*
   d. an oath.

   ANS: C DIF: E

7. The original homes of the Goths were in
   a. the Balkan Peninsula.
   b. southern Gaul.
   c. the North African coast.
   d. central Asia.

   ANS: A DIF: C

8. In order to occupy Spain, the West Goths drove out
   a. the Ostrogoths.
   b. Spaniards and Gauls.
   c. Gauls and Romans.
   d. Romans and Vandals.

   ANS: D DIF: C

9. The Vandals gained their reputation for destructiveness as
   a. Mediterranean pirates.
   b. invaders from central Asia.
   c. conquerors of Spain.
   d. soldiers in the Roman army.

   ANS: A DIF: E

10. After 476, Rome and Italy were ruled by
    a. emperors chosen by the army.
    b. generals and leaders of Germanic groups.
    c. emperors chosen by the Eastern Roman Empire.
    d. Germans who had invaded from North Africa.

    ANS: B DIF: E

11. The Germans were attracted to Rome because of its
    a. forests and marshes.
    b. wealth and culture.
    c. beautiful Danube Valley.
    d. feasting, dancing, and drinking.

    ANS: B DIF: A

12. Germans took over the Roman alphabet to
    a. replace their language.
    b. write their own language.
    c. learn Latin.
    d. change their language to modern German.

    ANS: B DIF: A

13. German men made a living
    a. through barter and trade.
    b. building thatched-roof huts.
    c. raising cattle, farming, and raiding.
    d. making shields and spears.

    ANS: C DIF: A

14. Unlike the disciplined armies of many other civilizations, German warriors
    a. planned their attacks very carefully.
    b. attacked in small bands and by surprise.
    c. developed better weapons and battle gear.
    d. fought only for honor and life after death.

    ANS: B DIF: A

15. The Germanic groups found Rome weak and easy to fight because
   a. Roman leaders were fighting over politics and money.
   b. many Romans had become Christians and did not want to fight.
   c. Rome had lost all of its provinces.
   d. Attila the Hun had killed thousands of Rome's legionnaires.

   ANS: A   DIF: A

MATCHING

Match each item with the correct statement below.

a. Attila	f. Ostrogoths
b. Odoacer	g. Visigoths
c. Thor	h. Vandals
d. Valhalla	i. Theodoric
e. Alaric	j. Wodan

1. German general who ruled Italy after the last Roman emperor
2. Germanic people also known as East Goths
3. Chief Germanic god of war, poetry, learning, and magic
4. Germanic people known for their acts of destruction
5. In Germanic belief, the place where spirits of warriors would feast and fight forever
6. Ostrogoth leader who became ruler of Italy
7. Visigoth chieftain who captured Rome in 410
8. Leader of Asian invaders called Huns
9. Germanic god of thunder and war
10. Germanic people who defeated the Romans at Adrianople

1. ANS: B   DIF: A
2. ANS: F   DIF: A
3. ANS: J   DIF: A
4. ANS: H   DIF: A
5. ANS: D   DIF: A
6. ANS: I   DIF: A
7. ANS: E   DIF: A
8. ANS: A   DIF: A
9. ANS: C   DIF: A
10. ANS: G   DIF: A

SHORT ANSWER

1. What are some ways in which our modern civilization reflects ideas and practices of the early Germans?

   ANS:
   Answers will vary, but could include: law based on customs and approval of the people; oath-helpers like witnesses at modern trials.

   DIF: C

2. Study the map below. Name the Germanic groups that took over the Roman Empire, and tell where their territories were located. Use cardinal and intermediate directions.

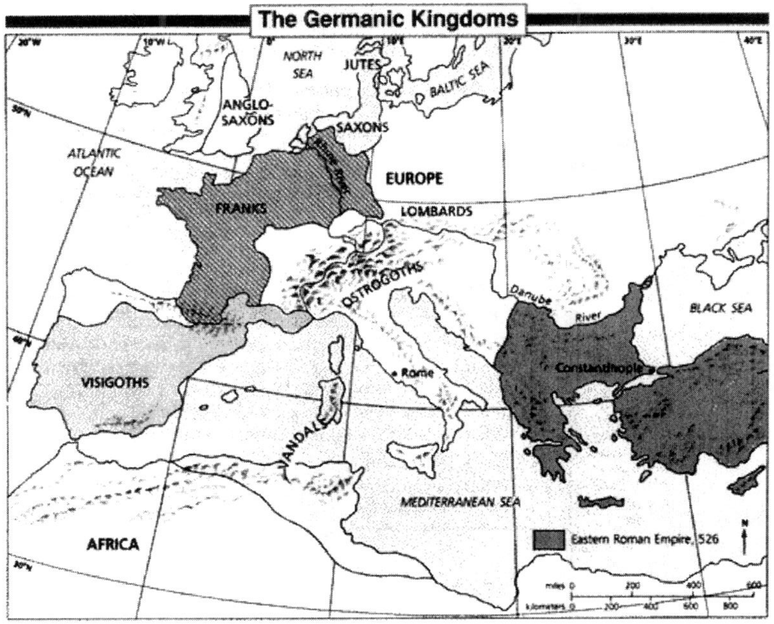

   ANS:
   Visigoths—southwestern part of the empire
   Vandals—southern part of the empire along the Mediterranean coast in Africa
   Ostrogoths—central northern part of the empire, west of the Danube river
   Jutes and Saxons—north of the Rhine River along the Baltic Coast
   Anglo-Saxons—northwestern corner of the empire on the British Isles

   DIF: C

SECTION QUIZ 17-1—VILLAGE LIFE

MULTIPLE CHOICE

1. German men were
   a. farmers.
   b. weavers.
   c. warriors.
   d. hunters.

   ANS: B   DIF: E

2. Which of the following was NOT true of German warrior bands?
   a. They had fixed plans for fighting.
   b. They made surprise raids on enemies.
   c. They wore suits of leather.
   d. They attacked while yelling to frighten their foes.

   ANS: A DIF: A

3. Wodan was
   a. the German god of learning.
   b. a German chieftain.
   c. a court-imposed fine.
   d. the German god of war.

   ANS: D DIF: E

4. Which of the following was NOT true of Thor?
   a. He was Wodan's son.
   b. He was the god of thunder.
   c. He was a god of war.
   d. He was a German military leader.

   ANS: D DIF: C

5. Blood feuds were
   a. fought between families.
   b. fought with knives.
   c. fought between two men.
   d. feuds between neighboring villages.

   ANS: A DIF: A

MATCHING

Match each item with the correct statement below.
a. ordeal
b. tunic
c. chieftain
d. *wergeld*
e. clan

1. military leader
2. group based on family ties
3. coat-like garment
4. fine
5. severe trial

1. ANS: C DIF: A
2. ANS: E DIF: A
3. ANS: B DIF: A
4. ANS: D DIF: A
5. ANS: A DIF: A

SHORT ANSWER

1. Why did German villagers allow farm animals to sleep in their houses?

   ANS:
   The animals helped heat the huts during the winter.

   DIF: A

2. What three major uses did the Germans have for their cattle?

   ANS:
   for food, clothing, and trade

   DIF: A

3. What did successful attacks give bands of German warriors?

   ANS:
   enslaved people, cattle, and treasure

   DIF: A

4. What ancient people were the Germans most like?

   ANS:
   Spartans

   DIF: A

SECTION QUIZ 17-2—THE CONQUERORS

MULTIPLE CHOICE

1. Odoacer was killed by
   a. East Goths.
   b. West Goths.
   c. Attila the Hun.
   d. Vandals.

   ANS: A DIF: C

2. The Battle of Adrianople was fought between
   a. the West Goths and the East Goths.
   b. the Vandals and the Huns.
   c. the West Goths and Rome.
   d. the West Goths and Constantinople.

   ANS: C DIF: C

3. The chieftain who captured and looted Rome in 410 was
   a. Theodoric.
   b. Alaric.
   c. Attila.
   d. Odoacer.

   ANS: B DIF: A

4. In the beginning, the Goths lived
   a. in Rome.
   b. in the Balkan Peninsula.
   c. in Palestine.
   d. near the Bering Strait.

   ANS: B DIF: A

5. In 472, Germanic people
   a. ruled Greece and Egypt.
   b. ruled Europe and Africa.
   c. controlled about 20 percent of the Roman Empire.
   d. controlled the entire Roman Empire.

   ANS: C DIF: E

MATCHING

Match each item with the correct statement below.

a. vandalism
b. Attila
c. Ostrogoths
d. Visigoths
e. Theodoric

1. East Goths
2. nicknamed "Little Daddy"
3. willful destruction of property
4. East Goth leader
5. West Goths

1. ANS: C DIF: A
2. ANS: B DIF: A
3. ANS: A DIF: A
4. ANS: E DIF: A
5. ANS: D DIF: A

SHORT ANSWER

1. What promises did the West Goths make to Rome in return for protection?

   ANS:
   They gave up their weapons and promised loyalty.

   DIF: A

2. Why did the West Goths rebel against the Romans?

   ANS:
   high prices of Roman food; Romans enslaved young West Goths

   DIF: A

3. Why did the Vandals leave Spain?

   ANS:
   They were driven out by the West Goths.

   DIF: A

CHAPTER 18—THE FRANKS

MULTIPLE CHOICE

1. The major river in the territory of the early Franks was the
   a. Tiber.
   b. Rhine.
   c. Danube.
   d. Thames.

   ANS: B DIF: E

2. During Clovis's reign, the Franks began to
   a. speak French and become Christians.
   b. speak a Germanic language much like English.
   c. send missionaries to convert the Saxons.
   d. destroy whatever remained of Roman culture.

   ANS: A DIF: A

3. The title held by Charles Martel was
   a. Emperor of the Romans.
   b. Mayor of the Palace.
   c. Mayor of Paris.
   d. King of the Franks.

   ANS: B DIF: E

4. Why was Charles Martel's victory at the Battle of Tours important?
   a. It united all the Franks under one king.
   b. It reestablished the Roman Empire.
   c. It protected Christianity in Europe against the spread of Islam.
   d. It created the modern nation of France.

   ANS: C DIF: C

5. After Pepin conquered the Lombards in Italy, their lands were given to
   a. the Frankish kingdom.
   b. the Pope.
   c. the Muslim invaders.
   d. the Roman emperor.

   ANS: B DIF: A

6. The most powerful people in Charlemagne's empire were
   a. scholars.
   b. serfs.
   c. minstrels.
   d. lords.

   ANS: D DIF: A

7. Charlemagne's most important goal was
   a. conquering the Eastern Roman Empire.
   b. building a Christian Roman Empire in western Europe.
   c. giving the Pope control over central Italy.
   d. reuniting the Eastern and Western Roman empires.

   ANS: B DIF: C

8. Which is the best description of Charlemagne's reign?
   a. A time of warfare and barbarian invasions
   b. A time of conflict between the Church and the king
   c. A period when nobles had more power than a weak king
   d. A revival of the arts and an emphasis on learning

   ANS: D DIF: C

9. Most of the people in Charlemagne's kingdom were
   a. farmers living in villages on a lord's estate.
   b. merchants and artisans living in towns.
   c. farmers with their own houses and fields.
   d. nomadic herders moving from place to place.

   ANS: A DIF: E

10. What was the effect of the Treaty of Verdun on Charlemagne's empire?
    a. His three grandsons ruled as co-emperors.
    b. Lothair, as emperor, ruled most of the territory.
    c. The land was divided into three unequal sections.
    d. A third of Charlemagne's territory went to the Church.

    ANS: C DIF: C

COMPLETION

1. Clovis set up the capital of the Frankish kingdom in ____________________.

   ANS: Paris DIF: E

2. Charles Martel led the Franks into battle against the Arabs in ____________________.

   ANS: Spain DIF: E

3. Pepin led the Frankish army into ____________________ to protect the Pope against invasion by a group of Germans.

   ANS: Italy DIF: A

4. Charlemagne first conquered Saxons in northern ____________________.

   ANS: Germany DIF: A

5. Scholars came from all over ____________________ to teach in Charlemagne's schools.

   ANS: Europe DIF: A

6. Frankish peasants lived in small ____________________ on the huge ____________________ of Frankish nobles.

   ANS: villages; estates DIF: A

MATCHING

Match each item with the correct statement below.

a. Franks
b. Roland
c. Lombards
d. Pepin
e. serfs
f. Clovis
g. Aachen
h. minstrels
i. counts
j. Lothair

1. Grandson of Charlemagne, given the title of emperor
2. People whose kingdom became modern Germany and France
3. Traveling entertainers
4. Warrior of Charlemagne who became a legend
5. First Germanic king to become a Christian
6. Capital and center of Charlemagne's empire
7. Poor people bound to the land
8. Germanic people living in central Italy
9. Officials of law courts
10. Son of Charles Martel, the first Frankish king to be anointed by the Pope

1. ANS: J DIF: A
2. ANS: A DIF: A
3. ANS: H DIF: A
4. ANS: B DIF: A
5. ANS: F DIF: A
6. ANS: G DIF: A
7. ANS: E DIF: A
8. ANS: C DIF: A
9. ANS: I DIF: A
10. ANS: D DIF: A

SHORT ANSWER

1. What difference do you think it makes to a society whether most of its people can read and write?

ANS:
Answers will vary, but could include: a society can build upon the thinking and development of earlier societies if its people can read the writing of the earlier people.

DIF: A

SECTION QUIZ 18-1—CLOVIS

MULTIPLE CHOICE

1. Early Franks lived
   a. in present-day Russia.
   b. on the Nile River.
   c. in present-day Germany.
   d. in Paris, France.

   ANS: C DIF: E

2. Another word for "warrior king" was
   a. Ghana.
   b. Goth.
   c. Clovis.
   d. Frank.

   ANS: A DIF: E

3. Which of the following was NOT true of Clovis?
   a. He brought all Franks under one rule.
   b. He made Paris the capital of his kingdom.
   c. He overthrew the Roman Empire.
   d. He made Latin the official language of his court.

   ANS: C DIF: A

4. The Franks
   a. converted to Judaism.
   b. mined salt.
   c. became farmers.
   d. were overthrown by the Vandals.

   ANS: C DIF: A

5. Clovis and 3,000 of his soldiers
   a. burned Rome.
   b. stormed Paris.
   c. converted to Christianity.
   d. died in a battle with the Vandals.

   ANS: C DIF: A

MATCHING

Match each item with the correct statement below.

a. converted
b. Paris
c. Clovis
d. Franks
e. Tunka Manin

1. a Germanic people
2. Frankish king
3. changed religion

4. warrior king
5. capital of Clovis's kingdom

1. ANS: D DIF: A
2. ANS: C DIF: A
3. ANS: A DIF: A
4. ANS: E DIF: A
5. ANS: B DIF: A

SHORT ANSWER

1. How did Clovis aid the Frankish groups?

   ANS:
   He united them.

   DIF: E

2. What did Clovis gain when he converted to Christianity?

   ANS:
   the support of Romans in his kingdom

   DIF: A

3. What gave the Franks a feeling of unity?

   ANS:
   They all spoke the same language and practiced the same religion.

   DIF: A

4. What was Clovis's duty in return for the Church's support?

   ANS:
   to protect the Church against non-believers

   DIF: A

SECTION QUIZ 18-2—CHARLES THE HAMMER

MULTIPLE CHOICE

1. Charles Martel was
   a. Pepin's son.
   b. Pepin's father.
   c. Pepin's brother.
   d. anointed by the Pope.

   ANS: B DIF: E

2. The Battle of Tours was won by
   a. the Arabs.
   b. the Berbers.
   c. the Franks.
   d. the Lombards.

   ANS: C DIF: E

3. Which of the following was NOT true of Charles Martel?
   a. He was known as "The Hammer."
   b. He led the Franks in the Battle of Tours.
   c. He served as Mayor of the Palace.
   d. His father was the Pope.

   ANS: D DIF: A

4. In 711 A.D.,
   a. Arabs and Berbers were conquered by the Franks.
   b. Arabs and Berbers conquered Spain.
   c. Pepin defeated the Lombards.
   d. Charles Martel conquered the Lombards.

   ANS: B DIF: E

5. The Frankish kings who followed Clovis
   a. were great warriors.
   b. were weak rulers.
   c. had many wives.
   d. traded salt for gold.

   ANS: B DIF: A

MATCHING

Match each item with the correct statement below.

a. anointed
b. Pepin
c. Lombards
d. Mayor of the Palace
e. Charles Martel

1. blessed with holy oil
2. government official
3. The Hammer"
4. ruler who was blessed by the Pope
5. their land given to the Pope

1. ANS: A DIF: A
2. ANS: D DIF: A
3. ANS: E DIF: A
4. ANS: B DIF: A
5. ANS: C DIF: A

SHORT ANSWER

1. How did Frankish rulers after Clovis weaken the Frank nation?

   ANS:
   They divided the kingdom among their sons.

   DIF: A

2. Why did the Frankish princes lose the loyalty of their people?

   ANS:
   They spent most of their time and energy fighting among themselves.

   DIF: A

SECTION QUIZ 18-3—CHARLEMAGNE

MULTIPLE CHOICE

1. Pepin's two sons were
   a. Carlos and Charles Martel.
   b. Roland and Louis.
   c. Louis and Charlemagne.
   d. Carloman and Charles.

   ANS: D DIF: E

2. The *Song of Roland* was a poem about
   a. Roland's victory over the Basques.
   b. Roland's defeat by the Basques.
   c. Charlemagne's victory over Roland.
   d. Roland's execution.

   ANS: B DIF: C

3. Charlemagne was made Roman emperor
   a. on Christmas Day of 800 A.D.
   b. by Pepin.
   c. in St. Michael's Church.
   d. by the Basques.

   ANS: A DIF: E

4. Which of the following was NOT true of Charlemagne?
   a. He was the son of Pepin.
   b. He appreciated learning.
   c. He was not in favor of the arts.
   d. He died in 814 A.D.

   ANS: C DIF: A

5. Charlemagne's son and heir was
   a. Lothair.
   b. Roland.
   c. Louis the Pious.
   d. Pepin.

   ANS: C DIF: A

MATCHING

Match each item with the correct statement below.

a. counts
b. minstrels
c. lords
d. serfs
e. Charlemagne

1. Charles the Great
2. nobles
3. court officials
4. people bound to the land
5. traveling musicians

1. ANS: E DIF: A
2. ANS: C DIF: A
3. ANS: A DIF: A
4. ANS: D DIF: A
5. ANS: B DIF: A

SHORT ANSWER

1. What countries did Charlemagne invade to reach his goal of ruling all of western Europe?

   ANS:
   Italy, northern Germany, and Spain

   DIF: A

2. Why did Charlemagne issue a great many laws?

   ANS:
   to bring justice to his kingdom

   DIF: A

3. What was the purpose of Charlemagne's annual meeting with his counts and warriors?

   ANS:
   to report troubles and discuss new laws

   DIF: A

4. How did scholars in the Frankish court change the Roman alphabet?

   ANS:
   They introduced lower-case letters.

   DIF: A

CHAPTER 19—THE IRISH AND THE ANGLO-SAXONS

MULTIPLE CHOICE

1. When did the last Roman legions leave Britain?
   a. 44 B.C., when Julius Caesar was killed
   b. 180 A.D., when the *Pax Romana* ended
   c. 410 A.D., when the Germans captured Rome
   d. 597 A.D., when Christian monks arrived

   ANS: C DIF: C

2. The Germanic people who migrated to Britain after the Romans left were the
   a. Celts.
   b. Angles, Saxons, and Jutes.
   c. Scots.
   d. Danes.

   ANS: B DIF: A

3. Ireland became a center for Celtic culture and Christianity because
   a. Roman influence remained strong there.
   b. arts and learning thrived in Irish cities.
   c. it was safe from attacks by the Germans.
   d. the Pope sent missionaries to help the Irish Church.

   ANS: C DIF: A

4. The centers of Irish life in the Early Middle Ages were
   a. nobles' estates.
   b. monasteries.
   c. the king's courts.
   d. palace schools.

   ANS: B DIF: C

5. In 597 Augustine and other monks were sent by Pope Gregory to convert the
   a. Danes.
   b. Romans.
   c. Celts.
   d. Anglo-Saxons.

   ANS: D DIF: E

6. As king of England, Alfred was ruler over
   a. the people of the Anglo-Saxon kingdoms.
   b. Anglo-Saxons, Romans, and Danes.
   c. Celts in Ireland.
   d. the people of England and Denmark.

   ANS: A DIF: E

7. Local government districts in Anglo-Saxon England were called
   a. estates.
   b. coracles.
   c. shires.
   d. sheriffs.

   ANS: C DIF: E

8. In Anglo-Saxon England, the Danelaw was
   a. the area of England where Danes lived and ruled.
   b. money paid to the Danes to keep peace.
   c. a part of Denmark granted to King Alfred.
   d. a history of the Danish people in Britain.

   ANS: A DIF: A

9. The government of Anglo-Saxon England centered on
   a. a council of lords.
   b. the king.
   c. the Pope.
   d. the witenagemot.

   ANS: B DIF: C

10. Which of the following was NOT one of the duties of a noble in Anglo-Saxon England?
    a. Keeping the peace locally
    b. Farming the estate lands
    c. Serving the king in war
    d. Attending the witenagemot

    ANS: B DIF: E

11. Irish monks did not follow the same practices as Christian monks in other countries because
    a. St. Patrick, the founder of the Irish church, did not want them to.
    b. the Irish did not fear attacks by the Germans.
    c. the Irish monasteries had little communication with other countries.
    d. they were too busy looking for new converts.

    ANS: C DIF: A

12. Because Irish monks could move from place to place more freely than other monks, many
    a. were related to Irish clans.
    b. became missionaries to northern England and Europe.
    c. followed no rules at all.
    d. lost contact with the Roman Church.

    ANS: B DIF: A

13. The Anglo-Saxons converted to Christianity, but they
    a. were not strong enough to convert the Danes as well.
    b. told many stories about St. George the Dragon Slayer.
    c. refused to obey Pope Gregory I.
    d. kept much of their old culture alive through songs and stories.

    ANS: D DIF: A

14. Alfred the Great based his laws on Anglo-Saxon customs that
    a. gave the nobles power to enslave the peasants.
    b. protected the weak and stressed honesty.
    c. kept the Danes away from Wessex.
    d. had been in force since Roman times.

    ANS: B DIF: A

15. Alfred was like the great Frankish king Charlemagne because he
   a. conquered much of Europe.
   b. drove the Danes out of England.
   c. set up a palace school to train the sons of noblemen.
   d. wrote many books in Latin.

   ANS: C DIF: A

16. Alfred had his scholars translate Latin books into English so that
   a. more officials could read them.
   b. the palace tutors did not have that chore.
   c. the English people could read about their history.
   d. all English citizens would know the new laws.

   ANS: C DIF: A

17. The territory of Danelaw eventually
   a. was given to the Archbishop of Canterbury.
   b. became part of Scotland.
   c. was taken from the Danes and became part of England.
   d. became the great English city of London.

   ANS: C DIF: A

MATCHING

Match each item with the correct statement below.

a. Wessex	f. Alfred
b. Iona	g. Patrick
c. Saxons	h. Gregory
d. sheriffs	i. Norselaw
e. Picts	j. witenagemot

1. One group of Germanic people who migrated to Britain
2. Native British people who resisted Roman rule
3. Pope who sent a mission of monks to convert Britain
4. Area of Britain originally ruled by Alfred
5. Legendary warrior of Anglo-Saxon literature
6. King who united England against the Danes
7. An advisory council of nobles and Church leaders
8. Nobles chosen by the king who administered the shires
9. Island near Scotland, where a monastery was built
10. Missionary bishop who converted Ireland

1. ANS: C DIF: A
2. ANS: E DIF: A
3. ANS: H DIF: A
4. ANS: A DIF: A
5. ANS: I DIF: A
6. ANS: F DIF: A
7. ANS: J DIF: A

8. ANS: D DIF: A
9. ANS: B DIF: A
10. ANS: G DIF: A

SHORT ANSWER

1. What was the major problem facec by the Irish Church during the Germanic invasions of the Roman Empire? How did the Church address the problem?

   ANS:
   Answers will vary, but could include: the Irish Church lost contact with Rome during the Germanic invasions, which led to Irish abbots leading the Church instead of the Pope.

   DIF: A

2. Study the map below. Which bodies of water isolate the British Isles from the rest of Europe?

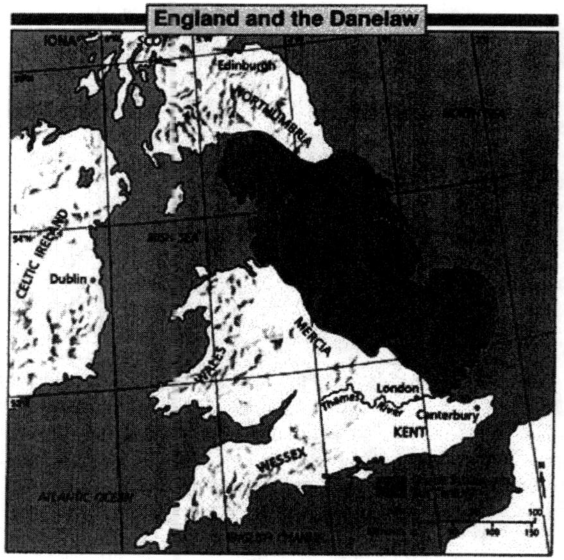

   ANS:
   the Atlantic Ocean, the Irish Sea, and the North Sea

   DIF: A

SECTION QUIZ 19-1—CELTIC IRELAND

MULTIPLE CHOICE

1. Which of the following was NOT true of Saint Patrick?
   a. He was born in Britain.
   b. He was kidnapped by Irish pirates.
   c. He studied to become a priest.
   d. He set up a monastery on an island.

   ANS: D DIF: A

2. The center of Irish culture became
   a. Iona.
   b. Ireland.
   c. France.
   d. Rome.

   ANS: B DIF: E

3. Many Irish monks chose to be
   a. archbishops.
   b. pirates.
   c. saints.
   d. hermits.

   ANS: D DIF: E

4. Monasteries became
   a. centers of Irish life.
   b. outlawed in the 400s.
   c. trading centers.
   d. burial grounds.

   ANS: A DIF: A

5. Coracles were built
   a. into stockades.
   b. of cowhide and wood.
   c. mainly for monks to use.
   d. to house church officials.

   ANS: B DIF: A

MATCHING

Match each item with the correct statement below.

a. Iona
b. coracle
c. Saint Columba
d. Saint Patrick
e. monastery

1. Irish boat
2. island off of Scotland
3. founder of Irish Church
4. Irish monk
5. home to monks

1. ANS: B DIF: A

2. ANS: A DIF: A
3. ANS: D DIF: A
4. ANS: C DIF: A
5. ANS: E DIF: A

SHORT ANSWER

1. Which Roman general invaded and conquered much of the British Isles?

   ANS:
   Julius Caesar

   DIF: E

2. What people refused the influence of Roman culture?

   ANS:
   the Celts

   DIF: E

3. Why did the Celts have no cities?

   ANS:
   Their people were divided into clans that lived in small villages.

   DIF: A

4. What geographic feature of Ireland protected the Celts from German invasion?

   ANS:
   the Atlantic Ocean

   DIF: A

SECTION QUIZ 19-2—CHRISTIANITY

MULTIPLE CHOICE

1. Alfred the Great
   a. was a Dane.
   b. became one of England's best-loved rulers.
   c. was a legendary warrior.
   d. was a sheriff in Anglo-Saxon England.

   ANS: B DIF: A

2. Beowulf was
   a. a well-known Anglo-Saxon writer.
   b. the ruler of England in 835 A.D.
   c. a great scholar.
   d. a legendary warrior.

   ANS: D DIF: C

3. Tapestries are
   a. paintings.
   b. woven wall hangings.
   c. ornate tablecloths.
   d. fences built around monasteries.

   ANS: B DIF: E

4. Alfred the Great was also known as
   a. King of Wessex.
   b. Beowulf.
   c. Archbishop of Canterbury.
   d. Charlemagne.

   ANS: A DIF: A

5. In the epic poem *Beowulf*, the monster's name is
   a. Gandalph.
   b. Goliath.
   c. Grindel.
   d. Beowulf.

   ANS: C DIF: A

MATCHING

Match each item with the correct statement below.

a. witenagemot
b. king's peace
c. witan
d. sheriff
e. shire

1. group of nobles and church leaders
2. royal protection
3. wiseman
4. district
5. noble chosen by the king

1. ANS: A DIF: A
2. ANS: B DIF: A
3. ANS: C DIF: A
4. ANS: E DIF: A
5. ANS: D DIF: A

SHORT ANSWER

1. What purpose did monasteries serve in England and Ireland?

   ANS:
   They were centers of religion and culture.

   DIF: A

2. What subjects did early European literature deal with?

   ANS:
   brave warriors who fought monsters and dragons

   DIF: A

3. Why did Alfred stop payments to the Danes?

   ANS:
   because his army had grown strong

   DIF: A

4. What did Alfred do so that the Anglo-Saxons would continue their loyalty and obedience to him?

   ANS:
   He established new laws based on Anglo-Saxon customs.

   DIF: A

CHAPTER 20—THE VIKINGS

MULTIPLE CHOICE

1. Which of these parts of the world was not visited by the Vikings?
   a. The Mediterranean
   b. Asia
   c. North America
   d. South America

   ANS: D DIF: C

2. One reason that the Vikings became seafarers was that
   a. Jutland had good farmland and harbors.
   b. they had no forests to supply wood for shipbuilding.
   c. their land was rocky, and the growing season was short.
   d. All of the above.

   ANS: C DIF: A

3. The Viking term for men who were warriors was
   a. *jarls.*
   b. *berserkers.*
   c. *runes.*
   d. sagas.

   ANS: B DIF: A

4. Which is the best description of a Viking village?
   a. Walled towns of stone houses on hilltops
   b. Wooden houses with porches and steep roofs
   c. Brick houses on straight, narrow streets
   d. Farmers' houses around the lord's estate

   ANS: B DIF: A

5. Stories of the Norse gods and goddesses were told in works called
   a. Norselaw.
   b. Danelaw.
   c. *Eddas.*
   d. epics.

   ANS: C DIF: E

6. The Danish, Norwegian, Swedish, and Icelandic languages are closely related to
   a. Latin-based languages.
   b. French.
   c. Germanic languages.
   d. Russian.

   ANS: C DIF: A

7. The Varangian Route was the Vikings'
   a. water route into Russia.
   b. route to North America.
   c. trading route to Italy.
   d. land route to Byzantium.

   ANS: A DIF: A

8. Norwegian Vikings established colonies in
   a. Greenland and Iceland.
   b. Normandy.
   c. Ireland and Scotland.
   d. England.

   ANS: A DIF: A

9. England became a part of the empire led by the Danish king
   a. Rollo.
   b. Erik the Red.
   c. Canute.
   d. Ethelred.

   ANS: C DIF: E

10. The people who came to be known as Normans were
    a. Danes living in the Danelaw area of England.
    b. Norwegians settled in an Iceland colony.
    c. Norsemen in a settlement that began the Russian nation.
    d. Danes living in an area on the coast of France.

    ANS: D DIF: E

MATCHING

Match each item with the correct statement below.

a. Norselaw
b. *jarl*
c. Leif Eriksson
d. Ethelred
e. Rurik
f. Vinland
g. fjord
h. Erik the Red
i. Jutland
j. Rollo

1. A deep, narrow bay along a coastline
2. Name of the place the Vikings discovered in North America
3. Norwegian Viking who established the Greenland colony
4. Danish leader who gained the right to live in France
5. Title given to a military chief who headed a group
6. Swedish chief who founded a settlement in what would be Kievan Rus
7. King of England nicknamed the Unready whose weakness encouraged Viking raids
8. Area of France later known as Normandy
9. Southern part of Viking lands used for farming
10. Viking leader who led the expedition to North America

1. ANS: G DIF: A
2. ANS: F DIF: A
3. ANS: H DIF: A
4. ANS: J DIF: A
5. ANS: B DIF: A
6. ANS: E DIF: A
7. ANS: D DIF: A
8. ANS: A DIF: A
9. ANS: I DIF: A
10. ANS: C DIF: A

SHORT ANSWER

1. How do you think life in the United States might be different today if the Vikings had established colonies where they landed in North America before the year 1000?

   ANS:
   Answers will vary, but could include: the United States might show more evidence of influence of Viking civilization and be about 500 years older.

   DIF: A

2. Study the chart below. How did the Vikings influence our calendar?

NORSE GODS

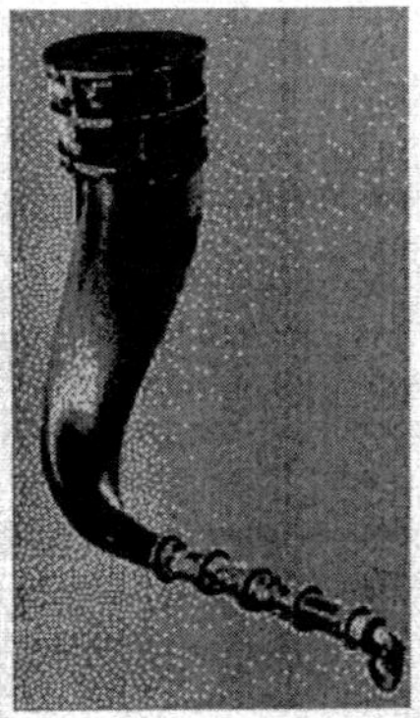

Name	Realm
Odin (or Wodan)	king of the gods; sky god; god of war and wisdom, *Wodan's day became Wednesday.*
Balder	god of light, joy, and spring
Bragi	god of poetry and stories
Freya	goddess of love and beauty
Freyr	god of rain, sunshine, and the harvest
Frigg	goddess of earth, marriages, and motherly love; Odin's wife; *Frigg's day became Friday.*
Hel (or Hela)	goddess of the dead
Idun	goddess of youth
Loki	god of fire; the mischief-maker
Njord	god of the sea
Thor	god of thunder, lightning, and the tides; *Thor's day became Thursday.*
Tyr	god of legal contracts and of truth; *Tyr's day became Tuesday.*

   ANS:
   The Vikings gave us the names of the days Tuesday, Wednesday, Thursday, and Friday.

   DIF: A

SECTION QUIZ 20-1—THE LAND

MULTIPLE CHOICE

1. Viking sailors slept in
   a. hammocks.
   b. beds.
   c. tents.
   d. leather bags.

   ANS: D DIF: C

2. Which of the following was NOT true of the Vikings?
   a. They traveled after their crops were harvested.
   b. They were successful at trade.
   c. They sailed in ships made of wood.
   d. They were also known as fjords.

   ANS: D DIF: E

3. The *jarls* served as
   a. the central government.
   b. leaders of small groups.
   c. the king's henchmen.
   d. laborers and slaves.

   ANS: B DIF: A

4. Viking houses had
   a. many floors.
   b. indoor plumbing.
   c. carved dragons on the roof.
   d. *jarls* on the porch.

   ANS: C DIF: E

5. Viking towns usually had
   a. two main streets.
   b. a mayor and a city council.
   c. a palace in which the *jarls* lived.
   d. a central plaza with many fountains.

   ANS: A DIF: E

MATCHING

Match each item with the correct statement below.
a. dragons
b. *jarls*
c. Vikings
d. fjords
e. Jutland

1. narrow bays
2. military chiefs
3. in the past, a name for Denmark
4. Viking roof decorations
5. Norsemen

1. ANS: D DIF: A
2. ANS: B DIF: A
3. ANS: E DIF: A
4. ANS: A DIF: A
5. ANS: C DIF: A

SHORT ANSWER

1. Why was the Scandinavian coastline particularly suited for making a living from the sea?

   ANS:
   It had many bays and natural harbors.

   DIF: A

2. Why did Vikings carve dragon heads on the bows of their ships?

   ANS:
   to frighten their enemies and evil sea spirits

   DIF: C

3. How did the Vikings spend their winters?

   ANS:
   by repairing boats and weapons

   DIF: A

4. What ancient traders were the Vikings like?

   ANS:
   the Phoenicians

   DIF: C

SECTION QUIZ 20-2—DAILY LIFE

MULTIPLE CHOICE

1. Which of the following was NOT true of the Vikings?
   a. They liked fine clothes.
   b. They were warriors.
   c. They wore their hair long.
   d. They disapproved of facial hair.

   ANS: D DIF: E

2. A Viking groom
   a. met his wife on their wedding day.
   b. bought his wife on their wedding day.
   c. fought for his wife on their wedding day.
   d. courted his wife for several days.

   ANS: B DIF: E

3. To call their warriors to battle, the Vikings
   a. went berserk.
   b. lit bonfires on mountaintops.
   c. blew through large horns.
   d. sailed close to the coastline.

   ANS: B DIF: A

4. Most Viking households had
   a. 10-20 members.
   b. 20-30 members.
   c. 30-40 members.
   d. more than 50 members.

   ANS: B DIF: A

5. Calling a Viking man "beardless"
   a. was an insult.
   b. was a joke.
   c. was a compliment.
   d. meant he was part of the family.

   ANS: A DIF: A

MATCHING

Match each item with the correct statement below.

a. magic charm
b. *runes*
c. *berserkers*
d. *Eddas*
e. sagas

1. Viking warriors
2. poems about the gods' deeds
3. long tales
4. letters
5. one use of *runes*

1. ANS: C DIF: A
2. ANS: D DIF: A
3. ANS: E DIF: A
4. ANS: B DIF: A
5. ANS: A DIF: A

SHORT ANSWER

1. Why did Viking families feud?

   ANS:
   to defend their honor

   DIF: A

2. How did the Vikings finally end the practice of feuding?

   ANS:
   by forcing feuding people to pay fines

   DIF: A

3. What protective gear did Vikings wear in battle?

   ANS:
   metal helmets and shirts made of iron rings

   DIF: A

4. What happened to the Viking sagas?

   ANS:
   People lost interest in them; many were forgotten or forbidden by the Church.

   DIF: A

5. What happened to the Viking runes?

   ANS:
   Vikings began to write with Roman letters instead.

   DIF: A

SECTION QUIZ 20-3—RAIDERS AND ADVENTURERS

MULTIPLE CHOICE

1. Ethelred, who was nicknamed the Unready,
   a. was the king of France in 871.
   b. was king of the Danes until 1016.
   c. became king of England in 978.
   d. was a nervous and sickly man.

   ANS: C DIF: E

2. In 911, the French king
   a. made Ethelred a knight.
   b. made Rollo a knight.
   c. signed a treaty with Rollo.
   d. signed a treaty with Alfred the Great.

   ANS: C DIF: A

3. Erik the Red was
   a. Leif Eriksson's father.
   b. Leif Eriksson's only son.
   c. Rollo's head general.
   d. Rollo's father.

   ANS: A DIF: A

4. The Viking settlement founded by Rurik
   a. is in present-day Africa.
   b. later became Sweden.
   c. became the basis of the Russian nation.
   d. was attacked by Native Americans.

   ANS: C DIF: C

5. In 1035, Canute
   a. began raiding Ethelred.
   b. conquered England.
   c. converted to Christianity.
   d. died.

   ANS: D DIF: A

MATCHING

Match each item with the correct statement below.

a. Rurik
b. Canute
c. Newfoundland
d. historical routes
e. Varangian

1. historically traveled roads
2. formerly known as Vinland
3. Swedish chief
4. Viking water route
5. Danish king

1. ANS: D DIF: A
2. ANS: C DIF: A
3. ANS: A DIF: A
4. ANS: E DIF: A
5. ANS: B DIF: A

SHORT ANSWER

1. How did the design of Viking ships aid the Vikings in raiding and exploring?

   ANS:
   The Vikings could safely sail both the deep water of the Atlantic and the shallow rivers of Europe.

   DIF: C

2. On what continent did some Swedish Vikings establish a settlement?

   ANS:
   Asia

   DIF: A

3. To what continent did some Norwegian Vikings travel?

   ANS:
   North America

   DIF: A

4. Where did most Vikings carry out their raids?

   ANS:
   western and southern Europe

   DIF: A

CHAPTER 21—THE BYZANTINE EMPIRE

MULTIPLE CHOICE

1. Which of these was NOT an advantage of the site of Constantinople?
   a. Trade routes between Europe and Asia crossed there.
   b. The sea protected the city on three sides.
   c. The city was surrounded by rich delta farmland.
   d. Great trade centers were to the east.

   ANS: C DIF: A

2. The most important factor in unifying the Byzantine Empire was
   a. the Latin language.
   b. distrust of the Romans.
   c. Eastern Christianity.
   d. fear of Germanic invaders.

   ANS: C DIF: C

3. The most important difference between Rome and the new Constantinople was in the
   a. religious atmosphere.
   b. popular entertainments.
   c. style of architecture.
   d. system of laws.

   ANS: A DIF: A

4. Which best describes the powers of a Byzantine emperor?
   a. Emperors chosen and controlled by the army
   b. Supreme power over government, Church, and law
   c. Power limited by rivalry with wealthy nobles
   d. Power shared equally by emperor and the patriarch

   ANS: B DIF: A

5. When a revolt threatened Justinian's rule, his best advice came from
   a. Tribonian.
   b. Theodora.
   c. Belisarius.
   d. Constantine.

   ANS: B DIF: A

6. The most important Byzantine influence on modern governments comes from
   a. Justinian's code of laws.
   b. the invention of Greek fire.
   c. Constantinople's defenses.
   d. the army's military tactics.

   ANS: A DIF: C

7. To regain the lands of the old Roman Empire, Justinian had to defeat
   a. Vikings in Scandinavia.
   b. Greeks in Asia Minor.
   c. the German kingdoms in western Europe and North Africa.
   d. Black Sea pirates.

   ANS: C DIF: E

8. The leader of the Church in the Byzantine Empire was
   a. the Pope in Rome.
   b. the emperor Charlemagne.
   c. the metropolitan of Antioch.
   d. the Patriarch of Constantinople.

   ANS: D DIF: E

9. When the empire no longer needed a large army in the 1100s, a change in policy lost the loyalty of
   a. metropolitans.
   b. rich landlords.
   c. farmers.
   d. merchants.

   ANS: C DIF: A

10. The Venetians harmed the Byzantines in the eleventh century by
    a. helping the Vikings attack Constantinople.
    b. taking over trade in their own ships.
    c. invading Asia Minor.
    d. attacking Byzantine territory in Italy.

    ANS: B DIF: A

MATCHING

Match each item with the correct statement below.

a. Byzantium
b. Cyril
c. Tribonian
d. Charlemagne
e. Theodora
f. Hagia Sophia
g. Justinian
h. theology
i. Constantine
j. icons

1. Religious images
2. Frankish emperor whose crowning angered Byzantines
3. Old Greek city, site of Constantinople
4. Empress and influential adviser to Justinian
5. Legal scholar who supervised writing of a legal code known as the Justinian Code
6. Missionary who gave Slavic peoples a new alphabet
7. Impressive church built by Justinian
8. Considered the greatest Byzantine emperor
9. Study of religion
10. Emperor who moved his capital out of Rome

1. ANS: J DIF: A
2. ANS: D DIF: A
3. ANS: A DIF: A
4. ANS: E DIF: A
5. ANS: C DIF: A
6. ANS: B DIF: A
7. ANS: F DIF: A

8. ANS: G DIF: A
9. ANS: H DIF: A
10. ANS: I DIF: A

SHORT ANSWER

1. What could be some uses of Greek fire in peacetime? How could its dangers to people be managed?

   ANS:
   Answers will vary, but could include: Greek fire could possibly be used to help clean up oil spills; its dangers to people might be managed by modern technology such as fire-resistant clothing.

   DIF: A

2. What three civilizations "blended" to make the Byzantine Empire?

   ANS:
   Greek, Roman, and Christian

   DIF: A

3. What civilization did the Byzantines see themselves as a part of?

   ANS:
   Roman

   DIF: E

4. What did the Church believe about the emperor's actions?

   ANS:
   that the emperor's actions were inspired by God

   DIF: A

5. What was the outstanding feature of Hagia Sophia?

   ANS:
   its huge, circular dome

   DIF: A

6. What supplies were lost to the Byzantines when the empire lost Asia Minor?

   ANS:
   food, materials, and soldiers

   DIF: A

7. Study the map below. What waterways did the Byzantines still control at the fall of their empire?

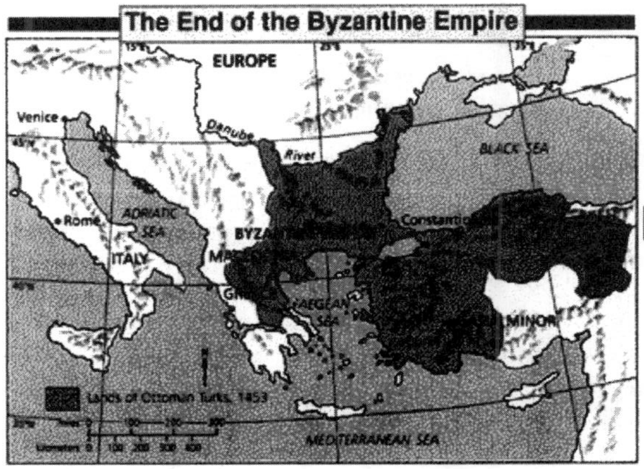

   ANS:
   the Aegean Sea and the Black Sea

   DIF: A

SECTION QUIZ 21-1—CONSTANTINOPLE

MULTIPLE CHOICE

1. Which of the following was NOT true of Constantinople?
   a. It took four years to build.
   b. It was modeled after Rome.
   c. It was nicknamed "New Rome."
   d. It had wide streets.

   ANS: D DIF: A

2. During Constantine's rule, Constantinople's population was
   a. 6,000.
   b. 16,000.
   c. 600,000.
   d. 6,000,000.

   ANS: C DIF: C

3. Among themselves, most Byzantines spoke
   a. Byzantine.
   b. Italian.
   c. Latin.
   d. Greek.

   ANS: D DIF: E

4. Relics were placed
   a. in shrines in people's homes.
   b. in public monuments, palaces, and churches.
   c. only in churches.
   d. only in Constantine's palace.

   ANS: B DIF: A

5. Constantine
   a. convinced wealthy Romans to move to Constantinople.
   b. converted to Judaism.
   c. modeled Constantinople after Paris.
   d. was French by birth.

   ANS: A DIF: A

MATCHING

Match each item with the correct statement below.

a. Latin
b. bodies of saints
c. family
d. relics
e. Byzantium

1. earlier name for Constantinople
2. center of Byzantine social life
3. official language of Constantinople
4. contents of Byzantine shrines
5. valued holy objects from the past

1. ANS: E DIF: A
2. ANS: C DIF: A
3. ANS: A DIF: A
4. ANS: B DIF: A
5. ANS: D DIF: A

SHORT ANSWER

1. What kinds of works did the officials of Constantinople oversee?

   ANS:
   They took charge of building roads, bridges, wells, and caravan shelters.

   DIF: A

2. How did Constantine convince wealthy Romans to move to Constantinople?

   ANS:
   They built palaces for them.

   DIF: E

3. Which of Constantinople's buildings were the most magnificent?

   ANS:
   the Christian churches

   DIF: A

SECTION QUIZ 21-2—JUSTINIAN I

MULTIPLE CHOICE

1. Who did Justinian hire to lead the Byzantine army?
   a. Tribonian
   b. Nicephorus
   c. Belisarius
   d. Hagia Sophia

   ANS: C DIF: A

2. The code of law developed by Tribonian and others was
   a. Tribonian's Law.
   b. the Hagia Sophia.
   c. the Justinian Code.
   d. the Byzantine Code.

   ANS: C DIF: C

3. Hagia Sophia was later called
   a. St. Justinian.
   b. St. Sophia.
   c. St. Hagia.
   d. the Byzantine Church of God.

   ANS: B DIF: E

4. Which of the following was NOT true of Greek fire?
   a. It was hard to put out.
   b. It burned the skin.
   c. It was made of acid and oil.
   d. It ignited when it came into contact with water.

   ANS: C DIF: A

5. Before becoming Justinian's wife, Theodora was
   a. a slave.
   b. a soothsayer.
   c. a Venetian princess.
   d. an actress.

   ANS: D DIF: A

MATCHING

Match each item with the correct statement below.

a. Greek fire
b. mosaics
c. theology
d. dowry
e. Hagia Sophia

1. chemical mix that ignites in water

2. wealth a woman brings to marriage
3. study of religion
4. made of colored glass or stone
5. "Holy Wisdom"

1. ANS: A DIF: A
2. ANS: D DIF: A
3. ANS: C DIF: A
4. ANS: B DIF: A
5. ANS: E DIF: A

SHORT ANSWER

1. What quality did Justinian prize in his officials?

   ANS:
   their abilities

   DIF: A

2. What action increased Justinian's power and control of the government?

   ANS:
   He put down a revolt by senators.

   DIF: A

3. Besides law, what other area of government was Justinian interested in?

   ANS:
   public works

   DIF: A

4. What areas of the military did Justinian improve?

   ANS:
   He set up a group of loyal cavalry soldiers, and he developed a series of battle moves.

   DIF: C

SECTION QUIZ 21-3—THE CHURCH

MULTIPLE CHOICE

1. The leader of the local Church in Constantinople
   a. was called the Pope.
   b. was called the Patriarch.
   c. was a metropolitan.
   d. had to be Greek.

   ANS: B DIF: C

2. Cyril was
   a. a missionary.
   b. a slave.
   c. a patriarch.
   d. an emperor.

   ANS: A DIF: E

3. A religious point that divided Byzantines for over 100 years
   a. concerned Charlemagne's right to be emperor.
   b. concerned the Cyrillic alphabet.
   c. concerned the use of icons.
   d. concerned Leo III's right to be emperor.

   ANS: C DIF: A

4. The Byzantines believed their emperor represented
   a. Moses.
   b. Christ on earth.
   c. Yahweh.
   d. Byzantine perfection.

   ANS: B DIF: A

5. In the Church in Constantinople, most priests
   a. were married.
   b. were missionaries.
   c. were hermits.
   d. were patriarchs.

   ANS: A DIF: A

COMPLETION

1. The emperor was the head of the government and of the ____________________.

   ANS: Church DIF: A

2. Monasteries sent ____________________ to other lands to keep peace.

   ANS: missionaries DIF: A

3. Missionaries translated parts of the ____________________ and Church ____________________ from Latin into other languages.

   ANS: Bible; services DIF: A

4. Church leaders in western Europe used icons a great deal because most people in the West could not ____________________.

ANS: read DIF: E

MATCHING

Match each item with the correct statement below.

a. metropolitans
b. Leo III
c. Charlemagne
d. icons
e. Cyril

1. helped create a new alphabet
2. church officials
3. Byzantine emperor
4. religious images
5. Emperor of the Romans"

1. ANS: E DIF: A
2. ANS: A DIF: A
3. ANS: B DIF: A
4. ANS: D DIF: A
5. ANS: C DIF: A

SECTION QUIZ 21-4—DECLINE OF THE EMPIRE

MULTIPLE CHOICE

1. What group conquered Byzantine lands in southern Italy in 1080?
   a. the Indians.
   b. the Venetians.
   c. the Vikings.
   d. the Turks.

   ANS: C DIF: C

2. In the 1100s, the Byzantine emperor cut costs by
   a. changing his policy toward Venice.
   b. changing his policy toward farmers.
   c. doing away with trade in Asia Minor.
   d. firing Viking mercenaries.

   ANS: B DIF: A

3. Which of the following was NOT true of the Byzantine Empire?
   a. It spread Christianity to peoples in the East.
   b. It gave the world new techniques in the fine arts.
   c. It lasted over a thousand years.
   d. It collapsed in 726.

   ANS: D DIF: E

4. The Byzantine emperor hired
   a. Vikings to stop the farmer's rebellion.
   b. Venetians to stop the Viking invasion.
   c. Muslims to stop the Viking invasion.
   d. Christians to stop the Muslim invasion.

   ANS: B DIF: A

5. By the time the Byzantine Empire fell,
   a. the emperor had killed himself.
   b. its farmland was ruined.
   c. its population had fallen to less than 100,000.
   d. its palaces had crumbled.

   ANS: C DIF: A

MATCHING

Match each item with the correct statement below.

a. Turks
b. Constantinople
c. Byzantine Empire
d. Venetians
e. Venice

1. Italian city-state
2. capital of Byzantine Empire
3. people from Venice
4. lasted 1,100 years
5. conquered the Byzantines in 1453

1. ANS: E DIF: A
2. ANS: B DIF: A
3. ANS: D DIF: A
4. ANS: C DIF: A
5. ANS: A DIF: A

SHORT ANSWER

1. What government service did farmers perform in the early years of the Byzantine Empire?

   ANS:
   They served in the army.

   DIF: A

2. Why were fewer soldiers needed during the later years of the empire?

   ANS:
   because the empire's borders were safe

   DIF: A

3. How did the decrease in a standing army affect the problems between the empire and the Vikings?

ANS:
The Byzantines got help from the Venetians, who helped them drive out the Vikings but then took over the empire's trade.

DIF: C

CHAPTER 22—THE SPREAD OF ISLAM

MULTIPLE CHOICE

1. Even before the founding of Islam, the holiest city in Arabia was
   a. Cairo.
   b. Makkah.
   c. Madina.
   d. Yathrib.

   ANS: B DIF: E

2. After his vision, Muhammad was convinced that
   a. the Arabs should worship only Allah.
   b. Abraham had been the ancestor of the Arabs.
   c. many gods should be worshiped in Makkah.
   d. the Arabs should follow the religion of Christianity.

   ANS: A DIF: A

3. Followers of Islam believe that Muhammad was
   a. a god.
   b. the only rightful caliph.
   c. the son of God.
   d. the prophet of Allah.

   ANS: D DIF: A

4. The first year of the Muslim calendar is
   a. 570 A.D., the year of Muhammad's birth.
   b. 622 A.D., the Anno Hijrah.
   c. 632 A.D., the year Muhammad died.
   d. 661 A.D., the death of Ali.

   ANS: B DIF: A

5. The capital of the Arab Empire was at Baghdad during the reign of
   a. the Abbasid caliphs.
   b. Abu Bakr.
   c. the Umayyad caliphs.
   d. the Rightly Guided Caliphs.

   ANS: A DIF: C

6. The Quran describes the five duties all Muslims must fulfill, called the
   a. Anno Hijrah.
   b. *Ka'bah.*
   c. revelation.
   d. pillars of faith.

   ANS: D DIF: E

7. What part of Europe had a rich Muslim culture for about 400 years?
   a. North Africa
   b. Southern Greece
   c. Spain
   d France

   ANS: C DIF: A

8. People in Europe learned about the numerals 0 to 9 from
   a. Arab mathematicians.
   b. Gupta mathematicians.
   c. Persian astronomers.
   d. Greek scientists.

   ANS: A DIF: E

9. One of the finest poems known is the *Rubaiyat*, written by the Persian poet
   a. Avicenna.
   b. Khad Ajuh.
   c. Omar Khayyam.
   d. Mu'awiya.

   ANS: C DIF: A

10. Islamic artists and scholars made valuable contributions in all of the following areas EXCEPT
    a. making maps of the world.
    b. painting pictures of people.
    c. writing histories.
    d. studying the stars.

    ANS: B DIF: C

11. Muhammad was able to return his government to Makkah
    a. because he signed a treaty with the citizens there.
    b. by defeating the government there.
    c. with the help of the pilgrims who visited the Ka'bah.
    d. with trade caravans from India and China.

    ANS: A DIF: A

12. Not only were goods from all over the known world exchanged at Baghdad, but so were
    a. territories and boundaries.
    b. leadership and battle skills.
    c. ideas and learning.
    d. fear and distrust.

    ANS: C DIF: A

13. During the Golden Age of Islam, trade increased to such an extent that
    a. the caliphs posted 24-hour guards around the markets.
    b. a banking system developed.
    c. people had to relax by playing polo and chess.
    d. the first private drugstores could be opened.

    ANS: B DIF: A

14. The rich culture of Muslim Spain produced
    a. swift Arabian horses.
    b. beautiful architecture and an increase in medical and philosophical studies.
    c. the first minted Arabic money.
    d. the highest taxes in the Arab empire.

    ANS: B DIF: A

15. Islam tried to help women by
    a. insisting that women travel.
    b. outlawing marriage to more than one woman.
    c. teaching that raising a female child guaranteed the parents a reward in heaven.
    d. entrusting their inheritance to their fathers or husbands.

    ANS: C DIF: A

16. Working together, Arab astronomers and geographers
    a. proved that blood circulates through the body.
    b. invented chemistry and geometry.
    c. changed tin, iron, and lead into gold.
    d. decided that the earth might be round.

    ANS: D DIF: A

MATCHING

Match each item with the correct statement below.

a.	Abbasids	f.	Avicenna
b.	Damascus	g.	*mosque*
c.	Abu Bakr	h.	Hejaz
d.	Quran	i.	Muhammad
e.	bedouins	j.	Islam

1. prophet whose teaching began the Islamic religion
2. Mountainous area in the western part of Arabian Peninsula
3. Muslim scriptures
4. Capital of Arab Empire under the Umayyad Dynasty
5. Muslim house of worship
6. Arabic word that means "the act of submitting to the will of God"
7. Persian doctor who discovered tuberculosis is contagious and wrote *Canon of Medicine*
8. Arab-speaking desert herders and warriors
9. First caliph, father-in-law of Muhammad
10. Islamic dynasty that favored non-Arab peoples

1. ANS: I DIF: A
2. ANS: H DIF: A
3. ANS: D DIF: A
4. ANS: B DIF: A
5. ANS: G DIF: A
6. ANS: J DIF: A
7. ANS: F DIF: A
8. ANS: E DIF: A
9. ANS: C DIF: A
10. ANS: A DIF: A

SHORT ANSWER

1. List three or four ways in which the development of Islam was similar to that of Christianity. What do you think are the major differences?

    ANS:
    Answers will vary, but could include: SIMILARITIES: faith in a single god; founded by one person whose preachings were initially laughed at; a single book (the Bible, the Quran) relating scriptures at the heart of the religion; DIFFERENCES: Islam requires pilgrimages, prayer five times daily, fasting.

    DIF: A

2. Study the map below. Which continent shown was the least affected by the religion of Islam? About what fraction of the known world would that continent be?

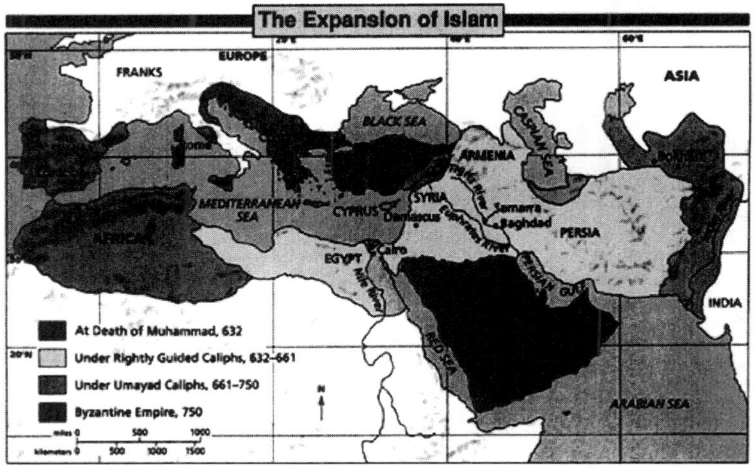

    ANS:
    Europe; about one-eighth

    DIF: C

SECTION QUIZ 22-1—ISLAM

MULTIPLE CHOICE

1. The book of Muslim scriptures is
   a. the *Ka'bah.*
   b. the Quran.
   c. the Ramadan.
   d. Makkah.

   ANS: B DIF: E

2. The Arabic word "Islam" means
   a. to journey to Makkah.
   b. the Year of Migration.
   c. submitting to the will of God.
   d. God.

   ANS: C DIF: E

3. The Islamic faith
   a. was founded by Allah.
   b. was founded by Muhammad.
   c. began in the city of Constantinople.
   d. uses scriptures known as *Anno Hijrah.*

   ANS: B DIF: A

4. The first year of the Muslim calendar was
   a. 570.
   b. 610.
   c. 622.
   d. 632.

   ANS: C DIF: A

5. In 610, Muhammad
   a. made a pilgrimage.
   b. built a mosque.
   c. had a revelation.
   d. wrote the Quran.

   ANS: C DIF: A

MATCHING

Match each item with the correct statement below.

a. pilgrims
b. *imam*
c. pillars of faith
d. *mosque*
e. *zakah*

1. the five Muslim duties
2. charity
3. prayer leader
4. Muslim house of worship
5. travelers to a religious shrine

1. ANS: C DIF: A

2. ANS: E DIF: A
3. ANS: B DIF: A
4. ANS: D DIF: A
5. ANS: A DIF: A

SHORT ANSWER

1. What were the two most powerful civilizations at the time that Islam was founded?

   ANS:
   Byzantium and Persia

   DIF: E

2. Why do Islamic pilgrims visit Makkah?

   ANS:
   It is the site of Arabia's holiest shrine.

   DIF: E

3. What belief does Islam have in common with Judaism and Christianity?

   ANS:
   that there is only one god

   DIF: A

4. Where did Muhammad first set up a government based on Islam?

   ANS:
   Madina

   DIF: A

5. Where did Muhammad relocate his rule?

   ANS:
   Makkah

   DIF: A

SECTION QUIZ 22-2—THE ARAB EMPIRE

MULTIPLE CHOICE

1. After Muhammad died, the first caliph was
   a. Mu'awiya.
   b. Shi'ah.
   c. a Persian engineer.
   d. Abu Bakr.

   ANS: D DIF: A

2. The first 100 years of Abbasid rule was known as
   a. the Umayyad Dynasty.
   b. the Golden Age of Islam.
   c. the Shi'ah.
   d. the Age of Viziers.

   ANS: B DIF: E

3. Mu'awiya
   a. was the first caliph.
   b. built the city of Baghdad.
   c. founded the Umayyad Dynasty.
   d. was the first vizier.

   ANS: C DIF: C

4. The first four caliphs after Muhammad's death
   a. were Abbasids.
   b. lived in Baghdad.
   c. were Muslim Arabs called Moors.
   d. were called the Rightly Guided Caliphs.

   ANS: D DIF: A

5. The Alhambra is
   a. a chief adviser.
   b. a Muslim sect.
   c. a palace in Granada.
   d. the capital of the Muslim world.

   ANS: C DIF: A

MATCHING

Match each item with the correct statement below.

a. Baghdad
b. Khazars
c. moat
d. vizier
e. caliph

1. successor
2. chief Abbasid adviser
3. city on the east bank of the Tigris
4. wide ditch filled with water
5. half-Mongolian people

1. ANS: E DIF: A
2. ANS: D DIF: A
3. ANS: A DIF: A
4. ANS: C DIF: A
5. ANS: B DIF: A

SHORT ANSWER

1. What did the Rightly Guided Caliphs acquire as they spread Islam?

   ANS:
   more territory and people to rule

   DIF: A

2. How did the Arabs treat people who surrendered to them?

   ANS:
   They made them pay taxes, but they could keep their lands.

   DIF: A

3. To where did the Umayyad Dynasty move the capital of the Arab empire?

   ANS:
   Damascus

   DIF: A

4. Over what did the Shi'ite and Sunni Muslims disagree?

   ANS:
   who should be their leader

   DIF: A

5. Why did the empire begin to break into independent kingdoms?

   ANS:
   It was too large for one caliph to control.

   DIF: A

SECTION QUIZ 22-3—ARAB CONTRIBUTIONS

MULTIPLE CHOICE

1. Arab alchemists tried to
   a. turn water into wine.
   b. turn base metals into gold and silver.
   c. use gold and silver as medicines.
   d. cure tuberculosis.

   ANS: B DIF: A

2. The poem *Rubaiyat*
   a. was written by Avicenna.
   b. was written by Ibn Khaldun.
   c. was written by Omar Khayyam.
   d. explains the contagious nature of tuberculosis.

   ANS: C DIF: C

3. The first accurate map of the world was drawn by
   a. ar-Razi.
   b. Ibn Khaldun.
   c. Avicenna.
   d. al-Idrisi.

   ANS: D DIF: A

4. Arab mathematicians
   a. invented the numerals 0-9.
   b. invented geometry.
   c. invented algebra.
   d. taught multiplication to Gupta mathematicians.

   ANS: C DIF: E

5. Which of the following is NOT true of the *Canon of Medicine*?
   a. It was written by Avicenna.
   b. It was an encyclopedia of medicine.
   c. It is considered one of the finest poems ever written.
   d. It was used in European medical schools for 500 years.

   ANS: C DIF: A

MATCHING

Match each item with the correct statement below.

a. Ibn Khaldun
b. ar-Razi
c. Omar Khayyam
d. contagious
e. tides

1. the rise and fall of oceans
2. can be passed from person to person

3. Muslim historian
4. Persian poet
5. Persian doctor

1. ANS: E DIF: A
2. ANS: D DIF: A
3. ANS: A DIF: A
4. ANS: C DIF: A
5. ANS: B DIF: A

SHORT ANSWER

1. How were Arab doctors different from doctors in other countries?

   ANS:
   Arab doctors had to pass a test.

   DIF: A

2. How does Islamic art differ from most other art?

   ANS:
   It shows no human figures or living creatures, and is made up mostly of geometric designs.

   DIF: C

3. How did Arab historians of the time present the history of the times?

   ANS:
   They wrote about events centered around rulers and peoples.

   DIF: A

CHAPTER 23—THE EASTERN SLAVS

MULTIPLE CHOICE

1. Which is the best description of an Eastern Slavic farm village in the 600s and 700s?
   a. Wooden cabins surrounded by a wall and a stockade
   b. Brick houses with white plastered walls
   c. Stone houses around a central fortress
   d. Wooden houses clustered around a monastery

   ANS: A DIF: A

2. To carry their goods to Byzantium, Kievan Rus traders used
   a. horse-drawn sleds.
   b. caravans on horseback.
   c. boats on the river.
   d. fast sailing ships.

   ANS: C DIF: A

3. The Viking warriors who helped defend the trade routes to Byzantium were also known as
   a. Russians.
   b. Varangians.
   c. Slavs.
   d. Dorians.

   ANS: B DIF: A

4. The first Rus state centered around the city of
   a. Kiev.
   b. Moscow.
   c. Novgorod.
   d. Byzantium.

   ANS: A DIF: E

5. In the Rus language, the term for wealthy landowning nobles was
   a. *veche*.
   b. boyars.
   c. *izbas*.
   d. khans.

   ANS: B DIF: A

6. One result of the Kievan Rus peoples' choice of Eastern Orthodox Christianity was
   a. more emphasis on Greek and Roman classical culture.
   b. the introduction of Byzantine culture.
   c. the destruction of the boyars' estates.
   d. closer ties with western Europe.

   ANS: D DIF: C

7. Which of these was NOT a result of the Mongol conquest of Kievan Rus?
   a. Ambitious princes made Muscovy the leading Rus state.
   b. The Church developed its own customs.
   c. The Muscovites paid tribute to the Mongol Khan.
   d. Boyars became more powerful than the czar.

   ANS: D DIF: E

8. By the reign of Ivan the Great, Muscovites believed that
   a. a council of the boyars should govern Muscovy.
   b. Byzantium was the center of Eastern Orthodox Christianity.
   c. the czar should head the government and the Church.
   d. the czar should retire and go to a monastery.

   ANS: C DIF: E

9. Under Ivan the Terrible, the *Oprichnina* were
   a. Mongol invaders.
   b. the czar's secret police.
   c. European engineers.
   d. the czar's enemies.

   ANS: B DIF: A

10. How did Ivan IV's way of governing affect peasants?
    a. Peasants were given land from the boyars' estates.
    b. Peasants were no longer free to move to other lands.
    c. Engineers from western Europe taught peasants new skills.
    d. The *Oprichnina* protected peasants from the Mongols.

    ANS: B DIF: C

MATCHING

Match each item with the correct statement below.

a. Vladimir I
b. Mongols
c. Dmitry
d. Sophia
e. Ivan the Terrible
f. Kiev
g. Yaroslav
h. Oleg
i. Volga
j. Ivan the Great

1. Prince of Moscow who first called himself czar: the official title of the Russian emperor
2. Prince of Kiev who adopted Eastern Orthodox Christianity
3. Early trading town on the Dnieper River
4. Asian people who conquered Kievan Rus
5. Byzantine princess who married a prince of Moscow
6. Prince of Moscow who defeated the Mongols in 1378
7. First Grand Prince of Kiev
8. River where first Kievan Rus settlements were made
9. Grand Prince of Kiev, called "the Wise" because of his interest in learning
10. Czar who broke the power of the boyars

1. ANS: J DIF: A
2. ANS: A DIF: A
3. ANS: F DIF: A
4. ANS: B DIF: A
5. ANS: D DIF: A
6. ANS: C DIF: A
7. ANS: H DIF: A
8. ANS: I DIF: A

9. ANS: G DIF: A
10. ANS: E DIF: A

Match the correct ending to the beginning of each sentence below.
a. by forming alliances with the Mongols.
b. whose people could not pay Mongol taxes or provide soldiers.
c. declined as its people fled to the north to escape invaders.
d. because Mongol chiefs, like the earlier Rus leaders, were fighting among themselves.
e. using guns and gunpowder, advanced weapons from Europe.
f. during the Mongol invasion.

11. After 250 years as a strong trading state, Kievan Rus _____
12. The people of Kievan Rus grew even more isolated _____
13. Muscovy princes added to the decline of Kievan Rus _____
14. Muscovy princes expanded their territories by taking over any Rus territory _____
15. Moscovite prince Dmitri was able to defeat the Mongols _____
16. Ivan IV took back territories from the Mongols _____

11. ANS: C DIF: A
12. ANS: F DIF: A
13. ANS: A DIF: A
14. ANS: B DIF: A
15. ANS: D DIF: A
16. ANS: E DIF: A

SHORT ANSWER

1. What do you think are the drawbacks of the slash-and-burn farming method?

ANS:
Answers will vary, but could include: slash-and-burn uses up farmland so that it cannot be reused, thus making a great deal of land necessary to continue growing crops. It also means the farmers must move whenever the land is used up, and ultimately would destroy the supply of trees.

DIF: A

2. Look at the map below. Use the scale of miles to figure a rough estimate of the area in square miles covered by Kievan Rus, as well as the additional area that paid tribute to the Rus princes.

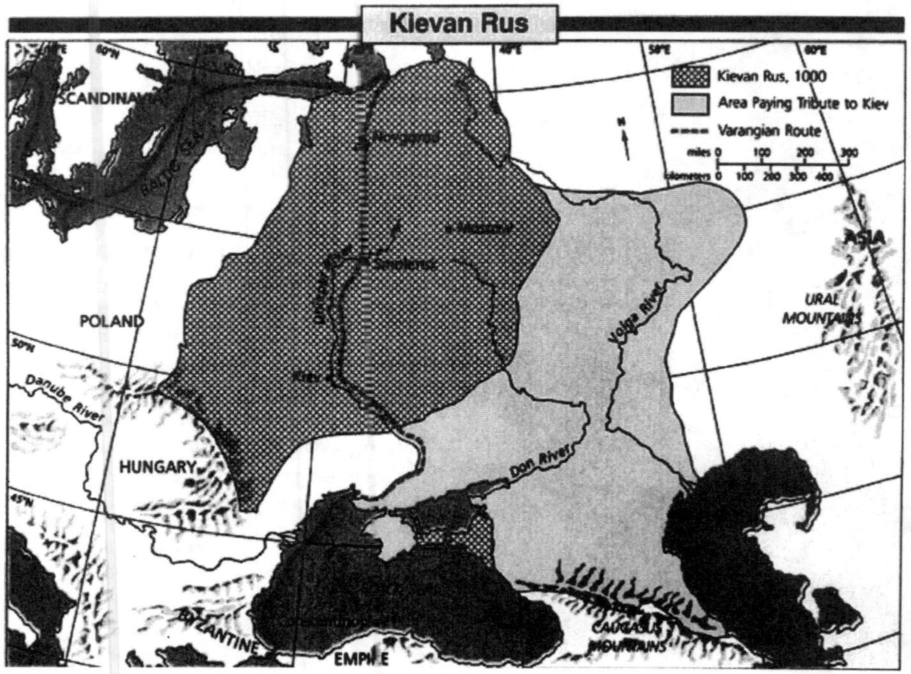

ANS:
Kievan Rus covered about 62,000 square miles of territory; about an additional 82,000 square miles paid tribute to the Rus princes.

DIF: C

SECTION QUIZ 23-1—EARLY EASTERN SLAVS

MULTIPLE CHOICE

1. Which of the following is NOT true of the Eastern Slavs?
a. They worshiped many gods.
b. They became skilled in building with wood.
c. They were mainly warriors.
d. They lived in *izbas*.

ANS: C DIF: C

2. To protect their trade route, the Eastern Slavs
   a. went to war with Rome.
   b. relied on the Varangians.
   c. closed the roads to travelers.
   d. built mighty fortresses.

   ANS: B DIF: A

3. Which of the following is NOT true of *izbas*?
   a. They had only one floor.
   b. They had fireplaces.
   c. They had gabled roofs.
   d. They had no windows.

   ANS: D DIF: A

4. The Eastern Slavs set up a trade route that ran
   a. halfway around the world.
   b. from the Baltic Sea to the Caspian.
   c. from the Volga River to Ukraine.
   d. the length of the Nile.

   ANS: B DIF: E

5. The Great Mother was
   a. the oldest woman in the village.
   b. the goddess of land and harvest.
   c. the goddess of military might.
   d. the goddess of wisdom and beauty.

   ANS: B DIF: A

MATCHING

Match each item with the correct statement below.

a. Varangians
b. Perun
c. slash-and-burn
d. *izbas*
e. Volos

1. one-room log cabins
2. god of thunder and lightning
3. protector of cattle and sheep
4. Viking warriors
5. method used to clear forests

1. ANS: D DIF: A
2. ANS: B DIF: A
3. ANS: E DIF: A
4. ANS: A DIF: A
5. ANS: C DIF: A

SHORT ANSWER

1. What was the relationship among people in early eastern Slav villages?

   ANS:
   They were related families.

   DIF: E

2. What were the ownership rights in these villages?

   ANS:
   Each family owned their own house.

   DIF: E

3. How did the slash-and-burn method of farming affect the lives of the East Slavs?

   ANS:
   They had to move every few years.

   DIF: A

4. Why did the East Slavs become skilled woodworkers?

   ANS:
   Their countryside was covered with large forests.

   DIF: A

5. How did trade with Byzantium help the East Slavs?

   ANS:
   They were able to live more comfortably and develop their civilization.

   DIF: A

SECTION QUIZ 23-2—KIEVAN RUS

MULTIPLE CHOICE

1. The term "Rus" means
   a. warrior band.
   b. farming state.
   c. grassland.
   d. ruled by boyars.

   ANS: A DIF: A

2. Which of the following was NOT true of Kiev?
   a. It overlooked the Dnieper River.
   b. It was a good location to protect merchant ships.
   c. It was the northernmost city on the Varangian trade route.
   d. It was the capital of Kievan Rus.

   ANS: C DIF: C

3. Yaroslav was
   a. father of Vladimir I.
   b. son of Vladimir I.
   c. the ruler of Byzantium.
   d. also known as Vladimir I.

   ANS: B DIF: A

4. In 988, Vladimir I
   a. went to war with Oleg.
   b. chose Byzantine Christianity as the official religion.
   c. converted to Islam.
   d. died.

   ANS: B DIF: E

5. Under Yaroslav's code of law
   a. the death penalty was used only in murder cases.
   b. physical punishment was severe.
   c. crimes against property were considered the most serious.
   d. criminals were never punished.

   ANS: C DIF: A

MATCHING

Match each item with the correct statement below.

a. steppe
b. boyars
c. Kievan Rus
d. *veche*
e. Yaroslav

1. assembly
2. state established by Oleg
3. grassland
4. landowning nobles
5. Grand Prince of Kiev

1. ANS: D DIF: A
2. ANS: C DIF: A
3. ANS: A DIF: A
4. ANS: B DIF: A
5. ANS: E DIF: A

SHORT ANSWER

1. How did Kiev's location affect Byzantium?

   ANS:
   Kiev controlled trade with Byzantium.

   DIF: A

2. What was the power structure in Kievan Rus?

   ANS:
   It was a group of small territories ruled by one main ruler.

   DIF: A

3. Who had the power to call a veche?

   ANS:
   any free man

   DIF: A

4. What did the Eastern Orthodox Church contribute to Kievan Rus culture?

   ANS:
   elements of Byzantine culture

   DIF: A

5. What two sources formed the basis for Kievan Rus laws?

   ANS:
   old Slavic customs and Byzantine law

   DIF: A

SECTION QUIZ 23-3—THE MONGOL CONQUEST

MULTIPLE CHOICE

1. Rus peasant men wore shoes made of
   a. leather.
   b. rags.
   c. paper.
   d. tree bark.

   ANS: D DIF: A

2. Which of the following was NOT true of Rus people?
   a. They did not eat much meat.
   b. They told stories for pleasure.
   c. They wore cotton stockings.
   d. They were mainly farmers.

   ANS: C DIF: E

3. Which of the following was NOT true of the Rus church?
   a. It united the people and made them proud of their culture.
   b. It forbade the eating of meat.
   c. It developed its own local rituals and practices.
   d. It was isolated from other Christian churches.

   ANS: A DIF: A

4. In 1240, Kievan Rus was taken over by
   a. the caftans.
   b. the Mongols.
   c. the Eastern Orthodox Church.
   d. the Rus people.

   ANS: B DIF: A

5. The Mongols made the Rus citizens pay tribute to
   a. Oleg.
   b. the caliph.
   c. the khan.
   d. the Mongolian sheriff.

   ANS: C DIF: C

MATCHING

Match each item with the correct statement below.

a. Mongols
b. caftans
c. khans
d. tunics
e. smocks

1. Mongol leaders
2. long robes that tied at the waist
3. group of united tribes
4. commonly worn by peasant men
5. commonly worn by peasant women

1. ANS: C DIF: A
2. ANS: B DIF: A
3. ANS: A DIF: A
4. ANS: D DIF: A
5. ANS: E DIF: A

SHORT ANSWER

1. Where did monks begin to set up monasteries during the Mongol invasion?

   ANS:
   deep in northern forests

   DIF: C

2. Why did towns and villages grow up around the monasteries?

   ANS:
   People looking for new land settled around the monasteries.

   DIF: A

3. Besides isolating the Rus people, what other important effect did Mongol rule have on them?

   ANS:
   It made them distrust ideas and practices from other countries.

   DIF: A

SECTION QUIZ 23-4—THE RISE OF MOSCOW

MULTIPLE CHOICE

1. In 1426, Ivan III, known as Ivan the Great,
   a. built Moscow's kremlin.
   b. ended Mongolian control of Moscow.
   c. became prince of Moscow.
   d. died.

   ANS: C DIF: A

2. Which of the following was NOT true of Ivan IV?
   a. He became czar of Muscovy when he was three years old.
   b. He was crowned czar in 1547, when he was 16 years old.
   c. His nickname became Ivan the Terrible.
   d. He died in 1505.

   ANS: D DIF: C

3. When Ivan IV died,
   a. his oldest son took the throne.
   b. his youngest son took the throne.
   c. the *Oprichnina* took over.
   d. he left no suitable heir.

   ANS: D DIF: A

4. To the Muscovites, Ivan IV was
   a. a great ruler who protected them.
   b. a cruel tyrant.
   c. feeble-minded.
   d. considered a god.

   ANS: A DIF: E

5. Which of the following was NOT true of the *Oprichnina*?
   a. It was made up of 5,000 of Ivan IV's most loyal supporters.
   b. Its members dressed in black.
   c. Its members killed thousands of people.
   d. It overthrew Ivan IV and took control of Moscow.

   ANS: D DIF: A

MATCHING

Match each item with the correct statement below.

a. czar
b. Dmitry
c. *Oprichnina*
d. Moscow
e. kremlin

1. Muscovy
2. fortress
3. secret police
4. emperor
5. a prince of Moscow

1. ANS: D DIF: A
2. ANS: E DIF: A
3. ANS: C DIF: A
4. ANS: A DIF: A
5. ANS: B DIF: A

SHORT ANSWER

1. Why did many Rus people move north past Moscow?

   ANS:
   They were trying to escape the Mongols.

   DIF: A

2. What kind of people settled near Moscow instead of continuing north?

   ANS:
   artisans

   DIF: A

3. How did the Muscovite princes handle succession to their thrones?

   ANS:
   It was passed from father to son.

   DIF: E

4. How did Ivan IV reward his advisers?

   ANS:
   with gifts of land and jobs as officials

   DIF: A

CHAPTER 24—FEUDAL SOCIETY

MULTIPLE CHOICE

1. The basis of power under the feudal system was
   a. money and gold.
   b. land ownership.
   c. military skill.
   d. the people's support.

   ANS: B DIF: A

2. In the 900s, peasants were willing to trade their land for protection from
   a. Germanic invaders.
   b. powerful kings.
   c. Viking raids.
   d. the Franks.

   ANS: C DIF: C

3. The most important duty of a feudal vassal was
   a. working the lord's farmlands.
   b. attending the lord's court.
   c. providing military service.
   d. protecting the lord's fief from attack.

   ANS: C DIF: A

4. The most common feudal agreements of lords and vassals established ties of loyalty and duty among
   a. clergy.
   b. nobles.
   c. serfs.
   d. kings.

   ANS: B DIF: E

5. In a castle, the noble's household quarters and great hall were located in the
   a. moat.
   b. palisade.
   c. *portcullis*.
   d. keep.

   ANS: D DIF: E

6. One of the duties of a page was to
   a. help knights care for their warhorses.
   b. rescue a knight who fell in battle.
   c. fight in tournaments and jousts.
   d. oversee the noble's different fiefs.

   ANS: A DIF: A

7. In general, noblewomen in the Middle Ages were expected to
   a. train pages in riding and fencing.
   b. pay a ransom if their lord was captured in battle.
   c. run the castle household and look after the poor.
   d. take care of the destriers.

   ANS: C DIF: C

8. On a manor, the person in charge of overseeing work in the fields was called
   a. a squire.
   b. a vassal.
   c. the seneschal.
   d. the bailiff.

   ANS: D DIF: E

9. Which of the following is NOT true about the life of a serf?
   a. Serfs could own their own land or house.
   b. Serfs could gain freedom by escaping to a town.
   c. Serfs had to have the noble's permission to marry.
   d. Serfs did not have to serve in the noble's army.

   ANS: A DIF: A

10. Toward the end of the Middle Ages, farming became more productive because
    a. feudal estates had grown larger.
    b. peasants could use oxen to pull their plows.
    c. heavier iron plows were invented.
    d. more serfs were free to move away from the land.

    ANS: C DIF: A

11. The kings who ruled western Europe after Charlemagne's death gave away more and more royal lands to
    a. invaders so that they would leave.
    b. the clergy so that they could build more monasteries.
    c. peasants and serfs to divide into manors.
    d. nobles who provided them with food, horses, and soldiers.

    ANS: D DIF: A

12. During the Viking invasions, people in western Europe
    a. fled to Asia Minor and Asia.
    b. wanted security and protection from their leaders.
    c. banded together to establish national governments.
    d. gave power back to the kings.

    ANS: B DIF: A

13. Nobles raised their own armies
    a. so they could develop feudalism.
    b. because they wanted to protect the poor and helpless.
    c. to protect their property, which included lands and people.
    d. because no national governments existed in western Europe.

    ANS: C DIF: A

14. European peasants traded their lands and freedom for
    a. a powerful noble's protection.
    b. the act of homage.
    c. the privilege of becoming knights.
    d. the trusted word of a powerful noble.

    ANS: A DIF: A

15. Along with land, a noble also received the right to
    a. make laws to govern the land and the people who lived on it.
    b. establish a manor village for farming.
    c. build castles with keeps for protection.
    d. send someone else in his place for military duty.

ANS: A DIF: A

MATCHING

Match each item with the correct statement below.

a. fiefs	f. act of homage
b. clergy	g. squire
c. serf	h. code of chivalry
d. joust	i. dubbing
e. palisades	j. seneschal

1. Rules governing a knight's behavior
2. Farm workers who could not leave the noble's land
3. Young nobleman who served a knight in battle
4. Estates given in return for military service
5. Social group made up of religious leaders
6. High wooden fences built for protection
7. A vassal's pledge of loyal service to a noble
8. Official of a manor who oversaw all the fiefs
9. Competition between two mounted knights
10. Ceremony by which a young noble became a knight

1. ANS: H DIF: A
2. ANS: C DIF: A
3. ANS: G DIF: A
4. ANS: A DIF: A
5. ANS: B DIF: A
6. ANS: E DIF: A
7. ANS: F DIF: A
8. ANS: J DIF: A
9. ANS: D DIF: A
10. ANS: I DIF: A

SHORT ANSWER

1. Why do you think the lives of noblewomen were so restricted? What advantages and disadvantages did their limited roles have for the society?

ANS:
Answers will vary, but could include: one reason the lives of noblewomen were so restricted may have been that the fighting and holding of territory was so important, and women did not take part in the fighting. Advantages of their limited roles may have included the fact that they and their children were more protected. Disadvantages clearly were that the society was deprived of possible contributions they could have made.

DIF: C

2. Study the map below. Then answer the following questions.

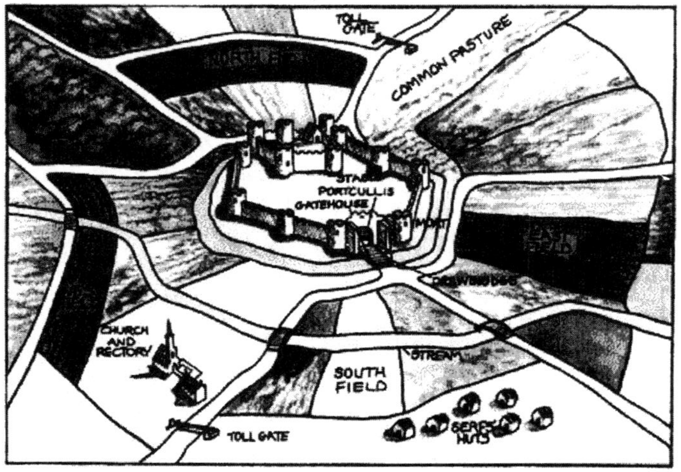

a. How does the map illustrate the three-field system of farming?
b. Which field is not sown?
c. Where does a village green belong?
d. What kind of dwelling does the noble of this manor have?
e. What kinds of standard protection does this castle provide?
f. What structures indicate that travelers through the noble's estate and manor pay for his protection?

ANS:

a. shows three fields as being planted
b. south field is lying fallow
c. in the middle of the serfs' huts
d. stone castle
e. stone wall and moat
f. toll gates

DIF: C

SECTION QUIZ 24-1—LAND AND GOVERNMENT

MULTIPLE CHOICE

1. In feudal times, the duty of the clergy was
   a. to teach Christianity and help the poor and sick.
   b. to govern, enforce laws, and protect people.
   c. to support the nobles by farming.
   d. to provide bread for the nobles.

   ANS: A DIF: A

2. When a vassal died,
   a. his fief usually passed to his wife.
   b. his fief usually passed to his son.
   c. his son became a knight.
   d. his son became a lord.

   ANS: B DIF: A

3. Vassals were expected to take part in military service
   a. 10-20 hours a month.
   b. 40-60 hours a month.
   c. 10-20 days a year.
   d. 40-60 days a year.

   ANS: D DIF: E

4. After Charlemagne's death in 814,
   a. kings became more powerful than ever.
   b. nobles became independent rulers.
   c. peasants farmed their own land.
   d. nobles were drafted to raise an army.

   ANS: B DIF: A

5. As part of the act of homage, a lord gave his vassal
   a. a written agreement.
   b. a glove, a stick, or a stone.
   c. his fastest horse.
   d. a bag of grain, a tunic, and a sword.

   ANS: B DIF: C

COMPLETION

1. In feudal times, land ownership brought ____________________ and wealth.

   ANS: power DIF: E

2. Kings who ruled after Charlemagne ignored their ________________.

ANS: responsibilities DIF: A

3. Nobles who grew more powerful than the kings became independent ________________ in their own areas.

ANS: rulers DIF: E

4. Peasants gave their ________________ to a noble in return for ________________.

ANS: land; protection DIF: A

5. Not much changed or ________________ because people believed that life was the way ________________ wanted it.

ANS: improved; God DIF: A

MATCHING

Match each item with the correct statement below.

a. feudalism
b. fiefs
c. knights
d. act of homage
e. vassals

1. estates
2. special ceremony
3. nobles who served a lord
4. warriors on horseback
5. government by landed nobles

1. ANS: B DIF: A
2. ANS: D DIF: A
3. ANS: E DIF: A
4. ANS: C DIF: A
5. ANS: A DIF: A

SECTION QUIZ 24-2—THE NOBILITY

MULTIPLE CHOICE

1. Which of the following is NOT a feature of castles?
   a. thick stone walls
   b. lookout towers
   c. moat
   d. thatched roof

ANS: D DIF: E

2. In feudal times, women often were married
   a. by the age of 12.
   b. on their 22nd birthday.
   c. after the age of 30.
   d. on their 30th birthday.

ANS: A DIF: E

3. The castle's drawbridge led to
   a. a watchtower.
   b. the *portcullis.*
   c. the keep.
   d. the dungeon.

ANS: B DIF: C

4. From the 800s to the 1000s, nobles lived
   a. in castles.
   b. in stone houses.
   c. in wooden houses.
   d. mainly on ships.

ANS: C DIF: A

5. In feudal castles, the household usually lived
   a. in the keep.
   b. in the great hall.
   c. in the dungeon.
   d. in the *portcullis.*

ANS: A DIF: A

COMPLETION

1. ________________ had more privileges and benefits than peasants or serfs.

ANS: Nobles DIF: E

2. When nobles were away fighting, they left servants and ________________ in charge to defend their castles.

ANS: officials DIF: A

3. Because of huge ________________ areas, most castles could be defended for months at a time.

ANS: storage DIF: A

4. Feudal marriages were planned to ________________ important families.

ANS: unite DIF: A

MATCHING

Match each item with the correct statement below.

a. keep
b. castles
c. palisades
d. ladies
e. *portcullis*

1. high wooden fences

2. tall tower with thick walls
3. stone houses
4. iron gate
5. noblewomen

1. ANS: C DIF: A
2. ANS: A DIF: A
3. ANS: B DIF: A
4. ANS: E DIF: A
5. ANS: D DIF: A

SECTION QUIZ 24-3—KNIGHTHOOD

MULTIPLE CHOICE

1. To become a knight, a squire had to
   a. polish armor.
   b. run errands for ladies.
   c. care for destriers.
   d. prove that he was a good fighter.

   ANS: D DIF: E

2. The ceremony used to make a squire a knight was called
   a. the code of chivalry.
   b. dubbing.
   c. the tournament.
   d. jousting.

   ANS: B DIF: C

3. A popular tournament event was
   a. scabbarding.
   b. dubbing.
   c. jousting.
   d. destriers.

   ANS: C DIF: E

4. A knight's sword holder was called his
   a. joust.
   b. armor.
   c. scabbard.
   d. destrier.

   ANS: C DIF: A

5. Which of the following was NOT part of the code of chivalry?
   a. honoring the Church
   b. showing bravery
   c. helping people
   d. speaking Latin

   ANS: D DIF: A

COMPLETION

1. A noble began training for knighthood as a ____________________, helping to care for a knight's horse and equipment.

   ANS: page DIF: E

2. As a ____________________, the young noble went with his knight into battle.

   ANS: squire DIF: E

3. After being knighted, the noble wore a ____________________ at his side to symbolize his promise to fight at his lord's side.

   ANS: sword DIF: E

MATCHING

Match each item with the correct statement below.
a. squire
b. destriers
c. code of chivalry
d. tournaments
e. page

1. rules for knights
2. warhorses
3. seven-year-old knight trainee
4. put under the care of one knight
5. contests of strength or skill

1. ANS: C DIF: A
2. ANS: B DIF: A
3. ANS: E DIF: A
4. ANS: A DIF: A
5. ANS: D DIF: A

SECTION QUIZ 24-4—THE MANOR

MULTIPLE CHOICE

1. Manors were isolated from one another by
   a. knights.
   b. bailiffs.
   c. seneschals.
   d. poor transportation and frequent fighting.

   ANS: D DIF: A

2. In feudal times, a major cause of disease was
   a. dirt.
   b. fire.
   c. warm weather.
   d. fleas.

   ANS: D DIF: E

3. Peasant furniture consisted of
   a. tables and stools.
   b. beds and chairs.
   c. sofas and tables.
   d. chairs only.

   ANS: A DIF: E

4. By the end of the Middle Ages, serfs
   a. no longer existed.
   b. had overthrown the nobles.
   c. could buy their freedom.
   d. had mostly become knights.

   ANS: C DIF: C

5. By the 1200s, which of the following was NOT true?
   a. Farmers could not grow as much as they had in the 1100s.
   b. Farmers used the three-field system.
   c. Farmers started to use heavy iron plows.
   d. The horse collar was invented.

   ANS: A DIF: A

MATCHING

Match each item with the correct statement below.

a. manors
b. freemen
c. village green
d. seneschals
e. bailiffs

1. farming communities
2. made sure peasants worked hard
3. visited each fief regularly
4. peasants who paid for farming rights
5. open area surrounded by cottages

1. ANS: A DIF: A
2. ANS: E DIF: A
3. ANS: D DIF: A
4. ANS: B DIF: A
5. ANS: C DIF: A

SHORT ANSWER

1. What two features of medieval life kept manors isolated?

   ANS:
   poor transportation and frequent fighting

   DIF: A

2. How did village animals contribute to poor health?

   ANS:
   They brought diseases and fleas into homes.

   DIF: A

3. What was the relationship between serfs and nobles?

   ANS:
   Serfs were the property of nobles.

   DIF: A

CHAPTER 25—THE CHURCH

MULTIPLE CHOICE

1. Which of these is NOT true of the Roman Catholic Church in the Middle Ages?
   a. High Church leaders were not part of the feudal system.
   b. Church leaders helped govern western Europe.
   c. The Church owned valuable lands and properties.
   d. Daily life in villages revolved around the Church.

   ANS: A DIF: C

2. People were tried by the Inquisition for
   a. committing crimes.
   b. breaking canon law.
   c. breaking the king's laws.
   d. believing in heresies.

   ANS: D DIF: A

3. The aim of the monastery at Cluny was
   a. to give kings more power over the Church.
   b. to gain more political power for Church leaders.
   c. to return the Church to honest, simple ways.
   d. to punish people whose beliefs were heresies.

   ANS: C DIF: A

4. The crusaders found it hard to fight against Saladin's soldiers, yet had help with a new weapon called the
   a. longbow.
   b. crossbow.
   c. emirs.
   d. scabbard.

   ANS: B DIF: A

5. Young noblemen could get a basic education in grammar, arithmetic, and five other subjects at a
   a. cathedral school.
   b. monastery.
   c. union.
   d. university.

   ANS: A DIF: E

6. Which event first triggered the Crusades?
   a. Venetians attacked Constantinople in 1202.
   b. Turkish armies threatened the Byzantines.
   c. Turks stopped Christian pilgrims from leaving Jerusalem.
   d. Saladin's armies captured Jerusalem in 1187.

   ANS: B DIF: A

7. The Crusade of Kings ended in failure with King Richard I, the Lionheart, signing a truce with
   a. the Pope.
   b. Emperor Frederick I.
   c. King Philip II Augustus.
   d. the Muslim leader.

   ANS: D DIF: A

8. The feudal kingdoms known as Outremer were
   a. set up in Palestine by crusaders.
   b. established in France by crusaders returning home.
   c. given to Saladin by European kings.
   d. made from lands taken from the Byzantines.

   ANS: A DIF: C

9. During the crusade in 1202, Constantinople was looted by
   a. Muslims.
   b. Venetians and crusaders.
   c. Turks and Saracens.
   d. French peasants.

   ANS: B DIF: A

10. The end of the Crusades is considered to be 1291, when
    a. Muslims captured Acre.
    b. Constantinople was burned.
    c. crusaders took Jerusalem
    d. the Children's Crusade ended.

    ANS: A DIF: C

11. What was the goal of the Roman Catholic Church during the Middle Ages?
    a. to remove its officials from political affairs
    b. to lead crusades against the Vikings
    c. to develop a civilization based on Christian ideals
    d. to strengthen the feudal system

    ANS: C DIF: A

12. Which of the following was Pope Gregory's goal for the Church?
    a. fewer orders of monks and nuns
    b. decreased power of kings and nobles
    c. increased power over Church officials
    d. more religious training for Church officials

    ANS: C DIF: A

13. Why did many monks and friars take vows of poverty?
    a. to prove to people that they were not in the Church to get rich
    b. to protect the natural world
    c. to save their families' money
    d. so the Church would not have to feed them

    ANS: A DIF: A

14. Which of the following was a reason for the increase in learning during the late Middle Ages?
    a. more secure governments and a stronger economy
    b. rebirth of Charlemagne's ideals
    c. more teachers available
    d. fewer, but better, classes

    ANS: A DIF: A

15. What did the Seljuq Turks do that angered European Christians?
   a. charged high prices for Eastern goods
   b. declared war on the Byzantine Empire
   c. threatened the Pope
   d. captured Christian shrines in the Holy Land

   ANS: D DIF: A

16. Which of the following did most of the remaining crusaders do after capturing Jerusalem?
   a. went home to Europe
   b. helped rebuild Jerusalem
   c. settled in Egypt
   d. set up trading centers in Asia Minor

   ANS: A DIF: A

17. Why did the crusaders finally lose the respect and support of many western Europeans?
   a. They changed their clothing and eating habits.
   b. Many did not share the wealth they brought back from Asia.
   c. A group sacked Constantinople instead of going to Jerusalem.
   d. They lost the land they had captured to the Muslims.

   ANS: A DIF: A

18. Which of the following was ***not*** a result of the Crusades?
   a. growth of trade and towns in Europe
   b. a united Church
   c. breakdown of the feudal system
   d. increase in the power of western European kings

   ANS: A DIF: C

MATCHING

Match each item with the correct statement below.

a. Thomas Aquinas	f. Saladin
b. Gregory VII	g. tithes
c. Urban II	h. chancellor
d. excommunicated	i. Innocent III
e. friars	j. Dominic

1. Pope who claimed power over kings and feudal nobles
2. Spanish monk who started an order of friars in 1216
3. Preachers who lived in the towns
4. Removed as a member of the Church
5. Pope who sent a crusade to help the Byzantine Empire
6. Military leader of Muslims in the Middle East
7. Offerings equal to 10 percent of income
8. Medieval religious scholar
9. Pope who called for a crusade in 1202, involving Venice
10. Church official who headed a university

1. ANS: B DIF: A
2. ANS: J DIF: A
3. ANS: E DIF: A
4. ANS: D DIF: A
5. ANS: C DIF: A
6. ANS: F DIF: A
7. ANS: G DIF: A
8. ANS: A DIF: A
9. ANS: I DIF: A
10. ANS: H DIF: A

SHORT ANSWER

1. Suppose you were a heretic, or a person who didn't share all the beliefs of the Church during the Inquisition. Would the fear of what might happen to you change your beliefs? Why or why not?

   ANS:
   Answers will vary, but could include: some students would feel that they would profess publicly to the beliefs despite their private thoughts in order to save themselves; others would feel that they would make every effort to believe the Church.

   DIF: A

2. Study the map below. What coordinates did the crusaders who were allies of the Venetians set out for?

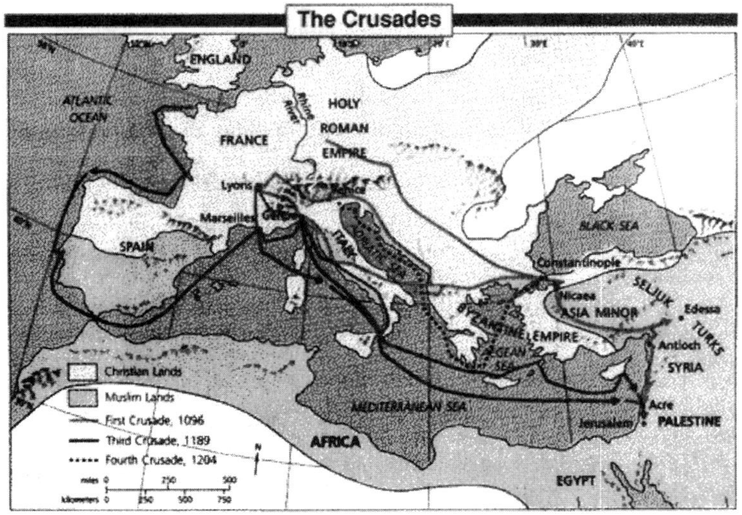

ANS:
41° N, 29° E

DIF: C

SECTION QUIZ 25-1—CATHOLIC INFLUENCE

MULTIPLE CHOICE

1. The Inquisition was set up in
   a. 1029.
   b. 1129.
   c. 1209.
   d. 1250.

   ANS: B DIF: A

2. Which of the following was NOT a duty of priests?
   a. recording births
   b. performing marriages
   c. delivering babies
   d. conducting burials

   ANS: C DIF: A

3. Heretics who confessed
   a. were punished and allowed back into the Church.
   b. were banished from the country.
   c. were burned at the stake.
   d. were hanged.

   ANS: A DIF: E

4. When people were excommunicated in the Middle Ages,
   a. they lost their political rights.
   b. they were put to death.
   c. their lives did not change very much.
   d. they were forced to leave the country.

   ANS: A DIF: A

5. The Church told people to obey the king's laws
   a. or be excommunicated.
   b. unless they contradicted canon laws.
   c. or leave the country.
   d. except regarding eating meat on Fridays.

   ANS: B DIF: C

MATCHING

Match each item with the correct statement below.
a. excommunicated
b. Roman Catholic Church
c. mass
d. the Inquisition
e. canon laws

1. the center of every village or town
2. Church laws
3. lost membership in the Church
4. Church court
5. worship service

1. ANS: B DIF: A
2. ANS: E DIF: A
3. ANS: A DIF: A
4. ANS: D DIF: A
5. ANS: C DIF: A

SHORT ANSWER

1. Under what conditions could a person disobey the king?

   ANS:
   if the king's laws went against the Church's laws

   DIF: A

2. What rights did excommunication take away?

ANS:
Church membership and all political rights

DIF: A

3. What problem within the Church did the Inquisition hope to stop?

ANS:
heresy

DIF: A

SECTION QUIZ 25-2—ATTEMPTS AT REFORM

MULTIPLE CHOICE

1. In the Middle Ages, tithes
   a. were usually paid with food instead of money.
   b. were equal to 10 percent of a person's income.
   c. were not requested from nobles.
   d. were used to support the nobles.

   ANS: B DIF: A

2. One of the most important monasteries was in
   a. Italy.
   b. Egypt.
   c. France.
   d. Greece.

   ANS: C DIF: E

3. The Dominican order was started
   a. in 1216.
   b. in 1370.
   c. in 1400.
   d. by Francis of Assisi.

   ANS: A DIF: A

4. Which of the following was NOT true of the Franciscans?
   a. The order was founded in 1200.
   b. The order was founded by Francis of Assisi.
   c. They had a deep love of nature.
   d. They were also known as Dominicans.

   ANS: D DIF: C

5. Pope Gregory VII
   a. ruled from Rome.
   b. was the Roman Emperor in 1075.
   c. was a monk from Cluny.
   d. was a Dominican.

   ANS: A DIF: A

MATCHING

Match each item with the correct statement below.
a. orders
b. Gregory VII
c. tithes
d. devout
e. friars

1. monies donated to the Church
2. groups of friars
3. preachers
4. deeply religious
5. continued Church reforms

1. ANS: C DIF: A
2. ANS: A DIF: A
3. ANS: E DIF: A
4. ANS: D DIF: A
5. ANS: B DIF: A

SHORT ANSWER

1. How did unfit people often get appointed to Church positions?

   ANS:
   Nobles often appointed close relatives or friends to Church positions. These people were not fit for religious duties.

   DIF: A

2. Who did the monks of Cluny believe should appoint all Church officials?

   ANS:
   the Church

   DIF: A

3. According to Pope Gregory VII, when could people disobey Church officials?

   ANS:
   when they went against the Pope

   DIF: A

4. What was Gregory's position on the Pope's power?

ANS:
The Pope was above all kings and nobles; only the Pope could choose bishops and other Church leaders.

DIF: A

SECTION QUIZ 25-3—LEARNING

MULTIPLE CHOICE

1. Cathedral schools
   a. were run by friars.
   b. taught seven subjects.
   c. were only open to priests.
   d. were only open to peasants.

   ANS: B DIF: A

2. By the 1200s, universities
   a. had lost their appeal.
   b. had spread all through Europe.
   c. required teachers to have studied at least 15 years.
   d. were taught by sponsors.

   ANS: B DIF: A

3. Thomas Aquinas wrote
   a. *Summa Theologica.*
   b. *Summa Biblio.*
   c. *Summa Universite.*
   d. over 20 philosophical works.

   ANS: A DIF: C

4. Universities were headed by
   a. lecturers.
   b. chancellors.
   c. priests.
   d. nuns.

   ANS: B DIF: E

5. At universities, all students
   a. had to be at least 21 years old.
   b. trained to become priests.
   c. had to pass certain tests.
   d. had to serve as lecturers.

   ANS: C DIF: A

MATCHING

Match each item with the correct statement below.

a. universities
b. chancellor
c. unions
d. Thomas Aquinas
e. cathedrals

1. Church official
2. noted scholar
3. groups devoted to learning
4. people joined in a common cause
5. churches headed by bishops

1. ANS: B DIF: A
2. ANS: D DIF: A
3. ANS: A DIF: A
4. ANS: C DIF: A
5. ANS: E DIF: A

SHORT ANSWER

1. What was the primary purpose of cathedral schools?

   ANS:
   to prepare the sons of nobles for Church work

   DIF: A

2. Why did cathedral schools broaden the range of subjects they offered?

   ANS:
   not every boy wanted to be a priest or monk

   DIF: A

3. Where were the majority of university students from?

   ANS:
   Europe

   DIF: E

SECTION QUIZ 25-4—THE CRUSADES

MULTIPLE CHOICE

1. The Nobles' Crusade began in
   a. 908.
   b. 1097.
   c. 1104.
   d. 1201.

   ANS: B DIF: C

2. Outremer
   a. was made up of four feudal kingdoms.
   b. was the primary reason for the Crusades.
   c. was governed by Emperor Frederick Barbarossa.
   d. was a great emir during the Crusades.

   ANS: A DIF: A

3. Which of the following was NOT true of Richard I?
   a. He was king of England.
   b. He was called "the Lionheart."
   c. He defeated Saladin.
   d. He was a brave warrior.

   ANS: C DIF: A

4. Which of the following is NOT the name of an emperor or king?
   a. Innocent III
   b. Richard I
   c. Philip II
   d. Frederick Barbarossa

   ANS: A DIF: E

5. Stephen of Cloyes
   a. led the Nobles' Crusade.
   b. led the Peasants' Crusade.
   c. led the Children's Crusade.
   d. conquered the city of Zara.

   ANS: C DIF: A

MATCHING

Match each item with the correct statement below.

a. Outremer
b. *Deus vult*
c. coordinates
d. emirs
e. grids

1. set of numbers
2. patterns of intersecting lines
3. soldier leaders
4. the kingdom beyond the sea"
5. It is the will of God"

1. ANS: C DIF: A

2. ANS: E DIF: A
3. ANS: D DIF: A
4. ANS: A DIF: A
5. ANS: B DIF: A

SHORT ANSWER

1. What goal for the Church did Urban II have when he urged crusades?

   ANS:
   He wanted the Eastern Orthodox Church to reunite with the Roman Catholic Church.

   DIF: A

2. How did the Peasants' Crusade end? The Nobles' Crusade?

   ANS:
   The peasant armies were almost completely wiped out by Turks in Asia Minor; the nobles captured Jerusalem and looted and killed Turks, Jews, and Christians alike.

   DIF: C

3. What was Saladin's goal?

   ANS:
   to take Persia back from the Christians

   DIF: C

4. What agreement did King Richard and Saladin make?

   ANS:
   crusaders kept parts of Palestine; Muslims controlled Jerusalem

   DIF: A

5. Who finally won control of Jerusalem?

   ANS:
   Muslims

   DIF: E

CHAPTER 26—RISE OF TRADE AND TOWNS

MULTIPLE CHOICE

1. Spices and other luxuries from the Near East came to western Europe by way of
   a. Scandinavia.
   b. Venice.
   c. Constantinople.
   d. North Africa.

   ANS: C DIF: A

2. The people of Flanders became most famous for
   a. making woollen cloth.
   b. setting up banks.
   c. trading in wheat.
   d. making salt from seawater.

   ANS: A DIF: A

3. By 1300, England became Flanders' most important trading partner by supplying
   a. skilled weavers.
   b. wool.
   c. sugar and spices.
   d. wheat.

   ANS: B DIF: E

4. Which of the following was NOT a result of the growth of fairs?
   a. Towns grew up around merchant settlements.
   b. People bartered goods instead of using gold or coins.
   c. People could buy goods from distant countries.
   d. The first banks were set up by moneychangers.

   ANS: B DIF: A

5. During the 1300s, diseased rats came to Europe on trading ships from the Middle East carrying a plague called the
   a. Flanders plague.
   b. burghers.
   c. pack rat plague.
   d. Black Death.

   ANS: D DIF: A

6. Townspeople came into conflict with feudal nobles because
   a. they were more loyal to the Church than to the noble.
   b. the nobles encouraged towns to grow too fast.
   c. they resented many feudal laws.
   d. Church leaders encouraged them to make larger profits.

   ANS: C DIF: C

7. The main interest of medieval guilds was
   a. securing town charters.
   b. sponsorship of trade fairs.
   c. protection for members.
   d. training for new artisans.

   ANS: C DIF: A

8. An artisan had to demonstrate skill by making a "masterpiece" in order to qualify as
   a. an apprentice.
   b. a burgher.
   c. a journeyman.
   d. a master.

   ANS: D DIF: E

9. Feudalism declined by the 1400s because of
   a. growing wealth and power of merchants and townspeople.
   b. increasing opposition by leaders of the Church.
   c. weaknesses of monarchies and central government.
   d. poverty and economic problems in towns.

   ANS: A DIF: C

10. One unusual feature of both Dante's *Divine Comedy* and Chaucer's *Canterbury Tales* is that
    a. they are written in people's native languages.
    b. their stories are very similar.
    c. both are written in Latin.
    d. they are modeled after Homer's *Odyssey*.

    ANS: A DIF: A

MATCHING

Match each item with the correct statement below.

a. master
b. journeyman
c. burg
d. charters
e. guild
f. communes
g. burghers
h. apprentice
i. fairs
j. wares

1. Person highly skilled in a trade, craft, or business
2. Association of merchants, artisans, and skilled workers
3. Person in training to learn a trade or craft
4. Goods offered for sale by merchants
5. Name given to a town near a castle
6. Gatherings for merchants sponsored by feudal nobles
7. Documents giving townspeople charge of their own affairs
8. In Italy, political groups seeking self-government
9. Person paid daily wages to work for an expert
10. Rich merchants who lived in town

1. ANS: A DIF: A
2. ANS: E DIF: A
3. ANS: H DIF: A
4. ANS: J DIF: A
5. ANS: C DIF: A
6. ANS: I DIF: A
7. ANS: D DIF: A
8. ANS: F DIF: A

9. ANS: B DIF: A
10. ANS: G DIF: A

SHORT ANSWER

1. During the 1000s and 1100s in western Europe, there were more births than deaths. Why was this an important contribution to progress at that time? In the world today, there are also more births than deaths. Is this still a positive factor? Why?

   ANS:
   Answers will vary, but could include: the increased birth rate was important in the 1000s and 1100s because the basic population at that time was comparatively small and more people were needed as workers as great trade and cultural changes took place. Today the higher rate of births is not as positive, as the world population is outgrowing the earth's resources and ability to support the population.

   DIF: A

2. Why did the population of western Europe increase during the 1000s and 1100s?

   ANS:
   There were more births than deaths and a better food supply.

   DIF: E

3. What part did the Italian navies play in the development of European trade?

   ANS:
   They made the Mediterranean Sea safe from attacks by Muslims.

   DIF: A

4. In addition to overcrowding, what other unhealthy conditions existed in towns?

   ANS:
   open sewers, dirty, streets filled with garbage, rats

   DIF: E

5. How did the Black Death affect trading and farming?

   ANS:
   It stopped them temporarily.

   DIF: E

6. What groups of people controlled business and trade in a town?

   ANS:
   merchants and artisans

   DIF: E

7. What were the town councils in northern Italy responsible for?

   ANS:
   tax collecting; setting the price for most goods; repairing streets; forming citizen armies; taking care of hospitals, orphanages, and homes for the poor

   DIF: A

8. How did guilds help and protect their members?

   ANS:
   They set wages, prices, and working conditions, and helped members who were sick or out of work.

   DIF: A

9. How did merchants, artisans, and bankers increase their power while decreasing the power of kings and nobles?

   ANS:
   They controlled business and trade, depended less on rulers for help, and developed loyalty toward their towns.

   DIF: A

10. Study the map below. Which European country appears to have fewer trade routes than the others? What were some of the important trading centers in the East? What is the most important trading center on the southern Mediterranean coast?

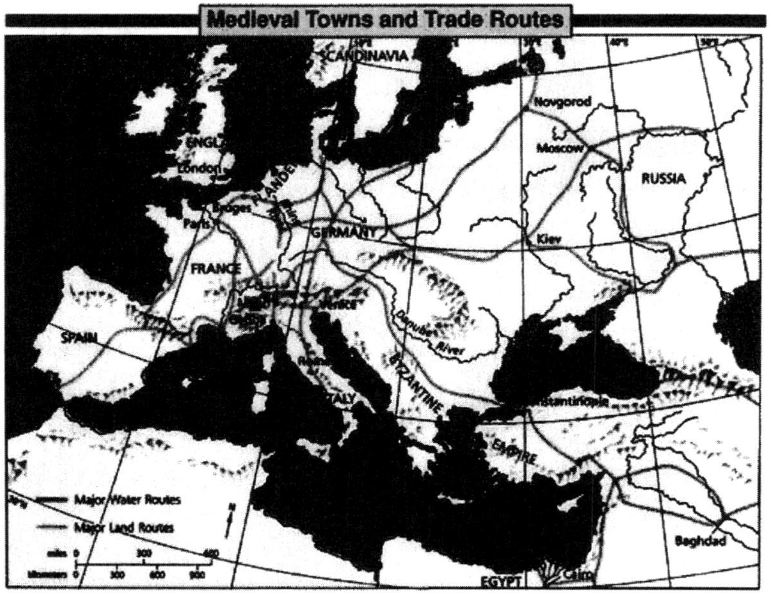

ANS:
Spain; Constantinople, Baghdad, Kiev, Moscow, Novgorod; Alexandria

DIF: C

SECTION QUIZ 26-1—TRADING CENTERS

MULTIPLE CHOICE

1. Which of the following was NOT true of Venice?
   a. It was founded in the 500s.
   b. It became a leading port in the 1100s.
   c. Its merchants developed a banking system.
   d. Its main industry was weaving.

   ANS: D DIF: A

2. Which of the following was NOT true of Flanders?
   a. It was the earliest Atlantic trade center.
   b. It was located on the Adriatic.
   c. Its main industry was weaving.
   d. By 1300, its most important partner was England.

   ANS: B DIF: C

3. The Flemish built harbors on
   a. the Indian Ocean.
   b. the Dead Sea.
   c. the Mediterranean Sea.
   d. the North Sea.

   ANS: D DIF: A

4. In the 1100s, many Venetians
   a. became weavers.
   b. were merchants.
   c. were shepherds.
   d. were farmers.

   ANS: B DIF: A

5. The Flemish developed an international industry with
   a. spices.
   b. salt.
   c. weaving.
   d. embroidery.

   ANS: C DIF: E

COMPLETION

1. Both Venice and Flanders were located on major ____________________.

   ANS: sea routes DIF: A

2. Towns on the Italian mainland made and sent ____________________ to Venice to be shipped to other areas.

   ANS: cloth DIF: A

3. While Italian trading towns were quarreling, towns along Europe's ____________________ coast developed trade routes.

   ANS: Atlantic DIF: E

4. The Flemish became famous for their ____________________.

   ANS: wool cloth DIF: A

MATCHING

Match each item with the correct statement below.

a. wool
b. England
c. Venice
d. Flanders
e. salt

1. island port in the Adriatic Sea
2. area on the northwest coast of Europe
3. Venetian trade product
4. Flemish trade product
5. Flanders trading partner by 1300

1. ANS: C DIF: A
2. ANS: D DIF: A
3. ANS: E DIF: A
4. ANS: A DIF: A
5. ANS: B DIF: A

SECTION QUIZ 26-2—MERCHANTS

MULTIPLE CHOICE

1. Fairs were sponsored by
   a. the Church.
   b. merchants.
   c. nobles.
   d. peasants.

   ANS: C DIF: E

2. At a fair, the area where the money changers sat was
   a. the *banc*.
   b. the wares.
   c. the palisades.
   d. the trade route.

   ANS: A DIF: A

3. The first merchants were mostly
   a. nobles who set up shop near the local castle.
   b. former members of the clergy.
   c. money changers.
   d. adventurers who traveled.

   ANS: D DIF: A

4. During the Middle Ages, merchants set up permanent shops
   a. as far from the monastery as possible.
   b. that eventually developed into towns.
   c. at fairs.
   d. surrounded by palisades.

   ANS: B DIF: A

5. In the Middle Ages, merchants began to use
   a. paper money to pay for things.
   b. sea salt to pay for things.
   c. precious metals to pay for things.
   d. the barter system.

   ANS: C DIF: C

COMPLETION

1. The overland trade route connecting Italy and Flanders went across the ____________________.

   ANS: Alps DIF: E

2. Trading fairs first appeared in eastern ____________________.

   ANS: France DIF: A

3. Merchants tried to locate their settlements along a ____________________ and close to ____________________ or monasteries.

   ANS: trade route; castles DIF: A

MATCHING

Match each item with the correct statement below.

a. wares
b. *banc*
c. fairs
d. burgs
e. trade

1. special trading gatherings
2. trade settlements
3. things for sale
4. bench
5. purpose of fairs

1. ANS: C DIF: A
2. ANS: D DIF: A
3. ANS: A DIF: A
4. ANS: B DIF: A
5. ANS: E DIF: A

SECTION QUIZ 26-3—LIVING CONDITIONS

MULTIPLE CHOICE

1. Experts think the number of Europeans who died from the plague was
   a. one in three.
   b. one in five.
   c. one in 20.
   d. one in 100.

   ANS: A DIF: C

2. In communes, stocks were used as
   a. punishment for major crimes.
   b. punishment for minor crimes.
   c. hitching posts for cattle and horses.
   d. merchant centers.

   ANS: B DIF: A

3. The major cause of the plague in the Middle Ages was
   a. foreign visitors.
   b. rotten food.
   c. diseased rats.
   d. polluted water.

   ANS: C DIF: E

4. Which of the following was NOT true of the burghers?
   a. They resented feudal laws.
   b. They worked together to build hospitals and schools.
   c. They were mostly nobles.
   d. They were taxed for using the marketplace.

   ANS: C DIF: A

5. Communes worked against the nobles and bishops by
   a. paying taxes.
   b. establishing self-government.
   c. putting them in stocks.
   d. repairing streets and running hospitals.

   ANS: B DIF: A

COMPLETION

1. As towns grew larger and wealthier, they replaced their palisades with stone ____________________.

   ANS: walls DIF: A

2. Buildings inside the town walls were crowded together to save ____________________.

   ANS: space DIF: A

3. Crowded conditions often made the towns ____________________ places to live.

   ANS: unhealthy DIF: A

4. Charters allowed townspeople to elect ____________________ to run the towns.

   ANS: officials DIF: E

5. ____________________ in some Italian towns were responsible for repairing streets and running hospitals, orphanages, and homes for the poor.

   ANS: Councils DIF: A

MATCHING

Match each item with the correct statement below.

a. charters
b. communes
c. burghers
d. stocks
e. "Black Death"

1. townspeople
2. Italian political groups
3. documents of town government
4. instrument of punishment
5. plague

1. ANS: C DIF: A
2. ANS: B DIF: A
3. ANS: A DIF: A
4. ANS: D DIF: A
5. ANS: E DIF: A

SECTION QUIZ 26-4—THE RISE OF GUILDS

MULTIPLE CHOICE

1. The guilds began around
   a. the 800s.
   b. the 1100s.
   c. 1400.
   d. the 1520s.

   ANS: B DIF: C

2. Apprentices trained
   a. for one to six months.
   b. for six months to a year.
   c. for two to seven years.
   d. for seven to ten years.

   ANS: C DIF: A

3. The journeyman who passed the guild's test
   a. became apprentices.
   b. became masters.
   c. became novices.
   d. became guild officials.

   ANS: B DIF: A

4. Which of the following was NOT true of guilds?
   a. They sponsored holy day celebrations.
   b. They paid for members' funerals.
   c. They controlled all business and trade in a town.
   d. They consisted of a maximum of 125 members.

   ANS: D DIF: A

5. Guild members who sold poorly made goods
   a. could be expelled from the guild.
   b. were sent to different guilds.
   c. were put in stocks.
   d. were made to leave the country.

   ANS: A DIF: E

COMPLETION

1. Guilds worked to see that their members were treated ____________________.

   ANS: equally DIF: A

2. Guild members usually lived and ____________________ in the same area of a town.

   ANS: worked DIF: E

3. Guilds were the centers of a town's ____________________ life, as well as the centers of trade and business.

   ANS: social DIF: A

MATCHING

Match each item with the correct statement below.

a. apprentice
b. master
c. guild
d. masterpiece
e. journeyman

1. business group
2. trainee
3. expert
4. worked for a daily wage
5. journeyman's proof of skill

1. ANS: C DIF: A

2. ANS: A DIF: A
3. ANS: B DIF: A
4. ANS: E DIF: A
5. ANS: D DIF: A

SECTION QUIZ 26-5—CULTURAL CHANGES

MULTIPLE CHOICE

1. In the 1400s, men began to wear
   a. jackets, stockings, and feather caps.
   b. tunics and pantaloons.
   c. caftans.
   d. knickers and tall boots.

   ANS: A DIF: A

2. Dante was a
   a. merchant.
   b. king.
   c. monk.
   d. scholar.

   ANS: D DIF: A

3. With the growth of their wealth, merchants
   a. had more leisure time.
   b. acquired many slaves.
   c. stopped working.
   d. married late.

   ANS: A DIF: E

4. Which of the following was NOT true of townspeople in the 1400s?
   a. They began to set clothing fashions.
   b. They hired private teachers for their children.
   c. They wanted strong central government.
   d. They wanted to overthrow their kings.

   ANS: D DIF: A

5. The growing power of the townspeople led to
   a. the decline of kings as rulers.
   b. the decline of feudalism.
   c. a decline in art and culture.
   d. the Inquisition.

   ANS: B DIF: C

COMPLETION

1. ____________________ loaned money to kings, nobles, and church officials.

   ANS: Bankers DIF: A

2. ____________________ turned their homes into mansions, or bought castles from poor nobles.

   ANS: Merchants DIF: A

3. Townspeople had ____________________ to enjoy paintings and books, and more ____________________ to buy them.

ANS: leisure time; money DIF: A

4. Books began to be written in the language of the townspeople instead of ____________________.

ANS: Latin DIF: A

5. Townspeople began to look to their ____________________ for strong central government to replace leadership by nobles.

ANS: kings DIF: A

MATCHING

Match each item with the correct statement below.

a. *Divine Comedy*
b. Dante
c. Geoffrey Chaucer
d. brocade
e. *Canterbury Tales*

1. woven cloth with raised designs
2. famous poem of the Middle Ages
3. collection of stories
4. wrote in English
5. wrote in Italian

1. ANS: D DIF: A
2. ANS: A DIF: A
3. ANS: E DIF: A
4. ANS: C DIF: A
5. ANS: B DIF: A

CHAPTER 27—RISE OF MONARCHIES

MULTIPLE CHOICE

1. Louis VI, Philip Augustus, and Louis IX were all kings in the line founded by
   a. Rudolf of Hapsburg.
   b. Philip the Fair.
   c. Hugh Capet, king of France.
   d. Ferdinand of Aragon.

   ANS: C DIF: C

2. To strengthen France, Philip IV took all of these actions EXCEPT
   a. forming the Estates-General.
   b. taking control of the cloth trade from the English.
   c. collecting taxes in an organized way.
   d. granting charters to win townspeoples' loyalty.

   ANS: B DIF: C

3. William the Conqueror gained his name by defeating
   a. Harold, king of England.
   b. William, Duke of Normandy.
   c. Louis, King of France.
   d. Edward the Confessor.

   ANS: A DIF: E

4. The *Domesday Book* was
   a. a list of King William's enemies in England.
   b. a description of the English court system.
   c. a census and land survey of England.
   d. a charter granting English nobles certain rights.

   ANS: C DIF: E

5. King Henry II of England's most important contribution to government was
   a. reforming law courts and beginning the jury system.
   b. establishing Parliament to represent the people.
   c. giving nobles rights through the Magna Carta.
   d. defeating France in the Hundred Years' War.

   ANS: A DIF: A

6. Joan of Arc's main goal was
   a. saving France from England.
   b. helping Charles become king.
   c. helping the French peasants.
   d. starting the Estates-General.

   ANS: A DIF: A

7. One important result of the Hundred Years' War was
   a. a stronger monarchy in England.
   b. more rights for farm workers and peasants.
   c. more power for the Pope and the Church.
   d. the establishment of the Holy Roman Empire.

   ANS: B DIF: A

8. The Holy Roman Emperors believed they were the leaders of Christianity and the true heirs of
   a. the Pope.
   b. Augustus.
   c. the Byzantine emperors.
   d. Charlemagne.

   ANS: D DIF: A

9. By the time Maximilian became Holy Roman Emperor, the Hapsburgs controlled land in most of Europe except
   a. England.
   b. Flanders.
   c. Italy.
   d. Germany.

   ANS: D DIF: A

10. To unify Spain as a Catholic country Ferdinand and Isabella depended most heavily on
    a. the educated Moors.
    b. the Spanish Inquisition.
    c. *corregidores*.
    d. the Holy Roman Empire.

    ANS: B DIF: A

11. Which of the following was ***not*** a result of the Norman invasion of England?
    a. The English learned French customs and language.
    b. Many English laws and government practices stayed in effect.
    c. William used feudal government to maintain control.
    d. William designated an heir so that there would not be any more fighting in England about who should rule.

    ANS: C DIF: A

12. Which of the following did ***not*** result from Henry II's rule?
    a. Order was restored.
    b. The English court system was reformed.
    c. Church officials came under the power of the king's courts.
    d. The king's law became common law all over England.

    ANS: C DIF: A

13. Which of the following did ***not*** result from the signing of the Magna Carta?
    a. a decrease of the king's power
    b. an increase of the nobles' power
    c. the end of feudal government in England
    d. a complete halt to the Great Council

    ANS: D DIF: A

14. Which of the following was ***not*** a result of the rules of Frederick I and II?
    a. Nobles regained their power.
    b. Italian city-states regained their freedom.
    c. German princes broke away from the king's rule.
    d. The Pope excommunicated Frederick II and called for a crusade against him.

    ANS: A DIF: A

15. Which of the following was ***not*** accomplished by Hapsburg rulers?
   a. The gained control of Flanders and other Low Countries.
   b. The had full control of the German princes.
   c. They gained lands and influence in Spain.
   d. The gained influence through marriages in the countries of Portugal, France, Denmark, and Austria.

   ANS: B DIF: A

16. Which of the following was ***not*** a result of the rule of Spain's Ferdinand and Isabella?
   a. There was weakness due to the lack of trained, educated people.
   b. Granada became part of Spain.
   c. Portugal surrendered to Spain.
   d. The country was united by religion.

   ANS: C DIF: A

MATCHING

Match each item with the correct statement below.

a.	Hapsburg	f.	Charles VII
b.	Ferdinand	g.	monarchies
c.	Isabella	h.	Thomas a Becket
d.	Magna Carta	i.	Otto I
e.	Philip the Fair	j.	*dauphin*

1. French ruler whose reign began national government
2. King of Germany named first Holy Roman Emperor
3. Family who served as Holy Roman emperors for about 650 years
4. Queen who used the Inquisition to unify Spain
5. Countries governed by one ruler
6. A document giving nobles certain rights
7. King who owed his throne to Joan of Arc
8. English clergyman who opposed the king's power
9. King of Aragon, one of the "Catholic Monarchs"
10. Eldest son of the French king

1. ANS: E DIF: A
2. ANS: I DIF: A
3. ANS: A DIF: A
4. ANS: C DIF: A
5. ANS: G DIF: A
6. ANS: D DIF: A
7. ANS: F DIF: A
8. ANS: H DIF: A
9. ANS: B DIF: A
10. ANS: J DIF: A

SHORT ANSWER

1. The story of Joan of Arc has been retold through the ages. It was performed as a play and made into a movie in modern times. Why do you think her story continues to interest audiences?

   ANS:
   Answers will vary, but could include: because the story is dramatic and exciting, with an unusual heroine who carried out almost magical deeds that saved a country.

   DIF: A

2. Study the map below. How many countries were able to unite feudal territories under one government ruled by a king? Were there fewer or more European countries in the late Middle Ages than there are today?

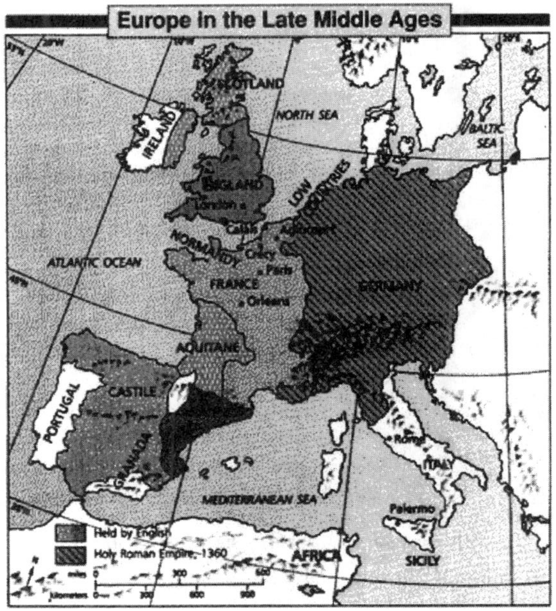

   ANS:
   About 10; fewer

   DIF: C

SECTION QUIZ 27-1—FRANCE

MULTIPLE CHOICE

1. Louis VI was also known as
   a. Louis the Frank.
   b. Louis the Fat.
   c. Louis the Fair.
   d. Louis of Loire.

   ANS: B DIF: E

2. Philip IV died in
   a. 1226.
   b. 1285.
   c. 1300.
   d. 1314.

   ANS: D DIF: C

3. The Capetian kings ruled for
   a. 100 years.
   b. 200 years.
   c. 300 years.
   d. 500 years.

   ANS: C DIF: A

4. Which of the following was NOT true of Louis VI?
   a. He stopped the raids of lawless vassals.
   b. He granted charters of freedom to many towns.
   c. He got rid of nobles who didn't fulfill their duties.
   d. His nickname was Louis the Fair.

   ANS: D DIF: A

5. After King Louis XI's death,
   a. Philip II became king.
   b. he was made a saint of the Roman Catholic Church.
   c. France was united under one ruler.
   d. Louis X took the throne.

   ANS: B DIF: A

MATCHING

Match each item with the correct statement below.

a. Estates-General
b. Philip the Fair
c. Philip Augustus
d. Hugh Capet
e. monarchies

1. countries ruled by one person
2. French noble made king in 987
3. as assembly of nobles
4. French ruler 1179-1223
5. French ruler 1285-1314

1. ANS: E DIF: A
2. ANS: D DIF: A
3. ANS: A DIF: A
4. ANS: C DIF: A
5. ANS: B DIF: A

SHORT ANSWER

1. How did Louis VI gain the loyalty of many French towns?

   ANS:
   by giving them charters of freedom

   DIF: A

2. Whom did Philip put in charge of his lands while he went on a crusade?

   ANS:
   He appointed royal agents.

   DIF: A

3. How did Louis IX make France more peaceful?

   ANS:
   He ordered nobles to stop feuding and forbade duels.

   DIF: A

4. Whose interests did Philip the Fair believe came first?

   ANS:
   those of the state (country)

   DIF: A

SECTION QUIZ 27-2—ENGLAND

MULTIPLE CHOICE

1. In 1066, Harold Godwinson
   a. conquered William, Duke of Normandy.
   b. died.
   c. introduced feudalism.
   d. became king of England.

   ANS: D DIF: A

2. Under William I, the witenagemot
   a. was disbanded.
   b. was called the Great Council.
   c. was recorded in the *Domesday Book*.
   d. killed Edward the Confessor.

   ANS: B DIF: A

3. Thomas a Becket
   a. murdered Henry II.
   b. wanted Church officials to be free of royal control.
   c. was murdered by William's knights.
   d. was forced to sign the Magna Carta.

   ANS: B DIF: E

4. Which of the following was NOT true of the Magna Carta?
   a. It decreased the king's power.
   b. It increased the nobles' power.
   c. It stated that freemen had a right to a trial by their peers.
   d. It was a census and survey of the land.

   ANS: D DIF: C

5. The Archbishop of Canterbury and good friend of Henry II was
   a. Harold Godwinson.
   b. Simon de Montfort.
   c. Thomas a Becket.
   d. Edward the Confessor.

   ANS: C DIF: A

MATCHING

Match each item with the correct statement below.

a. grand jury
b. *Domesday Book*
c. Magna Carta
d. circuit judges
e. trial jury

1. survey of the land and census record
2. presented criminals to judges
3. brought king's law to all the kingdom
4. decided on guilt or innocence
5. Great Charter

1. ANS: B DIF: A
2. ANS: A DIF: A
3. ANS: D DIF: A
4. ANS: E DIF: A
5. ANS: C DIF: A

SHORT ANSWER

1. Why could English nobles become powerful during the reign of Edward the Confessor?

   ANS:
   because Edward spent much time on religious duties, and not much time on his royal duties

   DIF: A

2. Why did William of Normandy challenge Harold Godwinson's claim to the English throne?

   ANS:
   William claimed that Edward the Confessor had promised the English throne to him.

   DIF: A

3. How did Henry II end unrest about the leadership of England?

   ANS:
   He assumed control of England, Ireland, Scotland, and Wales, and parts of France.

   DIF: A

4. Why did the reign of Richard I do little to help England's peace and unity?

   ANS:
   because Richard was off fighting in the Crusades

   DIF: A

5. Whom did Simon de Montfort and Edward I include in the Great Council?

   ANS:
   representatives of the common people

   DIF: A

SECTION QUIZ 27-3—THE HUNDRED YEARS' WAR

MULTIPLE CHOICE

1. Which of the following was NOT true of Joan of Arc?
   a. She led an attack against the English army.
   b. She spent a year in prison.
   c. She was burned at the stake.
   d. She only lived to the age of 16.

   ANS: D DIF: E

2. Henry Tudor became king in
   a. 1205.
   b. 1285.
   c. 1337.
   d. 1485.

   ANS: D DIF: A

3. The English owed their success at the Battle of Agincourt to
   a. cannons.
   b. longbows.
   c. horses.
   d. Joan of Arc.

   ANS: B DIF: A

4. In 1337,
   a. Henry Tudor became king of England.
   b. Joan of Arc was burned at the stake.
   c. Joan of Arc was proclaimed innocent.
   d. the Hundred Years' War began.

   ANS: D DIF: C

5. The city of Orleans was
   a. freed by Joan of Arc.
   b. where the Battle of Crecy was fought.
   c. the home of Henry Tudor.
   d. the home of the *dauphin* in 1429.

   ANS: A DIF: A

MATCHING

Match each item with the correct statement below.

a. Joan or Arc
b. Calais
c. longbow
d. Crecy
e. *dauphin*

1. eldest son of a king
2. "Maiden of Orleans"
3. weapon that shot arrows
4. French seaport
5. French battleground

1. ANS: E DIF: A
2. ANS: A DIF: A
3. ANS: C DIF: A
4. ANS: B DIF: A
5. ANS: D DIF: A

SHORT ANSWER

1. Why was the victory at Orleans important for the French?

   ANS:
   It gave the French a renewed sense of hope.

   DIF: A

2. How did the Hundred Years' War affect France's feudal government?

   ANS:
   It ended it.

   DIF: A

3. How did the Hundred Years' War affect England's feudal government?

   ANS:
   It ended it.

   DIF: A

4. Which country, France or England, had the stronger government centered on strong royal power?

   ANS:
   France

   DIF: A

SECTION QUIZ 27-4—GERMANY

MULTIPLE CHOICE

1. Frederick II was Frederick I's
   a. cousin.
   b. son.
   c. grandson.
   d. uncle.

   ANS: C DIF: E

2. Which of the following was NOT true of Frederick I?
   a. He was called Barbarossa, or "red beard."
   b. His armies were defeated by the Italian city-states.
   c. He drowned while leading the Third Crusade.
   d. He was also known as Rudolf.

   ANS: D DIF: E

3. Maximilian I
    a. became emperor in 1493.
    b. became emperor in 1439.
    c. married Mary, Queen of Scots.
    d. was also known as Rudolf.

    ANS: A DIF: C

4. In 1227, Frederick II
    a. was made Holy Roman Emperor.
    b. was excommunicated.
    c. married Mary of Burgundy.
    d. died.

    ANS: C DIF: A

5. In the 900s, the most important country in western Europe was
    a. Germany.
    b. Italy.
    c. France.
    d. England.

    ANS: A DIF: A

MATCHING

Match each item with the correct statement below.

a. Otto I
b. diet
c. Frederick I
d. Frederick II
e. Palermo

1. assembly
2. became king of Germany in 936
3. city in Sicily
4. was called Barbarossa
5. best-educated monarch of his time

1. ANS: B DIF: A
2. ANS: A DIF: A
3. ANS: E DIF: A
4. ANS: C DIF: A
5. ANS: D DIF: A

SHORT ANSWER

1. How did Otto I decrease the power of German nobles?

    ANS:
    He removed those who would not obey him.

    DIF: A

2. What role did Otto see for himself?

    ANS:
    heir of the Roman emperors

    DIF: A

3. What country did Otto I invade to increase German territory?

    ANS:
    Italy

    DIF: E

4. What empire did Otto I create?

    ANS:
    the Holy Roman Empire

    DIF: A

5. How did the Hapsburgs become rulers of the Holy Roman Empire?

    ANS:
    They were elected by German princes.

    DIF: A

SECTION QUIZ 27-5—SPAIN

MULTIPLE CHOICE

1. Ferdinand of Aragon married Isabella in
    a. 711.
    b. 1200.
    c. 1469.
    d. 1502.

    ANS: C DIF: A

2. Which of the following did NOT happen during the Inquisition?
    a. More than 2,000 people were killed.
    b. Jews were forced to convert or leave Spain.
    c. Catholicism was banned.
    d. Ferdinand and Isabella ruled Spain.

    ANS: C DIF: A

3. In 1502, Ferdinand and Isabella
   a. were married.
   b. were killed.
   c. surrendered Granada.
   d. ordered the Moors to convert or leave the country.

   ANS: D DIF: E

4. To keep order in the land, Isabella and Ferdinand
   a. sent *corregidores* to govern the towns.
   b. gave the Moors freedom of religion.
   c. surrendered Granada.
   d. split up their two kingdoms.

   ANS: A DIF: C

5. Isabella and Ferdinand
   a. believed in freedom of religion.
   b. believed that to be truly united, all of Spain had to be Catholic.
   c. were more interested in education than in religion.
   d. felt the Inquisition was wrong.

   ANS: B DIF: A

MATCHING

Match each item with the correct statement below.

a. Castile
b. *corregidores*
c. heresy
d. Ferdinand and Isabella
e. Moors

1. royal officials
2. Isabella's birthplace
3. major crime during the Inquisition
4. Catholic monarchs
5. conquered Spain in 711

1. ANS: B DIF: A
2. ANS: A DIF: A
3. ANS: C DIF: A
4. ANS: D DIF: A
5. ANS: E DIF: A

SHORT ANSWER

1. Who ruled Spain during the late Middle Ages?

   ANS:
   the Moors

   DIF: A

2. Who overthrew the Moors?

   ANS:
   Spanish Christians

   DIF: A

3. Why did Ferdinand and Isabella believe that Spain needed to be united?

   ANS:
   They thought that all Spaniards needed to be Roman Catholics.

   DIF: A

4. Why did many Jews convert to Christianity?

   ANS:
   so they would not be put to death

   DIF: A

5. How did Ferdinand and Isabella force the Moors out of Spain?

   ANS:
   They ordered the Moors to convert to Catholicism; and so most of the Moors left.

   DIF: A

CHAPTER 28—THE RENAISSANCE

MULTIPLE CHOICE

1. The term "Renaissance" refers to the period when
   a. monks took Christianity to all parts of Europe.
   b. scholars took a new interest in ideas and classical writings from Greece and Rome.
   c. European rulers began to build strong nations.
   d. scholars studied the ideas of the Middle Ages.

   ANS: B DIF: A

2. The wealth of the Italian city-states came mainly from
   a. the Church.
   b. trade.
   c. the Crusades.
   d. their empires.

   ANS: B DIF: E

3. The Renaissance artist who also was known as an inventor of clever machines was
   a. Lorenzo de Medici.
   b. Jan Van Eyck.
   c. Leonardo da Vinci.
   d. Lucretia Borgia.

   ANS: C DIF: A

4. During the Renaissance, the city of Venice was ruled by
   a. a council chosen from aristocratic merchants.
   b. the Byzantine emperor in Constantinople.
   c. a council chosen by the people of Venice.
   d. the Pope in Rome.

   ANS: A DIF: C

5. Which ruler encouraged Renaissance ideas in France?
   a. Cesare Borgia
   b. Philip II
   c. Henry VII
   d. Francis I

   ANS: D DIF: A

6. Johannes Gutenberg influenced the Renaissance by
   a. developing new techniques in oil painting.
   b. inventing a printing press to produce books quickly.
   c. establishing a strict government in Florence.
   d. portraying people realistically in his drawings.

   ANS: B DIF: A

7. The Renaissance author who wrote about the idealistic knight Don Quixote was
   a. Miguel de Cervantes Saavedra.
   b. Rabelais.
   c. Michelangelo.
   d. Erasmus.

   ANS: A DIF: C

8. From 1455 to 1485, the noble families of York and Lancaster quarreled over the English throne in the
   a. Thirty Years' War.
   b. Wars of the Roses.
   c. Hundred Years' War.
   d. Tudor Wars.

   ANS: B DIF: A

9. Which of these best represents the Renaissance in England?
   a. El Greco's paintings
   b. Rabelais's novels
   c. Shakespeare's plays
   d. Michelangelo's sculptures

   ANS: C DIF: A

10. The Renaissance reached its height in England during the reign of
    a. Elizabeth I.
    b. Philip II.
    c. Henry VIII.
    d. Mary Tudor.

    ANS: A DIF: A

COMPLETION

1. The Renaissance began in ____________________.

   ANS: Italy DIF: E

2. Personal ____________________ through proper behavior became a goal of many people during the Renaissance.

   ANS: improvement DIF: A

3. Italian traders and German merchants formed a new ____________________ class of people between the rich and powerful and the very poor.

   ANS: middle DIF: A

4. The ____________________ rebuilt Rome to prove to European leaders that Church leaders were still powerful.

   ANS: Pope DIF: E

5. After Rome was rebuilt, it became the center of the Italian ____________________.

   ANS: Renaissance DIF: A

6. Gutenberg's ____________________ helped spread the new ideas of the Renaissance.

   ANS: printing press DIF: A

7. The Renaissance lasted about ____________________ years.

   ANS: 200 DIF: A

MATCHING

Match each item with the correct statement below.

a. El Greco
b. Medici
c. Savonarola
d. *piazza*
e. El Escorial
f. Henry VII
g. Borgia
h. Jimenez
i. chateaux
j. *doge*

1. Monk who tried to bring a strict way of life to Florence
2. Palace, monastery, and church built for Spanish royalty
3. Central place and marketplace in an Italian city
4. First English king from the Tudor family
5. Castles built in France by Renaissance architects
6. Ruling family in the city of Florence
7. Church official who encouraged the Renaissance in Spain
8. Official ruler chosen from merchant nobles in Venice
9. Greek Renaissance artist who worked in Spain
10. Family name of Pope Alexander VI

1. ANS: C DIF: A
2. ANS: E DIF: A
3. ANS: D DIF: A
4. ANS: F DIF: A
5. ANS: I DIF: A
6. ANS: B DIF: A
7. ANS: H DIF: A
8. ANS: J DIF: A
9. ANS: A DIF: A
10. ANS: G DIF: A

SHORT ANSWER

1. Consider what you know about the role of art and literature in the United States today. How is it like the Renaissance? How is it different?

ANS:
Answers will vary, but could include: students may understand that today many people make their livings as artists and writers, and many people enjoy and appreciate their art. However, these artists are not as important to governments as they were during the Renaissance. Students may know that few artists today have the good fortune to be hired by wealthy individuals simply to pursue their art, as was common during the Renaissance.

DIF: C

2. Study the chart below. Which Renaissance people followed the study of science and the natural world? Which person might have written about rules of social behavior?

RENAISSANCE PEOPLE

Baldassare Castiglione	*1478–1529*	Italian writer; wrote book on rules of behavior for ladies and gentlemen
Benvenuto Cellini	*1500–1571*	Italian goldsmith; sculptor; wrote about his life and times.
Vittoria Colonna	*1492–1547*	Italian author; wrote religious and love poems
Nicolaus Copernicus	*1473–1543*	Polish astronomer; stated that Earth moves around the sun
Albrecht Dürer	*1471–1528*	German artist; painted and made woodcuts of religious and classical subjects
Beatrice d'Este	*1475–1497*	Italian noblewomen; sisters; honored for their learning;
Isabella d'Este	*1474–1539*	supported writers and artists
Galileo	*1564–1642*	Italian scientist; did experiments on the motion of objects; used telescope to discover new facts about universe
Niccolò Machiavelli	*1469–1527*	Italian politician; writer; wrote advice to rulers on how to keep power
Thomas More	*1477–1535*	English scholar; saint; government official; refused to accept king as Church head
Petrarch	*1304–1374*	Italian poet; scholar; restored study of classics; collected manuscripts; wrote letters and poems
Raphael	*1483–1520*	Italian religious painter and architect
Andreas Vesallus	*1514–1564*	Flemish surgeon; founder of modern medicine; wrote first full description of human body

ANS:
Copernicus, Galileo, and Vesalius; Baldassare Castiglione

DIF: C

SECTION QUIZ 28-1—THE ITALIAN CITY-STATES

MULTIPLE CHOICE

1. "Renaissance" means
   a. small, independent city-state.
   b. rebirth.
   c. artistic inspiration.
   d. showing objects as they appear at different distances.

   ANS: B DIF: A

2. Leonardo da Vinci is known for
   a. painting the Sistine Chapel's ceiling.
   b. painting the Mona Lisa.
   c. sculpting the Pieta.
   d. inventing perspective drawing.

   ANS: B DIF: A

3. Lorenzo de Medici
   a. became the ruler of Florence in 1478.
   b. was Savonarola's brother.
   c. was a monk.
   d. was hanged for heresy.

   ANS: A DIF: A

4. Rodrigo Borgia
   a. was a Renaissance sculptor and painter.
   b. overthrew the Medicis in 1494.
   c. became Pope Alexander VI.
   d. was hanged for heresy.

   ANS: C DIF: C

5. During the Renaissance, Venice
   a. was ruled by a few merchant aristocrats.
   b. was the home of the Pope.
   c. was ruled by the Medicis.
   d. was burned to the ground.

   ANS: A DIF: E

MATCHING

Match each item with the correct statement below.

a. classical writings
b. humanists
c. *doge*
d. *piazza*
e. Papal States

1. official ruler
2. central square
3. territories ruled by the Pope
4. Renaissance scholars
5. writings of ancient Greece and Rome

1. ANS: C DIF: A
2. ANS: D DIF: A
3. ANS: E DIF: A
4. ANS: B DIF: A
5. ANS: A DIF: A

Match the beginning of each sentence to the correct ending.

a. the Papal States and Venice.
b. emotions as well as appearance.
c. wisdom and generosity.
d. certain painters and sculptors.
e. muscular and filled with motion.

6. In addition to power, Italian leaders were interested in _____
7. Art was so important that Italian city-states competed for _____
8. Artists such as Leonardo da Vinci tried to paint people's _____
9. Michelango's sculptures present the human figure as _____
10. The Italian Renaissance began in Florence, then moved to _____

6. ANS: C DIF: A
7. ANS: D DIF: A
8. ANS: B DIF: A
9. ANS: E DIF: A
10. ANS: A DIF: A

SECTION QUIZ 28-2—FRANCE

MULTIPLE CHOICE

1. The French began invading Italy in
   a. 1424.
   b. 1449.
   c. 1494.
   d. the 1500s.

   ANS: C DIF: C

2. Rabelais was
   a. a Latin professor.
   b. the Holy Roman Emperor in 1494.
   c. a physician-monk.
   d. an Italian author.

   ANS: C DIF: C

3. The characters in *The Adventures of Gargantua and Pantagruel* were
   a. giants.
   b. dwarves.
   c. Romans.
   d. French authors.

   ANS: A DIF: A

4. Francis I had his chateaux built by
   a. French architects.
   b. Italian architects.
   c. Rabelais.
   d. French nobles.

   ANS: B DIF: A

5. French chateaux were often built
   a. along the Loire River.
   b. according to French design.
   c. according to Francis I's design.
   d. according to Greek design.

   ANS: A DIF: A

MATCHING

Match each item with the correct statement below.

a. *The Adventures of Gargantua and Pantagruel*
b. Rabelais
c. chateaux
d. Loire
e. Francis I

1. castles
2. French author
3. river in France
4. French king
5. popular Renaissance book

1. ANS: C DIF: A
2. ANS: B DIF: A
3. ANS: D DIF: A
4. ANS: E DIF: A
5. ANS: A DIF: A

SHORT ANSWER

1. How did the French become interested in Italian culture?

   ANS:
   The French kings became interested in Italian culture, and had their subjects copy many Italian things.

   DIF: A

2. How did Italian architects become influential in France?

   ANS:
   The king and many nobles hired Italian architects to design and build castles for them.

   DIF: A

SECTION QUIZ 28-3—GERMANY AND FLANDERS

MULTIPLE CHOICE

1. Erasmus
   a. was French.
   b. was German.
   c. translated the New Testament.
   d. developed the printing press.

   ANS: C DIF: E

2. The printing press was developed
   a. by the Van Eycks.
   b. about 1320.
   c. about 1440.
   d. by northern European artists.

   ANS: C DIF: A

3. *Praise of Folly*
   a. was very complimentary toward the Church.
   b. attacked Church corruption.
   c. was written by Gutenberg.
   d. was the first printed book.

   ANS: B DIF: A

4. Northern European artists mainly painted
   a. animals.
   b. portraits.
   c. scenes from the Bible and daily life.
   d. fantasy scenes of faraway places.

   ANS: C DIF: C

5. Oil paintings
   a. had deep, rich colors.
   b. had thin, watery colors.
   c. were first painted by Erasmus.
   d. were usually of animals.

   ANS: A DIF: E

MATCHING

Match each item with the correct statement below.

a. Hubert and Jan Van Eyck
b. printing press
c. Flanders
d. Johannes Gutenberg
e. Erasmus

1. wrote *Praise of Folly*
2. machine used to make books
3. German inventor
4. discovered oil painting
5. the Van Eycks' birthplace

1. ANS: E DIF: A
2. ANS: B DIF: A
3. ANS: D DIF: A
4. ANS: A DIF: A
5. ANS: C DIF: A

SHORT ANSWER

1. Why did religious leaders learn Greek and Hebrew?

   ANS:
   so they could understand the earliest versions of the Bible

   DIF: A

2. What did Erasmus attack in his book *Praise of Folly*?

   ANS:
   corrupt church leaders and church practices

   DIF: A

3. How did Northern artists make use of Italian Renaissance art?

   ANS:
   They studied Italian artists, and then developed their own styles.

   DIF: A

SECTION QUIZ 28-4—SPAIN

MULTIPLE CHOICE

1. Cardinal Jimenez's translation of the Bible was written in
   a. Greek, Latin, and Hebrew.
   b. Latin.
   c. Greek.
   d. Spanish.

   ANS: A DIF: A

2. Philip II became king of Spain in
   a. the late 1400s.
   b. 1505.
   c. 1555.
   d. 1605.

   ANS: C DIF: E

3. *Don Quixote*
   a. was a popular theater in Spain.
   b. is a tragedy.
   c. is about a comical knight.
   d. was banned during the Inquisition.

   ANS: C DIF: A

4. Some experts believe that El Greco
   a. copied his style from Byzantine artists.
   b. copied his style from Miguel de Cervantes Saavedra.
   c. was completely blind.
   d. was a noted Church official.

   ANS: A DIF: C

5. El Escorial
   a. was the largest palace ever built.
   b. painted figures with very long bodies.
   c. wrote many plays and short stories.
   d. was a symbol of Spanish rulers' power and religious devotion.

   ANS: D DIF: A

MATCHING

Match each item with the correct statement below.

a. El Escorial
b. Cardinal Jimenez
c. Miguel de Cervantes Saavedra
d. El Greco
e. Toledo

1. Greek painter
2. palace of Philip II
3. center of painters and poets

4. wrote *Don Quixote*
5. leading Spanish Church official

1. ANS: D DIF: A
2. ANS: A DIF: A
3. ANS: E DIF: A
4. ANS: C DIF: A
5. ANS: B DIF: A

SHORT ANSWER

1. How did strong church and government control affect the arts in Spain?

   ANS:
   Painting and poetry flourished.

   DIF: A

2. For what were the paintings of El Greco noted?

   ANS:
   They were noted for portraying people with very long bodies and limbs that stretched beyond normal size.

   DIF: A

SECTION QUIZ 28-5—ENGLAND

MULTIPLE CHOICE

1. The Wars of the Roses
   a. were fought between the Yorks and the Lancasters.
   b. were fought between the Yorks and the Tudors.
   c. were also known as the Hundred Years' War.
   d. were fought over land used as English gardens.

   ANS: A DIF: A

2. The Tudors took over the English throne
   a. during the Hundred Years' War.
   b. in 1455.
   c. in 1485.
   d. in 1555.

   ANS: C DIF: A

3. Henry VIII was Elizabeth's
   a. son.
   b. brother.
   c. father.
   d. uncle.

   ANS: C DIF: E

4. Which of the following was NOT written by William Shakespeare?
   a. *Macbeth*
   b. *Hamlet*
   c. *Julius Caesar*
   d. *Don Quixote*

   ANS: D DIF: A

5. Shakespeare drew ideas for his plays from
   a. the histories of England and ancient Rome.
   b. the lives of the saints.
   c. Renaissance Italy.
   d. Church documents.

   ANS: A DIF: C

MATCHING

Match each item with the correct statement below.
a. white rose
b. Henry VIII
c. Henry VII
d. red rose
e. Elizabeth I

1. ruled England at 25 years old
2. first Tudor king
3. Yorkist symbol
4. Lancastrian symbol
5. became king of England in 1509

1. ANS: E DIF: A
2. ANS: C DIF: A
3. ANS: A DIF: A
4. ANS: D DIF: A
5. ANS: B DIF: A

SHORT ANSWER

1. Which Tudor monarch ruled during the peak of the English Renaissance?

   ANS:
   Elizabeth I

   DIF: A

2. Which art form was especially popular in Renaissance England?

   ANS:
   plays

   DIF: E

3. What kinds of music did people particularly like?

ANS:
folk songs and ballads

DIF: A

CHAPTER 29—THE REFORMATION

MULTIPLE CHOICE

1. According to Martin Luther, people could be saved from their sins by
   a. obeying the Pope.
   b. having faith in Jesus.
   c. buying indulgences.
   d. reading the Bible.

   ANS: B DIF: A

2. Martin Luther gained support for his ideas from
   a. Emperor Charles V.
   b. the king of England.
   c. Pope Leo X.
   d. the German princes.

   ANS: D DIF: A

3. The Peace of Augsburg was an agreement between
   a. the Pope and Emperor Charles V.
   b. Emperor Charles V and the German princes.
   c. Luther and the German princes who supported him.
   d. Luther and Pope Leo X.

   ANS: B DIF: A

4. The city where Reformed churches were most powerful was
   a. Canterbury, England.
   b. Rome, Italy.
   c. Geneva, Switzerland.
   d. Wittenberg, Germany.

   ANS: C DIF: E

5. Which of these was NOT a belief of Calvinism?
   a. People should be free to believe as they wish.
   b. People should work hard and save money.
   c. God is all-knowing and all-powerful.
   d. Ministers can interpret and enforce Bible teachings.

   ANS: A DIF: C

6. Ignatius of Loyola formed a group of teachers, scholars, and missionaries and the members of the group were known as
   a. Huguenots.
   b. Loyalists.
   c. Calvinists.
   d. Jesuits.

   ANS: D DIF: A

7. Which of these English rulers worked to create a Church of England that would appeal to both Protestants and Catholics?
   a. Elizabeth I
   b. Edward VI
   c. Henry VIII
   d. Mary I

   ANS: A DIF: E

8. Which of these European rulers tried to make England Catholic by marrying its queen and later sending an armada?
   a. Henry of Navarre
   b. Philip II of Spain
   c. Francis I of France
   d. Emperor Charles V

   ANS: B DIF: A

9. Spanish rule in the Low Countries resulted in all of the following EXCEPT
   a. religious freedom.
   b. rebellion by Protestants.
   c. heavy taxation.
   d. harsh laws.

   ANS: A DIF: A

10. What was one important result of the Thirty Years' War?
    a. More power for the Holy Roman Emperor
    b. The restoration of Roman Catholicism in most of Europe
    c. The establishment of the Church of England
    d. The growth of France as a major nation

    ANS: D DIF: C

11. During the Renaissance, the Roman Catholic Church
    a. appreciated the changes taking place.
    b. did not adjust to the changes.
    c. did not have any reason to change.
    d. busied themselves with political change.

    ANS: B DIF: A

12. Martin Luther's ideas eventually
    a. spread to the Near East and Far East.
    b. became Protestantism.
    c. brought the Low Countries back to the Church.
    d. spread to the Jesuit schools and monasteries.

    ANS: B DIF: A

13. The reformation of the English Church
    a. was the last and longest.
    b. started with Henry VIII.
    c. never really took place.
    d. was finished by Mary Tudor.

    ANS: B DIF: A

14. The people of the Low Countries did not like
    a. Protestants or Catholics.
    b. the revolt of the northern provinces.
    c. the heavy taxes and harsh laws of Philip of Spain.
    d. French Catholics from the southern provinces.

    ANS: C DIF: A

15. The southern and northern provinces of the Low Countries
    a. experienced almost 80 years of religious war.
    b. remained Catholic and under Spanish rule.
    c. overthrew Spanish rule.
    d. caused the breakup of the Holy Roman Empire.

    ANS: A DIF: A

16. After the Thirty Years' War, European countries
    a. admitted that France was stronger than Germany.
    b. began to form trade and exploration alliances.
    c. allowed all religions to exist peacefully.
    d. never again fought each other over religion.

    ANS: D DIF: C

MATCHING

Match each item with the correct statement below.

a. Peace of Augsburg
b. Reformed Church
c. seminary
d. Spanish Armada
e. Council of Trent
f. Edict of Nantes
g. Henry of Navarre
h. Peace of Westphalia
i. indulgences
j. Thomas Cranmer

1. Treaty ending the Thirty Years' War
2. Law granting religious freedom to French Protestants
3. Church pardons that lessen punishment for sins in return for money
4. Archbishop of Canterbury who encouraged the Church of England
5. Fleet of warships
6. Peace treaty between German Lutherans and Catholics
7. Meeting of Catholic bishops to make reforms
8. School for training Catholic priests
9. Name given to one group of Protestant churches
10. Ruler who became Catholic to unify France

1. ANS: H DIF: A
2. ANS: F DIF: A
3. ANS: I DIF: A
4. ANS: J DIF: A
5. ANS: D DIF: A
6. ANS: A DIF: A
7. ANS: E DIF: A
8. ANS: C DIF: A
9. ANS: B DIF: A
10. ANS: G DIF: A

SHORT ANSWER

1. Why do you think it was important to people to have church services conducted in their own language instead of Latin?

   ANS:
   Answers will vary, but could include: services in their own language helped people understand what the services were about, thus making them feel more a part of the religion.

   DIF: A

SECTION QUIZ 29-1—MARTIN LUTHER

MULTIPLE CHOICE

1. Martin Luther's family
   a. was upper class.
   b. wanted him to be a monk.
   c. wanted him to be a lawyer.
   d. was French.

   ANS: C DIF: A

2. In 1520, Martin Luther
   a. became a monk.
   b. built St. Peter's Church in Rome.
   c. was excommunicated.
   d. died.

   ANS: C DIF: E

3. Martin Luther posted a list of 95 theses
   a. on the door of St. Peter's Church.
   b. on the door of the castle church in Wittenberg.
   c. on walls throughout the city of Rome.
   d. on church walls throughout Kievan Rus.

   ANS: B DIF: A

4. Charles V betrayed Martin Luther by
   a. giving him a fair trial.
   b. secretly promising to condemn him.
   c. informing the Pope of Martin Luther's heresy.
   d. feeding him a diet of worms.

   ANS: B DIF: A

5. The German Diet of Worms
   a. tried Martin Luther.
   b. was considered nutritious.
   c. was headed by Charles V.
   d. was broken up in 1521.

   ANS: A DIF: C

MATCHING

Match each item with the correct statement below.

a. Martin Luther
b. heretic
c. reformation
d. theses
e. indulgences

1. change
2. documents for forgiveness of sins
3. statements about beliefs
4. person with unacceptable beliefs
5. German monk

1. ANS: C DIF: A
2. ANS: E DIF: A
3. ANS: D DIF: A
4. ANS: B DIF: A
5. ANS: A DIF: A

SHORT ANSWER

1. What were many Church leaders afraid of losing if the Church was reformed?

   ANS:
   their power

   DIF: A

2. How did Luther let Church leaders know about his feelings?

   ANS:
   He nailed a list of theses to a church door in Wittenburg.

   DIF: A

3. What was Luther's attack against the Pope?

   ANS:
   He said that the Pope's sale of indulgences made people think they could buy their way into heaven.

   DIF: A

SECTION QUIZ 29-2—A NEW RELIGION

MULTIPLE CHOICE

1. Ulrich Zwingli
   a. lived in the 1600s.
   b. was an assistant of John Calvin.
   c. was a Roman Catholic priest.
   d. led the Protestant movement in Switzerland.

   ANS: D DIF: E

2. The German Peace of Augsburg
   a. kept Lutherans and Catholics from fighting for almost 50 years.
   b. was written by John Calvin.
   c. was written by Ulrich Zwingli.
   d. was posted on a church wall by Martin Luther.

   ANS: A DIF: A

3. John Calvin believed
   a. God's will was written in the Bible.
   b. in parties and dances.
   c. Protestants should be persecuted.
   d. Ulrich Zwingli was a heretic.

   ANS: A DIF: A

4. Which of the following is NOT true of Calvinism?
   a. It taught people to work hard.
   b. It taught people to save money.
   c. It supported public cleanliness.
   d. It supported only one interpretation of the Bible.

   ANS: D DIF: C

5. Ulrich Zwingli was killed
   a. in a battle in 1531.
   b. in a battle in 1666.
   c. by Charles V.
   d. by John Calvin.

   ANS: A DIF: A

MATCHING

Match each item with the correct statement below.

a. ministers
b. Peace of Augsburg
c. Lutheran Church
d. John Calvin
e. Geneva

1. Protestant Church leaders
2. formed by Luther's supporters
3. religious treaty

4. very strict Protestant reformer
5. Swiss city

1. ANS: A DIF: A
2. ANS: C DIF: A
3. ANS: B DIF: A
4. ANS: D DIF: A
5. ANS: E DIF: A

SHORT ANSWER

1. What treaty kept Germany unified for some time after the Lutherans left the Roman Catholic Church?

   ANS:
   the Peace of Augsburg

   DIF: C

2. Where did the Protestant movement take hold following the German break?

   ANS:
   Scandinavia and Switzerland

   DIF: A

3. How did Swiss Protestants establish their church?

   ANS:
   They set up Reformed churches that spent more time teaching from the Bible, and they conducted church services in the language of the area.

   DIF: A

4. What Calvinist teachings helped improve living conditions in Geneva?

   ANS:
   the ideas of working hard and saving money

   DIF: A

SECTION QUIZ 29-3—CATHOLIC REFORM

MULTIPLE CHOICE

1. The leading countries of the Catholic reform movement were
   a. France and England.
   b. Greece and Egypt.
   c. Spain and Italy.
   d. India, China, and Japan.

   ANS: C DIF: E

2. Which of the following was NOT true of the Jesuits?
   a. They led simple lives.
   b. They served as advisers in royal courts.
   c. They formed the Council of Trent.
   d. They helped the poor.

   ANS: C DIF: C

3. The Council of Trent
   a. met every year from 1545 to 1563.
   b. met three times a year from 1545 to 1563.
   c. met three times between 1545 and 1563.
   d. still meets today.

   ANS: C DIF: A

4. The Council of Trent was set up
   a. by the Pope.
   b. to end Jesuit control.
   c. to end Protestant reform.
   d. to try Martin Luther.

   ANS: A DIF: E

5. Ignatius of Loyola
   a. was once a Spanish noble.
   b. was once a wealthy French landowner.
   c. died in 1563.
   d. was the Pope from 1545 to 1563.

   ANS: A DIF: A

MATCHING

Match each item with the correct statement below.
a. Ignatius of Loyola
b. Jesuit
c. seminary
d. Council of Trent
e. black robes

1. well-known Catholic reformer
2. Society of Jesus member
3. bishops who discussed reforms

4. Jesuit clothing
5. training school for priests

1. ANS: A DIF: A
2. ANS: B DIF: A
3. ANS: D DIF: A
4. ANS: E DIF: A
5. ANS: C DIF: A

SHORT ANSWER

1. What two defenses did the Jesuits use against criticisms of the Roman Catholic Church?

   ANS:
   reason and good deeds

   DIF: A

2. Where were Jesuits successful in bringing people back to the Roman Catholic Church?

   ANS:
   in Poland, Bohemia, and Hungary

   DIF: C

3. Who was responsible for calling the Council of Trent?

   ANS:
   the Pope

   DIF: E

SECTION QUIZ 29-4—A MIDDLE WAY

MULTIPLE CHOICE

1. Reformation of the Church in England started as
   a. a political quarrel between Henry VII and John Cranmer.
   b. a political quarrel between Henry VIII and Pope Clement VII.
   c. a domestic dispute between Anne Boleyn and Henry VIII.
   d. a war between the Puritans and the Roman Catholics.

   ANS: B DIF: A

2. Which of the following was NOT true of Henry VIII?
   a. His first wife was Catherine of Aragon.
   b. His second wife was Anne Boleyn.
   c. His third wife was known as "Bloody Mary."
   d. He had several children.

   ANS: C DIF: A

3. In 1558, Elizabeth
   a. became queen.
   b. was excommunicated.
   c. married Henry VIII.
   d. died.

   ANS: A DIF: E

4. Henry ended his marriage to Catherine of Aragon with the help of
   a. Anne Boleyn.
   b. the Pope.
   c. Thomas Cranmer.
   d. Edward VI.

   ANS: C DIF: C

5. When Edward VI died in 1553,
   a. Elizabeth I became queen.
   b. Mary I became queen.
   c. Edward VII became king.
   d. Henry VIII became king.

   ANS: B DIF: A

MATCHING

Match each item with the correct statement below.
a. Edward VI
b. John Cranmer
c. Mary I
d. Anne Boleyn
e. Puritans

1. Archbishop of Canterbury
2. Henry VIII's second wife
3. Henry VIII's son
4. Henry VIII's daughter
5. wanted to get rid of Catholic ways

1. ANS: B DIF: A
2. ANS: D DIF: A
3. ANS: A DIF: A
4. ANS: C DIF: A
5. ANS: E DIF: A

SHORT ANSWER

1. What situation caused problems between Henry VIII and the Roman Catholic Church?

   ANS:
   Henry wanted the Church to end his marriage to Catherine so that he could marry Anne Bolyn, but the Church refused to do this.

   DIF: A

2. How did Henry VIII become head of the Church in England?

   ANS:
   English Parliament passed a law making the king of England the head of the Church in England.

   DIF: A

3. What made the English people regret that they had insisted on Mary Tudor as Henry's successor?

   ANS:
   Mary tried to make Catholicism the official religion in England.

   DIF: A

4. Why was Elizabeth able to take the English throne when Mary died?

   ANS:
   Mary had no heirs.

   DIF: A

5. What mix was "the middle way" that Elizabeth found to set up the English Church?

   ANS:
   It consisted of Catholic practices and Protestant beliefs.

   DIF: A

SECTION QUIZ 29-5—WARS OF RELIGION

MULTIPLE CHOICE

1. By the middle 1500s, most northern Europeans were
   a. Catholics.
   b. Protestants.
   c. Huguenots.
   d. heretics.

   ANS: B DIF: E

2. Under Elizabeth I, England was
   a. the leading Protestant power in Europe.
   b. the leading Catholic power in Europe.
   c. one of the least powerful Protestant nations.
   d. split in half by a civil war.

   ANS: A DIF: A

3. Under Philip II, the Spanish Armada had
   a. 50 warships.
   b. 130 warships.
   c. nowhere to dock its ships.
   d. only Protestant sailors.

   ANS: B DIF: A

4. Which of the following is NOT true of Catherine de Medici?
   a. She was Charles IX's mother.
   b. She allowed Catholic nobles to kill leading Huguenots in Paris.
   c. She tried to keep peace.
   d. She was a Huguenot.

   ANS: D DIF: C

5. Philip II set up an Inquisition in the Low Countries
   a. to stamp out Catholicism.
   b. to stamp out Protestantism.
   c. and created the Edict of Nantes.
   d. and chose Sir Francis Drake as the chief Inquisitor.

   ANS: B DIF: A

MATCHING

Match each item with the correct statement below.
a. Edict of Nantes
b. galleons
c. armada
d. Henry VI
e. Huguenots

1. large groups of warships
2. heavy ships
3. gave Huguenots freedom to worship
4. French Protestants
5. Henry of Navarre

1. ANS: C DIF: A
2. ANS: B DIF: A
3. ANS: A DIF: A
4. ANS: E DIF: A
5. ANS: D DIF: A

SHORT ANSWER

1. What effect did the rise of different religions have on people and countries?

   ANS:
   It caused bitterness between peoples of different faiths and wars between countries.

   DIF: A

2. Why did Philip of Spain want to conquer England?

   ANS:
   He believed that control of England would lead to control of all Europe.

   DIF: A

3. How did religious differences cause disunity in France?

   ANS:
   They caused a civil war between Catholics and Protestants.

   DIF: A

4. How did Henry IV of France end fighting between Protestants and Catholics?

   ANS:
   He made Catholicism the national religion but allowed Huguenots freedom of worship.

   DIF: A

5. How did Philip II try to keep the Low Countries under Spanish rule?

   ANS:
   He set up the Inquisition and sent royal armies.

   DIF: A

SECTION QUIZ 29-6—THE THIRTY YEARS' WAR

MULTIPLE CHOICE

1. What did Ferdinand II do to win people back to the Roman Catholic Church?
   a. His armies invaded Sweden.
   b. His armies invaded Denmark.
   c. He sent Jesuits throughout Germany.
   d. He promised tracts of land to all converts.

   ANS: C DIF: C

2. The Peace of Westphalia was signed
   a. in 1643.
   b. in 1648.
   c. by the Pope.
   d. by Martin Luther.

   ANS: B DIF: E

3. The Protestant nobles of Bohemia revolted
   a. in 1618.
   b. in 1643.
   c. in 1648.
   d. in 1512.

   ANS: A DIF: A

4. Which of the following is NOT true of the Thirty Years' War?
   a. It began as a revolt in Bohemia.
   b. It ended in 1648.
   c. Ferdinand II was the German king.
   d. Ferdinand wanted everyone to convert to Protestantism.

   ANS: D DIF: A

5. France, a Catholic country, entered the Thirty Years' War
   a. in 1648.
   b. in 1666.
   c. on the Protestant side.
   d. because of a dispute with Spain.

   ANS: C DIF: A

MATCHING

Match each item with the correct statement below.
a. Thirty Years' War
b. Sweden
c. Peace of Augsburg
d. Ferdinand II
e. Peace of Westphalia

1. leader of the German Catholic alliance
2. grew out of revolt in Bohemia
3. treaty that ended the Thirty Years' War
4. treaty that led to religious quarrel
5. defeated by Germany in 1634

1. ANS: D DIF: A
2. ANS: A DIF: A
3. ANS: E DIF: A
4. ANS: C DIF: A
5. ANS: B DIF: A

SHORT ANSWER

1. What political goal did Protestant kings have during the Thirty Years' War?

   ANS:
   to stop the spread of Catholicism

   DIF: A

2. What did the French win from the Thirty Years' War?

   ANS:
   strength and unity

   DIF: A

CHAPTER 30—THE AGE OF DISCOVERY

MULTIPLE CHOICE

1. Which of the following was NOT a reason why Europeans wanted to find a sea route to Asia?
   a. Need for spices
   b. Wish to spread Christianity
   c. Overcrowding in large cities
   d. Shortage of silver and gold

   ANS: C DIF: A

2. In the 1300s, Italian merchants carried on trade with India and Asia by working through
   a. Muslim traders.
   b. Chinese merchants.
   c. merchants in Constantinople.
   d. Russian trading posts.

   ANS: A DIF: A

3. Prince Henry of Portugal was known as "the Navigator" because
   a. he sailed across the Atlantic Ocean.
   b. he invented the compass to improve navigation.
   c. he set up a school where experts taught Portuguese sailors.
   d. he led the first Portuguese expedition around Africa.

   ANS: C DIF: C

4. Where did the first Portuguese explorers travel?
   a. Through the Red Sea
   b. Westward across the Atlantic
   c. Down the west coast of Africa
   d. Northward to Britain

   ANS: C DIF: A

5. Which explorer led the first round-trip voyage to India?
   a. Christopher Columbus
   b. Giovanni da Verrazano
   c. Vasco da Gama
   d. Hernando de Soto

   ANS: C DIF: A

6. The area that Columbus actually explored included present-day
   a. Florida and the Gulf Coast.
   b. New York and New England.
   c. India and Arabia.
   d. Cuba and the Bahamas.

   ANS: D DIF: E

7. How did Pope Alexander VI's line of demarcation divide the non-Christian parts of the world?
   a. Equally among all the European nations
   b. West of the line to Spain and lands east to Portugal
   c. Between the Catholic and Protestant countries in Europe
   d. The south to Spain, the north to Portugal

   ANS: B DIF: A

8. The Spanish *conquistadores* led by Cortes conquered
   a. the Aztecs of Mexico.
   b. the Inca Empire in Peru.
   c. French settlements in Canada.
   d. Muslim towns in Africa.

   ANS: A DIF: A

9. French claims to land in eastern Canada were based on the explorations made by
   a. Giovanni da Verrazano.
   b. Sir Martin Frobisher.
   c. Jacques Cartier.
   d. Henry Hudson.

   ANS: C DIF: A

10. The original goal of European explorers in North America was
    a. conquest of Indian empires.
    b. a northwest passage to Asia.
    c. trade with Native Americans.
    d. land for colonies.

    ANS: B DIF: E

11. ___________ led to the great age of discovery in the 1400s.
    a. Better ships and equipment
    b. Silk, spices, and precious metals
    c. The search for new trade routes
    d. Fewer wars over religion

    ANS: C DIF: A

12. Portuguese explorers had gone part way down the west coast of ___________ when Prince Henry died.
    a. Italy
    b. North America
    c. India
    d. Africa

    ANS: D DIF: E

13. ________________ were Italian navigators.
    a. Chancellor, Hudson and Drake
    b. Cortes, Pizarro, and De Soto
    c. Columbus, Cabot, and Verrazano
    d. Dias, Da Gama, and Magellan

    ANS: C DIF: A

14. Educated people of the time believed the earth was round, but the voyage of ____________ actually proved it.
    a. Magellan
    b. Columbus
    c. Verrazano
    d. da Gama

    ANS: A DIF: A

MATCHING

Match each item with the correct statement below.

a. Bartolomeu Dias
b. caravel
c. Henry the Navigator
d. Magellan
e. Cape of Good Hope
f. Verrazano
g. Ponce de Leon
h. Henry Hudson
i. *conquistadores*
j. astrolabe

1. Portuguese sea captain whose expedition made the first round-the-world trip
2. English explorer hired by the Dutch to look for a northwest passage
3. Spanish soldiers who conquered the Americas
4. Instrument used by sailors to determine latitude
5. Portuguese prince who encouraged exploration
6. Fast-sailing ship built in Portugal
7. Spanish soldier who explored Florida
8. Southern tip of continent of Africa
9. Italian navigator who explored coast of North America for the French
10. Portuguese captain who first sailed around Africa

1. ANS: D DIF: A
2. ANS: H DIF: A
3. ANS: I DIF: A
4. ANS: J DIF: A
5. ANS: C DIF: A
6. ANS: B DIF: A
7. ANS: G DIF: A
8. ANS: E DIF: A
9. ANS: F DIF: A
10. ANS: A DIF: A

SHORT ANSWER

1. How are today's astronauts like the explorers of the 1400s? How are they different?

ANS:
Answers will vary, but could include: SIMILARITIES: all had courage to go into the unknown as well as great curiosity about what they might find there. All were supported by their governments; DIFFERENCES: astronauts have the advantage of modern science predicting almost exactly what they will find; they also may be safer than early explorers because of the careful support systems they enjoy.

DIF: A

SECTION QUIZ 30-1—THE PORTUGUESE

MULTIPLE CHOICE

1. Which of the following is NOT true of Prince Henry the Navigator?
   a. He worked with designers to build better ships.
   b. He opened the first school for navigators.
   c. His explorers discovered the Gold Coast and Cape Verde.
   d. His explorers searched for the fountain of youth.

   ANS: D DIF: A

2. What is scurvy?
   a. a disease
   b. a type of ship
   c. gold and silver
   d. a group

   ANS: A DIF: E

3. The Equator was crossed
   a. in 1473.
   b. in 1504.
   c. in 1550.
   d. in 1666.

   ANS: A DIF: A

4. Which of the following is NOT true of Vasco da Gama's 1497 voyage?
   a. Bartolomeu Dias was with the voyage as far as Cape Verde.
   b. Da Gama's ships landed at Calicut in 1498.
   c. Many of the sailors died.
   d. The trip from Calicut back to Lisbon took almost two years.

   ANS: D DIF: C

5. Bartolomeu Dias called the southern tip of Africa
   a. the Cape of Good Faith.
   b. the Cape of Storms.
   c. the Cape of Good Hope.
   d. Cape Dias.

   ANS: B DIF: A

MATCHING

Match each item with the correct statement below.

a. compass
b. bullion
c. astrolabe
d. caravel
e. Sagres

1. instrument with north-pointing needle
2. instrument for finding latitude
3. gold and silver for making coins
4. Portuguese town
5. Portuguese ship

1. ANS: A DIF: A
2. ANS: C DIF: A
3. ANS: B DIF: A
4. ANS: E DIF: A
5. ANS: D DIF: A

SHORT ANSWER

1. Where did early Portuguese explorers first go?

   ANS:
   south along Africa's east coast

   DIF: A

2. Why did Prince Henry need gold?

   ANS:
   to make coins

   DIF: A

3. How did Prince Henry help Portuguese sailors?

   ANS:
   He set up a school for navigators and brought together many European and Arab sea experts to teach the Portuguese everything they knew.

   DIF: A

4. How did Prince Henry's explorations make Portugal rich?

   ANS:
   Portugal set up a successful trade between its merchants and African leaders.

   DIF: A

SECTION QUIZ 30-2—THE SPANISH

MULTIPLE CHOICE

1. Which of the following was NOT true of Christopher Columbus?
   a. He was supported by Queen Isabella of Spain.
   b. He set sail in 1492 with three ships.
   c. He believed the world was flat.
   d. One of his ships, the *Santa Maria*, was wrecked.

   ANS: C DIF: E

2. Between 1519 and 1521, Hernando Cortes
   a. invaded Peru.
   b. sailed from Cuba to Florida.
   c. invaded Mexico.
   d. built the city of Lima, Peru.

   ANS: C DIF: A

3. Vasco Nunez de Balboa became the first European to
   a. set foot in Peru.
   b. look for the fountain of youth in Florida.
   c. see the Great South Sea.
   d. see the Great Salt Sea.

   ANS: C DIF: C

4. The Great South Sea is now known as
   a. the Pacific Ocean.
   b. the Indian Ocean.
   c. the Dead Sea.
   d. the Atlantic Ocean.

   ANS: A DIF: A

5. Circumnavigating means
   a. crossing the Equator.
   b. an imaginary line from the North Pole to the South Pole.
   c. navigating by the stars.
   d. sailing around the world.

   ANS: D DIF: A

MATCHING

Match each item with the correct statement below.

a. papal line of demarcation
b. Ferdinand Magellan
c. Treaty of Tordesillas
d. *pacifico*
e. *conquistadores*

1. sought western route to the Indies
2. imaginary line from North to South Poles
3. conquerors
4. allowed Portugal to claim Brazil
5. Spanish word for "peaceful"

1. ANS: B DIF: A
2. ANS: A DIF: A
3. ANS: E DIF: A
4. ANS: C DIF: A
5. ANS: D DIF: A

SHORT ANSWER

1. What were the Spanish doing during the 1400s while the Portuguese were exploring?

   ANS:
   fighting the Moors for their freedom

   DIF: A

2. What did Columbus believe he had discovered?

   ANS:
   an all-water route to Asia

   DIF: A

3. What fear made the Spanish ask the Pope for help?

   ANS:
   Spain feared that Portugal might try to take away the riches that Columbus had discovered.

   DIF: A

4. How did England, France, and the Netherlands react to the papal line of demarcation?

   ANS:
   They ignored it.

   DIF: A

SECTION QUIZ 30-3—NORTHWEST PASSAGE

MULTIPLE CHOICE

1. Jacques Cartier
   a. sailed up the St. Lawrence River as far as present-day Montreal.
   b. discovered the Hudson River.
   c. explored the coasts of Newfoundland and Nova Scotia.
   d. gave the Dutch their claim in the Americas.

   ANS: A DIF: A

2. Giovanni da Verrazano, an Italian navigator, was hired by
   a. the Italians.
   b. the Spanish.
   c. the French.
   d. the English.

   ANS: C DIF: C

3. All the explorers and navigators discussed in this section
   a. were searching for the fountain of youth.
   b. were working for the French.
   c. established claims in the Netherlands.
   d. failed to find a northwest passage.

   ANS: D DIF: A

4. On his second voyage to locate a northwest passage, Henry Hudson
   a. gave the Dutch their claim in the Americas.
   b. sailed to what is today Albany, New York.
   c. became lost in a storm and was never seen again.
   d. died of scurvy.

   ANS: C DIF: A

5. The English, French, and Dutch sought a northwest passage to
   a. the Mediterranean.
   b. the Far East.
   c. the Americas.
   d. Canada.

   ANS: B DIF: E

MATCHING

Match each item with the correct statement below.

a. Sir Martin Frobisher
b. Jacques Cartier
c. John Cabot
d. Henry Hudson
e. sea dog

1. term meaning ship's captain
2. Italian navigator
3. English sea captain
4. French navigator
5. sailed to what is now Albany, New York

1. ANS: E DIF: A
2. ANS: C DIF: A
3. ANS: A DIF: A
4. ANS: B DIF: A
5. ANS: D DIF: A

SHORT ANSWER

1. At the beginning of the 1500s, what countries controlled the sea routes south of Europe?

   ANS:
   Spain and Portugal

   DIF: A

2. How did England, France, and the Netherlands react to Spanish and Portuguese rule of the seas?

   ANS:
   They looked for a route farther to the north.

   DIF: A

3. Which explorers might have thought they had found a northwest water route to the Far East?

   ANS:
   John Cabot and Jacques Cartier

   DIF: A

CHAPTER 31—EXPANSION INTO THE AMERICAS

MULTIPLE CHOICE

1. The land in Brazil was divided into
   a. small 50-acre plots for each settler.
   b. large sugar plantations owned by those who settled there.
   c. 15 huge captaincies given to wealthy Portuguese families.
   d. areas owned by either the Church or the monarch.

   ANS: C DIF: C

2. During the 1500s and 1600s, the most important product of the plantations in Brazil was
   a. sugarcane.
   b. coffee.
   c. cotton.
   d. tobacco.

   ANS: A DIF: A

3. What made Brazil unusual among South American colonies?
   a. Women had complete equality in politics.
   b. Only a small percentage of its workers were enslaved.
   c. People of black African ancestry held important jobs.
   d. Many people were descended from Africans and Native Americans.

   ANS: D DIF: A

4. In the Spanish colonies, *mestizos* were most likely to hold positions as
   a. bishops and archbishops.
   b. high government officials.
   c. plantation laborers.
   d. merchants and artisans.

   ANS: D DIF: A

5. The Spanish monarch was represented in the colonies by
   a. the viceroy.
   b. *peninsulares*.
   c. the Council of the Indies.
   d. the Roman Catholic Church.

   ANS: C DIF: A

6. What caused Spain to finally lose its power in the Atlantic?
   a. Attacks by English pirates
   b. A shortage of gold in Peru
   c. The defeat of the Armada
   d. Portugal's claims on Brazil

   ANS: C DIF: E

7. The aim of settling English colonies in North America was
   a. to obtain gold, silver, and raw materials.
   b. to extend the English system of laws and government.
   c. to give freedom of worship to English Separatists.
   d. to claim enough land for sugar plantations.

   ANS: A DIF: C

8. The first successful English settlement was at
   a. Plymouth.
   b. Jamestown.
   c. Massachusetts Bay.
   d. New Amsterdam.

   ANS: B DIF: E

9. The two nations who fought over colonial territory in India and North America were
   a. Britain and the Netherlands.
   b. Britain and France.
   c. Spain and France.
   d. Spain and the Netherlands.

   ANS: B DIF: A

10. The first universities in the Americas were opened in
    a. Massachusetts.
    b. Mexico and Lima.
    c. Virginia and Louisiana.
    d. Quebec.

    ANS: B DIF: A

MATCHING

Match each item with the correct statement below.

a. Powhatan
b. Bartholome de Las Casas
c. viceroyalties
d. Pedro Alvares Cabral
e. Separatists
f. burgesses
g. William Penn
h. Creoles
i. *bandeirantes*
j. Samuel de Champlain

1. Quaker leader who founded a colony in North America
2. Explorer who claimed Brazil for Portugal
3. Native Americans living near Jamestown colony
4. Districts in Spanish colonial government
5. Priest who tried to improve conditions for Native Americans in Spanish colonies
6. Fortune-hunters who explored the Brazilian frontier
7. Explorer who founded French settlement at Quebec
8. Colonists of Spanish descent born in the Americas
9. Representatives to first assembly in Virginia
10. English Protestants who wanted to leave the Anglican Church

1. ANS: G DIF: A
2. ANS: D DIF: A
3. ANS: A DIF: A
4. ANS: C DIF: A
5. ANS: B DIF: A
6. ANS: I DIF: A
7. ANS: J DIF: A
8. ANS: H DIF: A
9. ANS: F DIF: A
10. ANS: E DIF: A

Match each colonial empire with its mother country.

a. England
b. France
c. the Netherlands
d. Portugal
e. Spain

11. southern North America through central America and the West Indies down the west coast of South America; the Phillipine Islands
12. along the southeastern coast of South America; coastal posts in Africa, India, Southeast Asia, and the Spice Islands
13. along the Atlantic coast of North America; trading posts in India, Malaya, and the East and West Indies
14. West Indies islands, upper South American coast, island of Manhattan on the Atlantic coast; Capetown on the southern tip of Africa
15. around the Great Lakes; at points along the Mississippi River and its tributaries; West Indies; India

11. ANS: E DIF: A
12. ANS: D DIF: A
13. ANS: A DIF: A
14. ANS: C DIF: A
15. ANS: B DIF: A

SHORT ANSWER

1. Compare the colonization of the Americas by Portugal, Spain, England, the Netherlands, and France. How were they similar? How were they different? What influences from each of them do you think still exist in the Americas?

ANS:
Answers will vary, but could include: SIMILARITIES: all took advantage of the Native Americans and assumed that European cultures were superior to those they found; DIFFERENCES: one example is that of Portugal, whose territories already had large populations, making them difficult for Portugal to rule; influences: the languages of French, Portuguese, Spanish, and English are still spoken in areas those countries colonized. Many cultural influences should be obvious to students who consider how little our cultures reflect those of Native Americans.

DIF: C

SECTION QUIZ 31-1—PORTUGAL

MULTIPLE CHOICE

1. After the king of Portugal died in 1580,
   a. Isabella became queen.
   b. Philip II of Spain claimed the throne.
   c. Portugal had no ruler for 50 years.
   d. Pedro Alvares Cabral became king.

   ANS: B DIF: C

2. The main crop of Portuguese plantations in Brazil was
   a. sugarcane.
   b. corn.
   c. cotton.
   d. wheat.

   ANS: A DIF: E

3. Pedro Alvares Cabral was
   a. a Brazilian noble.
   b. a Portuguese explorer.
   c. the king of Portugal.
   d. a *bandeirante*.

   ANS: B DIF: A

4. Portugal had claimed all of Brazil by
   a. 1512.
   b. 1620.
   c. 1676.
   d. 1700.

   ANS: A DIF: C

5. In the 1690s, Portuguese interest in Brazil grew because
   a. settlers brought enslaved Africans.
   b. gold was discovered.
   c. Pedro Alvares Cabral told stories of Brazilian wealth.
   d. the Brazilian climate was so mild.

   ANS: B DIF: A

COMPLETION

1. By 1532, Portugal had a Brazilian ____________________, and it also had ____________________ in Africa, India, and Southeast Asia.

   ANS: colony; trading posts DIF: A

2. Portugal relied on its ____________________ power and the cooperation of conquered ____________________ to rule its territories.

   ANS: sea; leaders DIF: A

3. Brazil had no deposits of precious ____________, but it did have forests of valuable ____________.

ANS: metals; brazilwood DIF: A

4. While it was under Spanish rule, Portugal lost most of its lands to the ____________ and the ____________.

ANS: English; Dutch DIF: A

MATCHING

Match each item with the correct statement below.

a. brazilwood
b. *bandeirantes*
c. colonize
d. Spice Islands
e. captaincies

1. build permanent settlements
2. territorial strips
3. fortune-hunters
4. the Moluccas
5. used to make dyes

1. ANS: C DIF: A
2. ANS: E DIF: A
3. ANS: B DIF: A
4. ANS: D DIF: A
5. ANS: A DIF: A

SECTION QUIZ 31-2—SPAIN

MULTIPLE CHOICE

1. In the early 1500s, Spain conquered the Native American empires of
   a. Mexico and Peru.
   b. the United States.
   c. the United States and Canada.
   d. Portugal and Brazil.

ANS: A DIF: A

2. Two Spanish viceroyalties were
   a. Portugal and Brazil.
   b. Africa and Southeast Asia.
   c. New Peru and North America.
   d. New Spain and New Castile.

ANS: D DIF: A

3. Most of the enslaved Africans brought to the Americas by the Portuguese
   a. picked cotton for the viceroyalties.
   b. worked in the gold mines.
   c. worked on sugar plantations.
   d. were freed after three years' service to the viceroyalties.

ANS: C DIF: A

4. Creoles were
   a. Spaniards born in Spain.
   b. people of mixed European and Native American ancestry.
   c. of Spanish descent but born in the Americas.
   d. Native Americans.

ANS: C DIF: E

5. Which of the following was NOT true of the Spanish colonists?
   a. They sent large amounts of gold and silver back to Spain.
   b. They ran plantations.
   c. They were mostly of Native American descent.
   d. They were divided into clear-cut social groups.

ANS: D DIF: C

MATCHING

Match each item with the correct statement below.

a. viceroyalties
b. viceroy
c. *peninsulares*
d. asylum
e. *mestizo*

1. districts
2. king's representative
3. Spaniards born in Spain
4. mix of European and Native American
5. places for the mentally ill

1. ANS: A DIF: A
2. ANS: B DIF: A
3. ANS: C DIF: A
4. ANS: E DIF: A
5. ANS: D DIF: A

SHORT ANSWER

1. What was Spain's position in the Americas?

ANS:
It had the largest colonial empire of all the European powers.

DIF: A

2. How did Spain's large population help colonization?

ANS:
Spain had plenty of people to send to populate the colonies.

DIF: A

3. Why did Spain have little industry?

ANS:
It had driven out most of the classes that produced goods.

DIF: C

4. How did Spain lose its power in the Atlantic?

ANS:
The Spanish Armada was defeated by England.

DIF: A

SECTION QUIZ 31-3—ENGLAND

MULTIPLE CHOICE

1. Which of the following is NOT the name of a Native American nation?
   a. Roanoke
   b. Papago
   c. Cherokee
   d. Comanche

   ANS: A DIF: A

2. The Native Americans who lived near Jamestown were
   a. the Papago.
   b. the Comanche.
   c. the Powhatan.
   d. the Creeks.

   ANS: C DIF: A

3. When a country has a balance of trade,
   a. it buys more from other countries than it sells to them.
   b. it sells more to other countries than it buys from them.
   c. it sells exactly the same amount it buys.
   d. its money is tied up in shipping.

   ANS: B DIF: C

4. Separatists were looking for a place
   a. to mine gold and silver.
   b. where they could have free land.
   c. where they could have religious freedom.
   d. where people did not have to obey laws.

   ANS: C DIF: E

5. The Pilgrims were
   a. burgesses.
   b. Separatists.
   c. Quakers.
   d. Native Americans.

   ANS: B DIF: E

MATCHING

Match each item with the correct statement below.
a. burgesses
b. Cecilius Calvert
c. William Penn
d. Roanoke Island
e. indentured servants

1. representatives
2. worked to pay off ship passage
3. "Lost Colony"
4. Quaker leader
5. the second Lord Baltimore

1. ANS: A DIF: A
2. ANS: E DIF: A
3. ANS: D DIF: A
4. ANS: C DIF: A
5. ANS: B DIF: A

SHORT ANSWER

1. What did the English hope to get from the Americas to help their trade balance?

ANS:
gold, silver, and raw materials

DIF: A

2. After Roanoke disappeared, where did the English turn their attention?

ANS:
to India

DIF: A

3. To increase the number of colonists coming to Jamestown, what did the Virginia Company of London do?

   ANS:
   It gave land to anyone who paid their own way to the colonies.

   DIF: A

4. How many colonies did England's empire in the Americas consist of?

   ANS:
   13

   DIF: E

SECTION QUIZ 31-4—THE NETHERLANDS

MULTIPLE CHOICE

1. The Dutch bought Manhattan
   a. from the Native Americans.
   b. from the Spaniards.
   c. from the French.
   d. in 1684.

   ANS: A DIF: A

2. The Dutch bought Manhattan
   a. with 300 gold pieces.
   b. with goods worth about $24.
   c. with goods worth about $300.
   d. with animal skins.

   ANS: B DIF: A

3. New Amsterdam was the capital of
   a. Manhattan.
   b. the Netherlands.
   c. Australia.
   d. the New Netherlands.

   ANS: D DIF: C

4. New Amsterdam was later renamed
   a. New York.
   b. Manhattan.
   c. Pennsylvania.
   d. Amsterdam.

   ANS: A DIF: E

5. In 1602, the Dutch had a fleet of
   a. 1,000 ships.
   b. 5,000 ships.
   c. 10,000 ships.
   d. 15,000 ships.

   ANS: C DIF: C

MATCHING

Match each item with the correct statement below.

a. New Amsterdam
b. Manhattan
c. Dutch East India Company
d. Boers
e. New Netherlands

1. founded in 1602
2. Dutch colonists in Capetown
3. Dutch city founded in 1624
4. island bought by the Dutch in 1624
5. Dutch colonies in North America

1. ANS: C DIF: A
2. ANS: D DIF: A
3. ANS: A DIF: A
4. ANS: B DIF: A
5. ANS: E DIF: A

SHORT ANSWER

1. Where did the Dutch first establish colonies in the Americas?

   ANS:
   in the West Indies, along the coast of South America, and on the island of Manhattan

   DIF: A

2. What did the Dutch call their colonies?

   ANS:
   New Netherlands

   DIF: E

3. What was the capital of the Dutch colonies?

   ANS:
   New Amsterdam

   DIF: A

SECTION QUIZ 31-5—FRANCE

MULTIPLE CHOICE

1. Which of the following was NOT traded to the Native Americans by the French?
   a. wine
   b. guns
   c. beaver skins
   d. blankets

   ANS: C DIF: A

2. Which of the following was NOT true of the Treaty of Paris?
   a. It was signed in 1743.
   b. It was signed after four wars between the French and the English.
   c. Under the treaty, the French lost their North American colonies.
   d. Under the treaty, the French lost most of their settlements in India.

   ANS: A DIF: C

3. Rene-Robert Cavelier
   a. claimed the Mississippi River valley for France.
   b. claimed Quebec for Canada.
   c. was the first explorer to travel up the Mississippi River.
   d. was killed by Native Americans in 1763.

   ANS: A DIF: A

4. The French gained great wealth from
   a. the fur trade in the Americas.
   b. the fur trade in the West Indies.
   c. the cheeses they exported to the Americas.
   d. the beef products they imported from the Americas.

   ANS: A DIF: E

5. When Rene-Robert Cavelier claimed Louisiana,
   a. Louis VI was the king of France.
   b. Louis IX was the king of France.
   c. Louis XIV was the king of France.
   d. Philip II was the king of France.

   ANS: C DIF: C

MATCHING

Match each item with the correct statement below.

a. Samuel de Champlain
b. Quebec
c. beaver
d. New France
e. Louisiana

1. French explorer
2. popular fur for French hats

3. first French colony in the Americas
4. French colonies in the Americas
5. named for the French king

1. ANS: A DIF: A
2. ANS: C DIF: A
3. ANS: B DIF: A
4. ANS: D DIF: A
5. ANS: E DIF: A

SHORT ANSWER

1. What was the occupation of most French colonists?

   ANS:
   fur traders

   DIF: E

2. What bodies of water did the French explore?

   ANS:
   the Great Lakes and the Mississippi River

   DIF: A

3. In what places did France and England wage war?

   ANS:
   Europe, the Americas, and India

   DIF: A

4. To whom did the French lose their American colonies?

   ANS:
   the English

   DIF: E

SECTION QUIZ 31-6—THE INFLUENCE OF EMPIRES

MULTIPLE CHOICE

1. Empires in the Americas
   a. took away much of Europe's power.
   b. influenced fashion in Europe.
   c. increased the wealth and power of western Europe.
   d. led to war between Protestants and Roman Catholics.

   ANS: C DIF: C

2. Empires in the Americas introduced western Europeans to
   a. summer fashions.
   b. new laws.
   c. new foods.
   d. a new way to process potatoes.

   ANS: C DIF: E

3. Because of the increased growing of corn and potatoes,
   a. many western Europeans died of famine.
   b. fewer western Europeans died of famine.
   c. western Europeans stopped growing other crops.
   d. many western Europeans were able to spend time in cafes.

   ANS: B DIF: A

4. Which of the following was NOT a new food to Europeans?
   a. avocados
   b. lima beans
   c. peanuts
   d. butter

   ANS: D DIF: A

5. Because Europeans were so fond of a drink made from cocoa,
   a. many opened cafes.
   b. some tried to create an instant form of the drink.
   c. many moved to the Americas.
   d. some lived on nothing but the drink.

   ANS: A DIF: E

MATCHING

Match each item with the correct statement below.
a. cafe
b. potatoes
c. chocolate
d. famine
e. corn

1. drink made from roasted cocoa beans
2. small European restaurant

3. Ireland's main crop
4. cause of many European deaths
5. one of Italy's main crops

1. ANS: C DIF: A
2. ANS: A DIF: A
3. ANS: B DIF: A
4. ANS: D DIF: A
5. ANS: E DIF: A

SHORT ANSWER

1. How did corn and potatoes help the European population?

   ANS:
   Population increased because both were easy to grow.

   DIF: A

2. Which European nations ended up in control of the Americas?

   ANS:
   England and Spain

   DIF: A

CHAPTER 32—POLITICAL REVOLUTIONS

MULTIPLE CHOICE

1. The conflict between James I and Parliament was due mainly to
   a. Parliament's wish to abolish the Anglican Church.
   b. James's belief in the divine right of kings to rule.
   c. James's attempts to restore the Roman Catholic Church.
   d. Parliament's attempts to raise taxes.

   ANS: B DIF: A

2. In 1629, Charles I dismissed Parliament, which violated the agreement made in
   a. the Bill of Rights.
   b. the Star Chamber.
   c. the Petition of Right.
   d. the Commonwealth.

   ANS: C DIF: A

3. The Anglicans and Catholics who backed the king in the English civil war were known as
   a. Calvinists.
   b. Cavaliers.
   c. Roundheads.
   d. the New Model Army.

   ANS: B DIF: E

4. In the Glorious Revolution, Parliament took the important step of
   a. ending the monarchy and setting up a commonwealth.
   b. beheading a monarch and making his daughter the queen.
   c. replacing a ruler by choosing another king and queen.
   d. restoring the monarchy with another Tudor king.

   ANS: C DIF: A

5. Under the theory of mercantilism, American colonists were supposed to
   a. provide raw materials and buy English products.
   b. develop factories to supply England with goods.
   c. expand English trade by buying goods from European countries.
   d. develop a strong navy and large merchant fleet.

   ANS: A DIF: A

6. The first time that Parliament taxed the American colonists directly was through the
   a. Townshend Acts.
   b. Declaration of Rights.
   c. Tea Act.
   d. Stamp Act.

   ANS: D DIF: C

7. The new American Constitution included the principle that government receives its power from the people, also called
   a. representative democracy.
   b. popular sovereignty.
   c. limited government.
   d. natural rights.

   ANS: B DIF: A

8. Under the Old Regime in France, who paid taxes?
   a. Feudal nobles
   b. Bourgeoisie and city workers
   c. All French citizens
   d. High Church officials

   ANS: B DIF: A

9. Which of these was NOT a problem facing France in the 1780s?
   a. Religious wars between Catholics and Huguenots
   b. Shortage of money and large war debts
   c. Unequal distribution of lands
   d. Food shortages and unemployment in the cities

   ANS: A DIF: A

10. By the end of the French Revolution, the government of France was
    a. a republic.
    b. a constitutional monarchy.
    c. a popular democracy.
    d. an absolute monarchy.

    ANS: B DIF: A

11. Which of the following is ***not*** true about new ideas of government at the beginning of the 1700s?
    a. People did not want kings or Popes telling them what to do.
    b. People wanted their natural rights—life, liberty and property.
    c. People wanted a voice in their government.
    d. People wanted equal justice under the law.

    ANS: B DIF: A

12. How did the English monarchy change after the Glorious Revolution?
    a. Roman Catholics were no longer persecuted.
    b. The monarchy's power was greatly limited by Parliament.
    c. The Crown became hereditary.
    d. Royal power was always shared between king and queen.

    ANS: B DIF: A

13. What angered England's American colonies?
    a. Parliament boycotted American goods.
    b. Only English sailors could sail colonial ships.
    c. England got deeply into debt for fighting wars.
    d. The king and Parliament tightened their control over colonial governments.

    ANS: D DIF: A

14. How did the American Revolution influence the French people?
    a. The Third Estate made the king and queen pay the government's debt.
    b. The American war made the First and Second Estates think about reforms.
    c. The French people disagreed violently with the idea of revolution.
    d. The American revolt pointed out that French government needed political change.

    ANS: D DIF: A

15. Why was the American Revolution partly responsible for the French Revolution?
  a. The French government had given a great deal of money to the American colonies.
  b. The new American government could not afford to pay back the money it had borrowed from France.
  c. Outfitting ships and soldiers had increased France's deficit.
  d. French clergy and nobles followed the American example of refusing to pay their taxes.

ANS: A DIF: A

16. What did members of the Third Estate disagree about?
  a. the idea that the right to vote should depend on how much money or how much land a person had
  b. the fact that the bourgeoisie did not want to share the little power they had
  c. whether or not too many aristocrats had been executed
  d. the issue of city workers wanting a republican government

ANS: A DIF: A

17. What ideal did the French Revolution support?
  a. People should be able to change government whenever they want.
  b. People have the right to life, liberty, and property.
  c. People do not need to follow rules made up by kings.
  d. People have the right to choose their own government.

ANS: D DIF: A

MATCHING

Match each item with the correct statement below.

a. bourgeoisie	f. Charles I
b. John Locke	g. *emigres*
c. Voltaire	h. Marie Antoinette
d. Bastille	i. Robespierre
e. Oliver Cromwell	j. Mary

1. Military leader who headed the Commonwealth
2. Queen chosen by the English Parliament
3. French political leader during the "Reign of Terror"
4. People who fled France during the revolution
5. Prison fortress in Paris that symbolized royal tyranny
6. Philosophe who advocated freedom of speech
7. Top of the Third Estate, which included merchants, lawyers, and doctors
8. Queen called Madame Deficit, who was executed during the French Revolution
9. King beheaded during the English civil war
10. English philosopher who defended the idea of natural rights

1. ANS: E DIF: A
2. ANS: J DIF: A
3. ANS: I DIF: A
4. ANS: G DIF: A
5. ANS: D DIF: A

6. ANS: C DIF: A
7. ANS: A DIF: A
8. ANS: H DIF: A
9. ANS: F DIF: A
10. ANS: B DIF: A

SHORT ANSWER

1. Do you think revolutions require war and fighting? Why or why not?

ANS:
Answers will vary, but many students will define revolutions as violent ones; however, others may see that revolutions in political thought can take place through communication.

DIF: A

2. Study the map below. What two countries did not take part in the English Civil War? How did the territories of the two opposing sides differ?

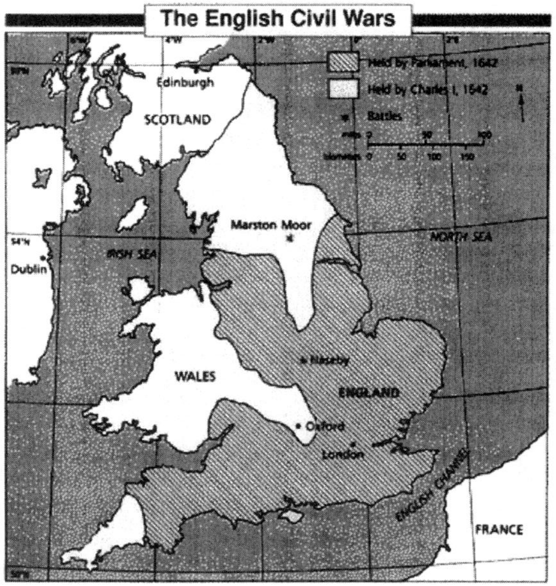

ANS:
Scotland and Ireland; the territory held by Parliament was unified, while the territory held by Charles I was divided into two sections.

DIF: C

SECTION QUIZ 32-1—REVOLUTION IN ENGLAND

MULTIPLE CHOICE

1. Which of the following was NOT true of Elizabeth I?
   a. She was the last Tudor monarch.
   b. She died in 1603.
   c. After her death, the Crown was passed to James VI of Scotland.
   d. She had two sons.

   ANS: D DIF: E

2. King Charles I was
   a. son of Elizabeth I.
   b. father of Elizabeth I.
   c. son of James I.
   d. father of James I.

   ANS: C DIF: A

3. The Star Chamber was
   a. the king's bedroom.
   b. a high-powered telescope developed by James I.
   c. a royal court that tried people without a jury.
   d. another name for Oliver Cromwell's army.

   ANS: C DIF: E

4. In the war between the Crown and the Parliament,
   a. those who backed the Crown were called Roundheads.
   b. those who backed the Crown were called Cavaliers.
   c. those who backed the Parliament were called Anglicans.
   d. those who backed the Parliament were called the Star Chamber.

   ANS: B DIF: C

5. Which of the following was NOT true of Oliver Cromwell?
   a. He was a Puritan leader.
   b. He took over the rule of England after the death of Charles I.
   c. He put down a rebellion in the Americas.
   d. After his death, his son Richard ruled England.

   ANS: C DIF: A

COMPLETION

1. The Stuart monarchs believed in rule by ____________________.

   ANS: divine right DIF: A

2. James I and Charles I dismissed ____________________ whenever that body objected to the kings' behavior.

   ANS: Parliament DIF: A

3. Oliver Cromwell and his supporters tried and executed Charles I for the crime of ____________________.

   ANS: treason DIF: A

4. Cromwell ruled as a military ____________________, representing only the Puritan minority in England.

   ANS: dictator DIF: A

5. Under the rule of William and Mary, Parliament was stronger and the ____________________ of the English people were protected

   ANS: rights DIF: A

MATCHING

Match each item with the correct statement below.

a. foreign policy
b. governing body
c. repealed
d. martial law
e. revolution

1. an attempt to overthrow the government
2. Parliament
3. rule by the army
4. abolished
5. relations with other countries

1. ANS: E DIF: A
2. ANS: B DIF: A
3. ANS: D DIF: A
4. ANS: C DIF: A
5. ANS: A DIF: A

SECTION QUIZ 32-2—THE AMERICAN REVOLUTION

MULTIPLE CHOICE

1. Which of the following was NOT true of the Stamp Act?
   a. It called for a tax on newspapers and legal documents.
   b. It was passed in 1675.
   c. It hurt merchants, lawyers, and those in the newspaper business.
   d. It was repealed in 1766.

   ANS: B DIF: A

2. The colonists called the British soldiers
   a. turncoats.
   b. traitors.
   c. redcoats.
   d. bootblacks.

   ANS: C DIF: E

3. Which of the following was NOT true of the Coercive Acts?
   a. They were passed in 1774.
   b. They closed Boston harbor.
   c. They put Massachusetts under military rule.
   d. They made the colonists build houses for the military.

   ANS: D DIF: C

4. The First Continental Congress
   a. met in September 1776.
   b. called for the repeal of the Stamp Act.
   c. was made up of 12 colonies.
   d. met in Boston.

   ANS: C DIF: C

5. The United States Constitution was adopted in
   a. 1774.
   b. 1776.
   c. 1783.
   d. 1789.

   ANS: D DIF: A

COMPLETION

1. Under mercantilism, English colonies were supposed to supply England with ____________________ that were scarce.

   ANS: goods DIF: A

2. Colonial legislatures lost power after the ____________________War.

   ANS: French and Indian DIF: A

3. A major colonial objection to Parliamentary control was that the colonies had no ____________________ in Parliament.

   ANS: representatives DIF: A

4. Some colonial leaders, such as George Washington, hoped to ____________________ with England and not go to war.

   ANS: settle the differences DIF: A

5. The American colonists finally won the war with England due to help from ____________________.

   ANS: France DIF: E

MATCHING

Match each item with the correct statement below.

a. popular sovereignty
b. monopoly
c. direct tax
d. mercantilism
e. amendments

1. government power from the people
2. formal changes
3. sole right
4. economic system
5. paid directly to the government

1. ANS: A DIF: A
2. ANS: E DIF: A
3. ANS: B DIF: A
4. ANS: D DIF: A
5. ANS: C DIF: A

SECTION QUIZ 32-3—THE FRENCH REVOLUTION

MULTIPLE CHOICE

1. In France in the 1600s and early 1700s, the First Estate was
   a. the clergy.
   b. the nobility.
   c. the monarch.
   d. the bourgeoisie.

   ANS: A DIF: A

2. Francois Marie Arouet was also known as
   a. Marie-Antoinette.
   b. Voltaire.
   c. Louis XVI.
   d. Bloody Mary.

   ANS: B DIF: A

3. The attack on the Bastille took place on
   a. May 5, 1755.
   b. July 14, 1769.
   c. July 4, 1776.
   d. July 14, 1789.

   ANS: D   DIF: C

4. Sans-culottes were
   a. members of the French legislature.
   b. members of the bourgeoisie.
   c. city workers.
   d. peasants.

   ANS: C   DIF: E

5. The Committee of Public Safety was led by
   a. Voltaire.
   b. Domingo Sarmiento.
   c. Maximilien de Robespierre.
   d. the sans-culottes.

   ANS: C   DIF: A

COMPLETION

1. In France, members of the Third Estate paid all the ____________ but had no power.

   ANS: taxes   DIF: E

2. The major problem of the French government was lack of ____________.

   ANS: money   DIF: E

3. The conditions that led to uprisings in France included poor crop ____________, high ____________ of food, and high ____________ among city workers.

   ANS: harvests; cost; unemployment   DIF: A

4. Many European countries declared war on France after ____________ and ____________ were executed.

   ANS: Louis XVI; Marie Antoinette   DIF: A

5. The French Revolution changed French government from a constitutional ____________ to a Directory with five leaders and a ____________.

   ANS: monarchy; legislature   DIF: A

MATCHING

Match each item with the correct statement below.
a. constitutional monarchy
b. guillotine
c. tyranny
d. estates
e. bourgeoisie

1. unjust use of power
2. Third Estate in France
3. machine used for beheading
4. classes
5. power limited by laws

1. ANS: C   DIF: A
2. ANS: E   DIF: A
3. ANS: B   DIF: A
4. ANS: D   DIF: A
5. ANS: A   DIF: A

CHAPTER 33—RISE OF INDUSTRY

MULTIPLE CHOICE

1. The idea that the sun is the center of the universe was published in 1543 by
   a. Ptolemy.
   b. Copernicus.
   c. Galileo.
   d. Newton.

   ANS: B DIF: E

2. For the 1500s and 1600s, what is meant by the term "Scientific Revolution"?
   a. A rediscovery of scientific ideas from Greece and Rome
   b. Changes in science that followed political revolutions
   c. The use of scientific method to form new ideas and theories
   d. A revolt by the scientists at major European universities

   ANS: C DIF: A

3. Which of the following was NOT a result of the enclosure movement in Great Britain?
   a. Smaller harvests of crops
   b. More profit for landowners
   c. Unemployment for many farm workers
   d. Migration to cities

   ANS: A DIF: C

4. The Industrial Revolution began in Great Britain in what industry?
   a. Cotton-growing
   b. Textile-making
   c. Railroads
   d. Iron and steel

   ANS: B DIF: A

5. By the middle of the Industrial Revolution, the most important source of power for factories was
   a. steam power.
   b. electricity.
   c. water power.
   d. gasoline engines.

   ANS: A DIF: E

6. Which of these inventors did NOT play a part in improving transportation in the late 1700s and early 1800s?
   a. John McAdam
   b. James Hargreaves
   c. Robert Fulton
   d. George Stephenson

   ANS: B DIF: C

7. The first product made using an assembly line process was
   a. Daimler's automobile.
   b. cotton cloth.
   c. the Colt revolver.
   d. the Bell telephone.

   ANS: C DIF: A

8. In Great Britain, the people who gained the most in comfort and influence from the Industrial Revolution were
   a. factory workers.
   b. the middle class.
   c. farmers and peasants.
   d. the nobility.

   ANS: B DIF: A

9. Which of these nations was the last to industrialize?
   a. Germany
   b. United States
   c. France
   d. Belgium

   ANS: A DIF: C

10. All of the following inventions depend on electricity EXCEPT
    a. the Morse telegraph.
    b. Marconi's wireless.
    c. Edison's light bulb.
    d. Daimler's engine.

    ANS: D DIF: A

COMPLETION

1. The Industrial Revolution shifted work from animal and human power to ____________________ power.

   ANS: machine DIF: A

2. The Industrial Revolution changed most Western societies from mostly agricultural to more ____________________.

   ANS: industrial DIF: A

3. The Agricultural Revolution paved the way for the Industrial Revolution by increasing the ____________________.

   ANS: population DIF: E

4. Machines helped fewer ____________________ produce more ____________________ in less ____________________.

   ANS: workers; goods; time DIF: A

5. When ____________________ replaced water as a major power source, factories could be built near raw materials.

   ANS: steam DIF: A

6. Finding inexpensive ways to smelt iron and make steel meant that building materials for machines were ____________________.

   ANS: cheaper DIF: A

7. The working class could not change poor working and living conditions because they could not ____________________ or form ____________________.

ANS: vote; unions DIF: A

MATCHING

Match each item with the correct statement below.

a. Galileo Galilei
b. James Watt
c. Bessemer process
d. Samuel F. B. Morse
e. spinning jenny
f. Guglielmo Marconi
g. automation
h. Samuel Colt
i. domestic system
j. Gottlieb Daimler

1. Inventor of the internal combustion engine
2. Italian astronomer and inventor who used his telescope to study the stars and planets
3. Process in which machines replace human labor
4. Scottish mechanic who perfected the steam engine
5. Inventor who developed the assembly line in his factory
6. Work is done at home
7. Inventor of the wireless telegraph known as radio
8. Machine used to speed up textile-making
9. Process for manufacturing steel
10. Inventor of the electric telegraph

1. ANS: J DIF: A
2. ANS: A DIF: A
3. ANS: G DIF: A
4. ANS: B DIF: A
5. ANS: H DIF: A
6. ANS: I DIF: A
7. ANS: F DIF: A
8. ANS: E DIF: A
9. ANS: C DIF: A
10. ANS: D DIF: A

SHORT ANSWER

1. Why do you think the Industrial Revolution took place in the areas of the world in which it did? Are all countries in the world now industrialized? How do you know?

ANS:
Answers will vary, but could include: the Industrial Revolution centered in western Europe as an outgrowth of the Scientific Revolution. Many countries today are not industrialized or developed, as students should understand from current countries who do not have enough industry to support themselves.

DIF: A

2. Study the chart below. Whose discoveries probably helped Gottlieb Daimler and Rudolf Diesel invent their combustion engines? Which scientists were probably part of the Agricultural Revolution?

SCIENTISTS

NAME	FIELD	ACCOMPLISHMENTS
Johannes Kepler *Germany*	*Astronomy*	announced laws of movement of planets, 1609
William Harvey *England*	*Medicine*	published theory on human blood circulation, 1628
Sir Isaac Newton *England*	*Physics*	stated laws of motion and theory of gravitation, 1687
Antoine–Laurent Lavoisier *France*	*Chemistry*	discovered nature of combustion, 1777
John Dalton *England*	*Chemistry*	announced atomic theory, 1803
Maria Mitchell *United States*	*Astronomy*	discovered new comet, 1847
Charles Darwin *England*	*Biology*	advanced theory on development of plants and animals, 1858
Gregor Mendel *Austria*	*Botany*	discovered principles of heredity, 1866
Louis Pasteur *France*	*Medicine*	advanced germ theory of disease, 1876; successfully vaccinated against rabies, 1885
Pierre Curie **Marie Curie** *France*	*Chemistry*	discovered radium and polonium, 1898

ANS:
Lavoisier; Darwin, Pasteur, and Mendel

DIF: C

SECTION QUIZ 33-1—SCIENTIFIC REVOLUTION

MULTIPLE CHOICE

1. Copernicus was the first to explain
   a. astronomy.
   b. that Earth revolves around the sun.
   c. that Earth is round.
   d. the theory of gravitation.

   ANS: B   DIF: E

2. Which of the following was NOT true of Galileo?
   a. He learned that the sun rotates on its axis.
   b. He was criticized by the Roman Catholic Church.
   c. He learned that the Milky Way has many stars.
   d. He thought the moon's surface was smooth.

   ANS: D   DIF: A

3. Galileo died in
   a. 1572.   c. 1642.
   b. 1602.   d. 1712.

   ANS: C   DIF: C

4. The technology for today's rockets and satellites
   a. is based on the work of Copernicus.
   b. is based on the work of Galileo.
   c. is based on the work of Sir Isaac Newton.
   d. is based on the work of Ptolemy.

   ANS: C   DIF: A

5. Galileo got the idea for his telescope from
   a. Copernicus.   c. French telescope makers.
   b. Ptolemy.   d. Dutch eyeglass makers.

   ANS: D   DIF: A

MATCHING

Match each item with the correct statement below.
a. Scientific Revolution   d. Galileo
b. Sir Isaac Newton   e. Copernicus
c. Industrial Revolution

1. began in the 1400s
2. shift toward human and machine power
3. Polish astronomer

4. Italian astronomer
5. explained the theory of gravitation

1. ANS: A   DIF: A
2. ANS: C   DIF: A
3. ANS: E   DIF: A
4. ANS: D   DIF: A
5. ANS: B   DIF: A

SHORT ANSWER

1. What did the studies of Nicholas Copernicus prove?

   ANS:
   The sun is at the center of the universe.

   DIF: A

2. What natural phenomena did Sir Isaac Newton explain?

   ANS:
   gravity

   DIF: A

3. How did scientists in Great Britain and France help the spread of scientific knowledge?

   ANS:
   formed organizations for the sharing and discussion of information

   DIF: A

SECTION QUIZ 33-2—AGRICULTURAL REVOLUTION

MULTIPLE CHOICE

1. The Agricultural Revolution
   a. set the stage for the Scientific Revolution.
   b. set the stage for the Industrial Revolution.
   c. left most landowners penniless.
   d. began with the invention of the tractor.

   ANS: B   DIF: A

2. Under the strip system, each small section of land
   a. could be used to grow a different crop.
   b. was the property of a tenant farmer.
   c. was three square acres.
   d. had a house and barn.

   ANS: A DIF: A

3. Most tenant farmers during the Agricultural Revolution
   a. were landowners.
   b. stayed on as paid workers.
   c. moved to the cities and became industrial workers.
   d. were enslaved.

   ANS: C DIF: A

4. Which of the following was NOT true of the Agricultural Revolution?
   a. New ways of breeding animals developed.
   b. There was greater production of food.
   c. The average life expectancy went down.
   d. The population increased.

   ANS: C DIF: E

5. In Great Britain, enclosure was being used
   a. by the 1600s.
   b. by the 1700s.
   c. by about 1810.
   d. by about 1880.

   ANS: B DIF: C

MATCHING

Match each item with the correct statement below.

a. population growth
b. enclosure
c. tenant farmers
d. Agricultural Revolution
e. landowners

1. result of greater food production
2. system of land division
3. new developments in farming
4. with enclosure, they grew prosperous
5. with enclosure, they were less needed

1. ANS: A DIF: A
2. ANS: B DIF: A
3. ANS: D DIF: A
4. ANS: E DIF: A
5. ANS: C DIF: A

SHORT ANSWER

1. What three results did the enclosure system produce for landowners?

   ANS:
   larger harvests, fewer workers, and more profit

   DIF: A

2. How were crops affected by the Agricultural Revolution?

   ANS:
   There was greater production of food.

   DIF: A

3. How were domesticated animals affected by the Agricultural Revolution?

   ANS:
   There were better breeding methods.

   DIF: A

SECTION QUIZ 33-3—INDUSTRIAL REVOLUTION

MULTIPLE CHOICE

1. Under the domestic system,
   a. most work was done in workers' cottages.
   b. work was done by machines.
   c. work was done in factories.
   d. people did not have to work very hard.

   ANS: A DIF: A

2. The factory system
   a. used only machines.
   b. brought workers and machines together in one place.
   c. was a result of an invention by James Watt.
   d. helped to bring about the Scientific Revolution.

   ANS: B DIF: A

3. In 1847, Samuel Colt
   a. invented the light bulb.
   b. invented the cotton gin.
   c. developed the assembly line.
   d. developed the factory system.

   ANS: C DIF: A

4. Which of the following does NOT describe the open-hearth process?
   a. It was invented by a Frenchman and a German.
   b. It was invented in 1863.
   c. It was used in the making of steel.
   d. It was faster than the Bessemer Process.

   ANS: A DIF: C

5. The steamboat was invented by
   a. Robert Fulton.
   b. Eli Whitney.
   c. James Watt.
   d. Thomas Telford.

   ANS: A DIF: E

MATCHING

Match each item with the correct statement below.

a. flying shuttle
b. textile
c. spinning jenny
d. automation
e. cotton gin

1. invented by John Kay
2. invented by James Hargreaves
3. invented by Eli Whitney
4. woven cloth
5. process in which machines do the labor

1. ANS: A DIF: A
2. ANS: C DIF: A
3. ANS: E DIF: A
4. ANS: B DIF: A
5. ANS: D DIF: A

SHORT ANSWER

1. Name three inventions that revolutionized Great Britain's textile industry.

   ANS:
   flying shuttle, spinning jenny, and cotton gin

   DIF: A

2. How was the textile industry changed by the factory system?

   ANS:
   It brought workers and machines together in one place.

   DIF: A

3. Name three new ways of organizing production that led to huge increases in the amount of goods manufactured.

   ANS:
   system of interchangeable parts, automation, and assembly line

   DIF: A

4. How was steel an improvement over iron?

   ANS:
   It was harder and stronger.

   DIF: A

5. Name three ways Great Britain improved transportation during the Industrial Revolution.

   ANS:
   improved road surfaces; widened and deepened rivers; built railroads

   DIF: A

SECTION QUIZ 33-4—INDUSTRIAL IMPACT

MULTIPLE CHOICE

1. Until the Middle Ages, England's two social classes were
   a. the clergy and the nobility.
   b. the nobility and the bourgeoisie.
   c. the monarchy and the peasantry.
   d. the nobles and the peasants.

   ANS: D DIF: A

2. Which of the following was NOT true of the Industrial Revolution?
   a. It led to the growth of cities.
   b. The middle class gained political power.
   c. In the early days, working conditions were difficult.
   d. In the early days, workers had to be at least 16 years old.

   ANS: D DIF: E

3. During the early days of the Industrial Revolution,
   a. the working class had its own political party.
   b. only the nobles had trade unions.
   c. workers had no political power.
   d. all workers had to join trade unions.

   ANS: C DIF: A

4. In 1824, trade unions
   a. were banned.
   b. were opened to children.
   c. were headed by the monarch.
   d. were made legal.

   ANS: D DIF: A

5. Which of the following was NOT true of the reform movement?
   a. It cut the workday to ten hours.
   b. It started schools and orphanages.
   c. It prohibited all women and children from working.
   d. It worked to improve living conditions.

   ANS: C DIF: C

MATCHING

Match each item with the correct statement below.
a. trade unions
b. lower class
c. middle class
d. boaters
e. epidemic

1. widespread disease
2. stiff straw hats
3. peasant class
4. workers' associations
5. rich merchant class

1. ANS: E DIF: A
2. ANS: D DIF: A
3. ANS: B DIF: A
4. ANS: A DIF: A
5. ANS: C DIF: A

SHORT ANSWER

1. How did the Industrial Revolution affect the middle class?

   ANS:
   The middle class increased in number and grew richer.

   DIF: A

2. What new class developed during the Industrial Revolution?

   ANS:
   working class

   DIF: A

3. Who made up the working class?

   ANS:
   mostly peasants who could no longer make a living by farming

   DIF: A

4. Why did working-class people have to sell their labor?

   ANS:
   They could no longer sell crops from their land.

   DIF: A

5. What kind of labor did the Industrial Revolution need?

   ANS:
   unskilled

   DIF: A

SECTION QUIZ 33-5—SPREAD OF INDUSTRY

MULTIPLE CHOICE

1. The first successful electric telegraph was built by
   a. Americans.
   b. Germans.
   c. the French.
   d. the English.

   ANS: A DIF: E

2. The internal combustion engine was invented by
   a. Thomas Edison.
   b. Samuel F. B. Morse.
   c. Gottlieb Daimler.
   d. Guglielmo Marconi.

   ANS: C DIF: A

3. After Great Britain, the first country to industrialize was
   a. the United States.
   b. Belgium.
   c. France.
   d. Germany.

   ANS: B DIF: C

4. The unification of Germany did not take place until
   a. 1812.
   b. 1850.
   c. 1871.
   d. 1902.

   ANS: C DIF: C

5. Alfred Vail built the first successful electric telegraph with
   a. Thomas Edison.
   b. Guglielmo Marconi.
   c. Alexander Graham Bell.
   d. Samuel F. B. Morse.

   ANS: D DIF: A

MATCHING

Match each item with the correct statement below.

a. immigrants
b. industrialized
c. Thomas Edison
d. Guglielmo Marconi
e. internal combustion engine

1. permanent settlers in a new place
2. inventor of the radio
3. inventor of the electric light
4. built up industry
5. machine fueled by gasoline

1. ANS: A DIF: A
2. ANS: D DIF: A
3. ANS: C DIF: A
4. ANS: B DIF: A
5. ANS: E DIF: A

SHORT ANSWER

1. How did Great Britain's workers react to the laws forbidding them to leave the country?

   ANS:
   They ignored them and left anyway.

   DIF: A

2. What slowed industrialization in France? Germany?

   ANS:
   In France there was war and revolution; in Germany there was no unity.

   DIF: A

3. What inventions revolutionized communication?

   ANS:
   telegraph, telephone, and radio

   DIF: A

4. What two fuels did the new internal combustion engines use?

   ANS:
   gas and oil

   DIF: E

CHAPTER 34—THE AMERICAS

MULTIPLE CHOICE

1. Which of the following was NOT a feature of American government in the early 1800s?
   a. Political parties
   b. Stability in government
   c. Election campaigns
   d. Votes for all citizens

   ANS: D DIF: A

2. By acquiring the Louisiana Territory, the United States gained control of
   a. California and Texas.
   b. the Rio Grande.
   c. the Mississippi River.
   d. land along the Ohio River.

   ANS: C DIF: A

3. Which of these statements is true about the United States before the Civil War?
   a. Many immigrants lived in large cities in the South.
   b. Industry was important in the North.
   c. Southerners wanted a stronger central government.
   d. Crops in the North were grown on large plantations.

   ANS: B DIF: C

4. Which of these events caused the southern states to secede from the Union?
   a. Abraham Lincoln was elected President.
   b. Congress outlawed enslavement in the United States.
   c. Lincoln issued an order freeing enslaved people.
   d. War broke out between North and South.

   ANS: A DIF: A

5. The belief that the United States should expand westward to the Pacific was known as
   a. annexation.
   b. urbanization.
   c. manifest destiny.
   d. federalism.

   ANS: C DIF: E

6. Creoles became leaders in the movements for independence in Latin America because
   a. their ties with Europe were still strong.
   b. they had the poorest living conditions of any colonists.
   c. they had political power and education.
   d. they held the highest government positions.

   ANS: B DIF: C

7. The countries in the northern part of South America were led to freedom by
   a. Antonio Narino.
   b. Father Jose Maria Morelos.
   c. Maximilian.
   d. Simon Bolivar.

   ANS: D DIF: A

8. The first Mexicans to revolt against Spanish rule were
   a. Native Americans.
   b. *peninsulares*.
   c. Creoles.
   d. enslaved Africans.

   ANS: A DIF: A

9. A "strong-man" Latin American leader is also called a(n)
   a. federalist.
   b. emperor.
   c. caudillo.
   d. junta.

   ANS: C DIF: E

10. The Mexican leader who successfully made reforms and worked to establish democracy was
    a. Santa Anna.
    b. Agustin de Iturbide.
    c. Pedro I.
    d. Benito Juarez.

    ANS: D DIF: A

COMPLETION

1. By 1830, the government of ____________________ was one of the world's most democratic.

   ANS: the United States DIF: A

2. By 1867, the United States had tripled its size by acquiring new ____________________.

   ANS: territory DIF: E

3. Differences between the northern and southern states in political beliefs and ways of life caused ____________________.

   ANS: the Civil War DIF: A

4. During the late 1800s and early 1900s, many Americans moved from ____________________ to ____________________.

   ANS: farms; cities DIF: A

5. ____________________ Creoles led the fight for independence in South America.

   ANS: Educated DIF: A

6. Most ____________________ had the support of large landowners and church leaders.

   ANS: caudillos DIF: A

7. In the United States, change in government happened peacefully with ____________________; in Latin America, change in government usually happened as violent ____________________.

   ANS: elections; revolutions DIF: A

8. Throughout the 1800s, most Latin American governments were ruled as ____________________.

ANS: military dictatorships DIF: A

MATCHING

Match each item with the correct statement below.

a. Agustin de Iturbide
b. Louisiana Purchase
c. Bernado O'Higgins
d. Gadsden Purchase
e. Santa Anna
f. Gran Colombia
g. Saint Domingue
h. Miguel Hidalgo
i. Toussaint-L'Ouverture
j. Confederacy

1. Liberator of Chile, along with San Martin
2. Leader of independence in Haiti
3. Land agreement between the United States and Mexico
4. Army officer who ruled as emperor of Mexico
5. Priest who led rebellion by Mexican Native Americans
6. French colony that became Haiti
7. Government established by seceding southern states
8. Independent state set up by Simon Bolivar
9. Land agreement with France that doubled the size of the United States
10. Caudillo who lost Mexican lands to the United States

1. ANS: C DIF: A
2. ANS: I DIF: A
3. ANS: D DIF: A
4. ANS: A DIF: A
5. ANS: H DIF: A
6. ANS: G DIF: A
7. ANS: J DIF: A
8. ANS: F DIF: A
9. ANS: B DIF: A
10. ANS: E DIF: A

SHORT ANSWER

1. Why do you think women, enslaved people, and Native Americans were not allowed to vote in early governments?

ANS:
Answers will vary, but could include: society did not value these people, so it did not value their decisions.

DIF: C

SECTION QUIZ 34-1—THE UNITED STATES

MULTIPLE CHOICE

1. A stable government
   a. is ruled by nobility.
   b. is ruled by the people.
   c. is ruled by a monarch.
   d. rules from year to year without great changes.

   ANS: D DIF: E

2. The United States bought the Louisiana Territory from
   a. England.
   b. France.
   c. Mexico.
   d. Canada.

   ANS: B DIF: E

3. The United States took possession of Florida as part of
   a. manifest destiny.
   b. the Louisiana Purchase.
   c. the Adams-Onis Treaty.
   d. the Gadsden Purchase.

   ANS: C DIF: A

4. In 1800, the two political parties in the United States were
   a. the Republicans and the Democrats.
   b. the Nationalists and the Federalists.
   c. the Democrats and the Democrat-Republicans.
   d. the Federalists and the Democrat-Republicans.

   ANS: D DIF: C

5. The dates of the Civil War were
   a. 1721-1725.
   b. 1801-1805.
   c. 1861-1865.
   d. 1880-1891.

   ANS: C DIF: A

MATCHING

Match each item with the correct statement below.

a. annexation
b. tenements
c. urbanization
d. representative government
e. federal

1. the act of taking over territory
2. usually run-down apartments
3. national
4. officials elected by the people
5. growth of cities

1. ANS: A DIF: A
2. ANS: B DIF: A
3. ANS: E DIF: A
4. ANS: D DIF: A
5. ANS: C DIF: A

SHORT ANSWER

1. Why did the number of voters grow between 1800 and 1830?

   ANS:
   New laws granted most white males the right to vote.

   DIF: A

2. How did beliefs about land differ between American settlers and Native Americans?

   ANS:
   Native Americans believed that land belonged to no one; settlers claimed the land belonged to whomever settled it.

   DIF: A

3. What four countries sold their territorial claims to the United States?

   ANS:
   Mexico, Spain, England, and France

   DIF: A

4. Why did the southern states try to secede from the United States?

   ANS:
   They disagreed with the Union about states' rights and slavery.

   DIF: A

5. From what two places did people come to settle in cities of the United States?

   ANS:
   from American farms; from Europe

   DIF: A

SECTION QUIZ 34-2—LATIN AMERICA

MULTIPLE CHOICE

1. At one time, Haiti was known as
   a. the West Indies.
   b. Saint Domingue.
   c. Belize.
   d. mountainous.

   ANS: B DIF: E

2. Which of the following was NOT true of Simon Bolivar?
   a. He was called "the Liberator."
   b. He freed Peru from Spanish rule.
   c. He renamed Haiti.
   d. He became the first president of Gran Colombia, Ecuador, and Panama.

   ANS: C DIF: A

3. Father Luis Beltran
   a. melted down gold and silver to make guns.
   b. melted down church bells to make guns and bullets.
   c. used his church as a front for the revolution.
   d. worked with Benito Juarez.

   ANS: B DIF: A

4. In 1821, the people of Central America joined together to form
   a. the Central Independent States.
   b. the United Provinces of Central America.
   c. Gran Colombia.
   d. Haiti.

   ANS: B DIF: A

5. Mexico became a republic in
   a. 1709.
   b. 1789.
   c. 1824.
   d. 1889.

   ANS: C DIF: C

MATCHING

Match each item with the correct statement below.

a. Benito Juarez
b. Agustin de Iturbide
c. Simon Bolivar
d. junta
e. indigo

1. political committee
2. "the Liberator"
3. plant used to make blue dye

4. Creole soldier and emperor of Mexico
5. Native American ruler of Mexico

1. ANS: D DIF: A
2. ANS: C DIF: A
3. ANS: E DIF: A
4. ANS: B DIF: A
5. ANS: A DIF: A

SHORT ANSWER

1. Against which European power did Haiti successfully rebel?

   ANS:
   France

   DIF: A

2. Whose democratic ideals did colonists follow as they rebelled throughout Latin America?

   ANS:
   those of the United States and France

   DIF: A

3. Which European powers lost colonies in Latin America when Mexico and Central America rebelled?

   ANS:
   Spain, France, and Great Britain

   DIF: A

4. Against which European power did Brazil rebel?

   ANS:
   Portugal

   DIF: A

5. Why was democracy difficult for the newly independent countries to achieve?

   ANS:
   They had no training or education in self-government.

   DIF: A

CHAPTER 35—UNREST IN EUROPE

MULTIPLE CHOICE

1. Which of these statements about Napoleon is NOT true?
   a. Napoleon reorganized the French system of laws.
   b. Napoleon was a political leader in the French Revolution.
   c. His soldiers and the French people admired Napoleon.
   d. France became more prosperous under Napoleon's rule.

   ANS: D DIF: C

2. The country that was most successful in resisting Napoleon was
   a. the Austrian Empire.
   b. Spain.
   c. Great Britain.
   d. Germany.

   ANS: C DIF: E

3. What was the aim of the Russians' scorched-earth policy?
   a. To drive Napoleon's army away with fire
   b. To destroy shelters and food the French might use
   c. To make the French retreat before winter began
   d. To destroy French villages and crops

   ANS: B DIF: A

4. The allies finally defeated Napoleon at
   a. Paris, France.
   b. Waterloo, Belgium.
   c. Moscow, Russia.
   d. Elba, Italy.

   ANS: B DIF: E

5. One main goal of the Congress of Vienna was
   a. to spread the ideas of the French Revolution.
   b. to encourage new democratic governments.
   c. to keep a balance of power among European countries.
   d. to punish France for Napoleon's actions.

   ANS: C DIF: A

6. The idea that the people as a whole, or government, should own land and factories was held by
   a. socialists.
   b. nationalists.
   c. liberals.
   d. royalists.

   ANS: A DIF: A

7. Liberal reforms and more voting rights were gained by gradual change through laws, not revolution, in
   a. Germany.
   b. France.
   c. Belgium.
   d. Great Britain.

   ANS: D DIF: A

8. The statesman who guided unification in the northern part of the Italian peninsula was
   a. Count Camillo di Cavour.
   b. Louis Philippe.
   c. Klemens von Metternich.
   d. Louis Napoleon Bonaparte.

   ANS: A DIF: A

9. Bismarck's strategy for unifying Germany was
   a. to encourage liberal democratic ideas in all the states.
   b. to go to war so Germans would unite against an enemy.
   c. to make all the German states equal with Prussia.
   d. to establish a Grand Empire in Europe.

   ANS: B DIF: A

10. The influence of nationalist ideas in the Austrian Empire brought about
    a. independence movements by many different peoples.
    b. a new interest in Austrian history and traditions.
    c. a movement for greater unity in the empire.
    d. the establishment of many small states in the empire.

    ANS: A DIF: C

11. Napoleon was able to get France out of debt because he
    a. defeated Austria, Russia, and Great Britain.
    b. raised the taxes in France.
    c. allowed only the national government to collect taxes.
    d. set up a system of education.

    ANS: C DIF: A

12. Laws were different in different parts of France because
    a. France had been at war with so many countries.
    b. the revolutionary governments could not agree on new laws.
    c. Napoleon took away the people's right to make laws.
    d. France's economy was so weak.

    ANS: B DIF: A

13. Napoleon's conquests helped spread the ideals of the French Revolution throughout Europe because
    a. he set up the French educational system all over Europe.
    b. peace and order gave people more time to read.
    c. French citizens ruled the conquered governments with French laws.
    d. better transportation brought newspapers to towns regularly.

    ANS: C DIF: A

14. The Congress System eventually broke down because
    a. it did not treat all workers equally.
    b. political groups led revolutions against the System.
    c. Europe's communities did not cooperate with each other.
    d. most Europeans believed in Karl Marx's teachings.

    ANS: B DIF: A

15. Great Britain had no revolutions because
    a. it had already gone through "The Glorious Revolution."
    b. the British government made reforms that gave English citizens more rights.
    c. the country did not know the rest of Europe was having wars.
    d. its economy was stronger than any other in Europe.

ANS: B DIF: A

MATCHING

Match each item with the correct statement below.

a. Duke of Wellington
b. Victor Emmanuel II
c. Louis Blanc
d. Garibaldi
e. Goethe
f. Consulate
g. Jacques Louis David
h. Otto von Bismarck
i. junker
j. William I

1. Prussian king who became kaiser of German Empire
2. Leader of revolutionary forces called Red Shirts in southern Italy
3. French artist who established the "Empire" style throughout Europe
4. Wealthy upper-class German landowner
5. New government established by Napoleon in 1799
6. German writer influenced by nationalist ideas
7. First king of a united Italy
8. Socialist leader in France who began national workshops
9. Prime minister who united German states
10. British general who defeated Napoleon in 1815 at the Battle of Waterloo

1. ANS: J DIF: A
2. ANS: D DIF: A
3. ANS: G DIF: A
4. ANS: I DIF: A
5. ANS: F DIF: A
6. ANS: E DIF: A
7. ANS: B DIF: A
8. ANS: C DIF: A
9. ANS: H DIF: A
10. ANS: A DIF: A

SHORT ANSWER

1. What kind of person do you think Napoleon was? Explain why you think so.

ANS:
Answers will vary, but could include: Napoleon was eccentric, brilliant, and a tyrant. Students should be able to support their opinions with examples of his actions.

DIF: A

SECTION QUIZ 35-1—THE AGE OF NAPOLEON

MULTIPLE CHOICE

1. Which of the following was NOT true of Napoleon?
    a. He was very popular with the French people.
    b. He wanted to build a Grand Empire to replace the Holy Roman Empire.
    c. He invaded Russia in 1812.
    d. He died in the Battle of Waterloo.

ANS: D DIF: E

2. Napoleon
    a. forbade the countries in his empire to trade with Great Britain.
    b. called Russia a "nation of shopkeepers."
    c. was crowned emperor at the Louvre.
    d. became the Pope in 1806.

ANS: A DIF: A

3. Napoleon came to France from
    a. Italy.
    b. Corsica.
    c. England.
    d. Switzerland.

ANS: B DIF: A

4. One important outcome of the French campaign in Egypt was that
    a. soldiers accompanying Napoleon discovered the Rosetta Stone.
    b. France was able to build the Louvre there.
    c. France was able to take over the country.
    d. Napoleon drew up the Napoleonic Code.

ANS: A DIF: A

5. In 1814, Napoleon
    a. was chosen to lead French troops into Italy.
    b. formed the Confederation of the Rhine.
    c. invaded Spain and Portugal.
    d. was forced to abdicate.

ANS: D DIF: C

MATCHING

Match each item with the correct statement below.

a. Napoleonic Code
b. Louvre
c. scorched-earth policy
d. plebiscite
e. abdicate

1. popular vote
2. French national museum

3. war tactic
4. give up the throne
5. French law under Napoleon

1. ANS: D DIF: A
2. ANS: B DIF: A
3. ANS: C DIF: A
4. ANS: E DIF: A
5. ANS: A DIF: A

SHORT ANSWER

1. Why were the French ready for a strong leader by the end of the 1700s?

   ANS:
   They wanted a return to peace and order.

   DIF: A

2. What were Napoleon's goals for his new government?

   ANS:
   He wanted to make it strong and rich.

   DIF: A

3. What freedoms did Napoleon take away from the French people?

   ANS:
   freedom of speech, freedom of the press, and the right to criticize or disagree with the government

   DIF: A

4. Which were the only two European countries of the time that Napoleon could not conquer?

   ANS:
   Great Britain and Russia

   DIF: A

5. How did the conquered European countries win back their freedom?

   ANS:
   They formed an alliance and fought and captured Napoleon .

   DIF: A

SECTION QUIZ 35-2—REVOLUTION AND REFORM

MULTIPLE CHOICE

1. Which of the following was NOT true of liberals?
   a. They wanted political reform based on Marx's ideas.
   b. Most were members of the middle class.
   c. They wanted to improve their own lives.
   d. They wanted freedom of thought and religion.

   ANS: A DIF: C

2. Karl Marx was
   a. French.
   b. Russian.
   c. German.
   d. English.

   ANS: C DIF: E

3. The July Revolution was a victory for
   a. Charles X.
   b. the middle class.
   c. the Catholic Church.
   d. the Ottoman Empire.

   ANS: B DIF: A

4. Louis Blanc was
   a. the head of the Old Regime.
   b. one of the leaders of the Second French Republic.
   c. Napoleon Bonaparte's nephew.
   d. Napoleon Bonaparte's son.

   ANS: B DIF: A

5. Which of the following is NOT true of Louis-Napoleon Bonaparte?
   a. He was elected president of the Second French Republic.
   b. In 1851, he did away with the constitution.
   c. He was voted Emperor Napoleon III.
   d. He was emperor until 1780.

   ANS: D DIF: A

MATCHING

Match each item with the correct statement below.
a. universal male suffrage
b. proletariat
c. communism
d. balance of power
e. nationalists

1. Marxist socialism
2. right of all adult men to vote
3. wanted independence for nations

4. equal strength among countries
5. industrial working class

1. ANS: C DIF: A
2. ANS: A DIF: A
3. ANS: E DIF: A
4. ANS: D DIF: A
5. ANS: B DIF: A

SHORT ANSWER

1. What were the long-term results of the Congress of Vienna?

   ANS:
   It set the stage for revolution in some countries and reform in others.

   DIF: A

2. How did the Congress of Vienna try to balance power in Europe?

   ANS:
   It tried to divide Napoleon's empire equally among the European countries.

   DIF: A

3. How did different political groups try to bring down the Congress System?

   ANS:
   They led a number of revolutions against the governments in European countries.

   DIF: A

4. Which European country made liberal reforms without revolution?

   ANS:
   Great Britan

   DIF: E

5. What two conditions in France in 1848 touched off another round of European revolutions?

   ANS:
   no right to vote and high unemployment

   DIF: A

SECTION QUIZ 35-3—GROWTH OF NATIONALISM

MULTIPLE CHOICE

1. In 1861, Italy
   a. was taken over by Napoleon III.
   b. became the Kingdom of Italy, a constitutional monarchy.
   c. became the Sovereign State of Unified Italy, a dictatorship.
   d. invaded Germany.

   ANS: B DIF: C

2. Which of the following was NOT true of the Red Shirts?
   a. They practiced guerrilla warfare.
   b. Most of them wore red shirts.
   c. In 1860, they conquered Sicily within three months.
   d. Their leader was Camillo di Cavour.

   ANS: D DIF: A

3. Which of the following was NOT true of Otto von Bismarck?
   a. He formed the Bismarck Party of Northern Germany.
   b. In 1870, he found an excuse to go to war with France.
   c. He became the king of Prussia.
   d. He was a junker.

   ANS: A DIF: A

4. Francis Joseph, the Austrian emperor, was
   a. Czechoslovakian.
   b. Polish.
   c. German.
   d. French.

   ANS: C DIF: E

5. In 1867, Austria
   a. elected William I kaiser.
   b. elected Francis Joseph emperor.
   c. became part of France.
   d. agreed to a dual monarchy with Hungary.

   ANS: D DIF: C

MATCHING

Match each item with the correct statement below.
a. Giuseppe Garibaldi
b. guerrilla warfare
c. Camillo di Cavour
d. kaiser
e. junker

1. Sardinian prime minister
2. leader of the Red Shirts

3. surprise attacks
4. rich landowner
5. emperor

1. ANS: C DIF: A
2. ANS: A DIF: A
3. ANS: B DIF: A
4. ANS: E DIF: A
5. ANS: D DIF: A

SHORT ANSWER

1. What memories gave rise to nationalistic feelings in Italy?

   ANS:
   memories from the ancient Roman Empire

   DIF: A

2. What three areas formed the unified country of Italy?

   ANS:
   the northern Italian states, Lombardy, and Sardinia

   DIF: A

3. Why did some German princes refuse to unite?

   ANS:
   They did not want to lose political power.

   DIF: A

4. What areas formed the unified country of Germany?

   ANS:
   the German states and Prussia

   DIF: A

5. How did nationalism keep Austria from becoming a unified country?

   ANS:
   The Austrian Empire was made up of many nationalities that each wanted to rule themselves.

   DIF: A

CHAPTER 36—RISE OF IMPERIALISM

MULTIPLE CHOICE

1. Which of the following was NOT a cause for the rise of imperialism in the late 1800s?
   a. Ideas of democracy and individual rights
   b. A demand for raw materials for industry
   c. The need for food for growing populations
   d. Nationalist ambitions and a wish for power

   ANS: A DIF: A

2. In establishing a protectorate over Egypt, Great Britain gained control of
   a. the interior of Africa.
   b. the Cape-to-Cairo railroad.
   c. the Suez Canal.
   d. the Nile River.

   ANS: C DIF: E

3. The Boer War was fought between
   a. Dutch and British settlers in southern Africa.
   b. Boer farmers and diamond miners.
   c. German colonists and Boer farmers.
   d. Boer settlers and native Africans.

   ANS: A DIF: A

4. The largest colonial empire in Africa belonged to
   a. Great Britain.
   b. Portugal.
   c. Germany.
   d. France.

   ANS: D DIF: A

5. In the 1800s, Great Britain had to guard the northwest frontier of India against
   a. Russia.
   b. France.
   c. Persia.
   d. China.

   ANS: A DIF: A

6. Which of the following statements describes China's position in the late 1800s?
   a. Foreign nations had great control over China.
   b. China's natural resources gave it great power.
   c. China avoided foreigners and kept its own traditions.
   d. China tried hard to increase its trade with foreign nations.

   ANS: A DIF: C

7. When one country grants another certain special rights, such as the land for a naval base, these are called
   a. a protectorate.
   b. spheres of influence.
   c. concessions.
   d. right of extraterritoriality.

   ANS: C DIF: C

8. When Japan decided to modernize, it took all the following actions EXCEPT
   a. ending feudalism.
   b. rejecting western technology.
   c. writing a constitution.
   d. protecting new industries.

   ANS: B DIF: A

9. Colonies on the mainland of Southeast Asia belonged mainly to
   a. France and Great Britain.
   b. United States and Great Britain.
   c. Germany.
   d. Japan.

   ANS: A DIF: A

10. The United States gained Puerto Rico and the Philippines after winning a war with
    a. Spain.
    b. Colombia.
    c. Cuba.
    d. Great Britain.

    ANS: A DIF: E

MATCHING

Match each item with the correct statement below.

a. Transvaal
b. Boers
c. David Livingstone
d. Indochina
e. Boxer Rebellion
f. Cape Colony
g. Matthew Perry
h. Cecil Rhodes
i. Leopold II
j. Sepoy Mutiny

1. British official who dreamed of an English-speaking empire in Africa
2. Independent state set up by Dutch South African farmers
3. American naval officer who made a treaty with Japan
4. British-run colony at the southern tip of Africa
5. British missionary who explored the African interior
6. Name given to French colonies in Southeast Asia
7. Movement to drive foreigners from China
8. Belgian ruler who first ran the Congo
9. Dutch South African farmers
10. Rebellion by Indian soldiers in the British army

1. ANS: H DIF: A
2. ANS: A DIF: A
3. ANS: G DIF: A
4. ANS: F DIF: A
5. ANS: C DIF: A
6. ANS: D DIF: A
7. ANS: E DIF: A
8. ANS: I DIF: A
9. ANS: B DIF: A
10. ANS: J DIF: A

SHORT ANSWER

1. What are some of the positive and negative aspects of imperialism?

   ANS:
   Answers will vary, but could include: POSITIVE: industrialization, economic opportunity, establishment of power, setting up orderly government; NEGATIVE: taking advantage of native peoples and their countries, laying the groundwork for war between the colonizers.

   DIF: A

2. Which European nations had the largest empires in Africa?

   ANS:
   Great Britain and France

   DIF: E

3. Which European country assumed control of India?

   ANS:
   Great Britain

   DIF: E

4. Which nation did Great Britain fear might challenge its rule in India?

   ANS:
   Russia

   DIF: A

5. Which country took over most of the Muslim centers of civilization in central Asia?

   ANS:
   Russia

   DIF: A

6. How were the British able to defeat the Chinese in the Opium War?

   ANS:
   The British had cannons and steam-driven warships.

   DIF: A

7. Why did the Open Door Policy aggravate China?

   ANS:
   The Open Door Policy meant that foreign powers were still trying to control China.

   DIF: A

8. What war made the United States an imperialist power?

   ANS:
   the Spanish-American War

   DIF: A

9. Why did the European powers take notice of the mainland in Southeast Asia?

   ANS:
   The mainland was a source of cash crops and raw materials.

   DIF: A

10. For what three purposes could many Pacific islands be used?

    ANS:
    sugar and pineapple plantations; mineral supplies; bases for ship repair and refueling

    DIF: A

SECTION QUIZ 36-1—GROWTH OF IMPERIALISM

MULTIPLE CHOICE

1. One reason for the rise of imperialism was that
   a. many countries wanted to find an ideal religion.
   b. factories needed raw materials.
   c. countries' populations were getting too large.
   d. factory owners were too rich.

   ANS: B DIF: C

2. Japan and the United States wanted to
   a. become as important as Africa.
   b. become as important as the colonial powers of western Europe.
   c. become trading partners.
   d. spread Christianity everywhere.

   ANS: B DIF: A

3. Many industrial leaders and merchants believed that
   a. raw materials could be found in areas that were not industrialized.
   b. factory workers should be "backward" people.
   c. new markets were unnecessary.
   d. all workers should be made to join trade unions.

   ANS: A DIF: A

4. Which of the following was NOT industrialized in the late 1800s?
   a. Great Britain
   b. France
   c. Africa
   d. Germany

   ANS: C DIF: E

5. Many Westerners believed that it was their duty to
   a. spread Christianity throughout the world.
   b. feed the hungry and sick in other countries.
   c. read the complete works of Rudyard Kipling.
   d. set up trade unions in countries that were not industrialized.

   ANS: A DIF: A

6. Which of the following is ***not*** a result of industrialism?
   a. a need for new markets
   b. a need for increased profits
   c. a mission to spread Christianity
   d. growing demand for raw materials and foods

   ANS: C DIF: A

7. The two major causes for imperialism were
   a. industrialism and revolution.
   b. nationalism and industrialism.
   c. liberalism and conservativism.
   d. communism and socialism.

   ANS: B DIF: A

8. Which of the following was ***not*** a result of nationalism?
   a. Some people believed that colonies made a country powerful.
   b. Some people believed that it was the duty of industrialized countries to industrialize those that were not.
   c. Italy, Germany, Japan, and the United States wanted to become colonial powers.
   d. European powers wanted to aid undeveloped countries.

   ANS: D DIF: A

MATCHING

Match each item with the correct statement below.

a. imperialism
b. factories
c. invest
d. nationalism
e. Rudyard Kipling

1. places where goods are produced
2. British author
3. put money into
4. one reason for colonial expansion
5. the policy of building empires

1. ANS: B DIF: A
2. ANS: E DIF: A
3. ANS: C DIF: A
4. ANS: D DIF: A
5. ANS: A DIF: A

SECTION QUIZ 36-2—AFRICA

MULTIPLE CHOICE

1. A protectorate is
   a. a country under the protection of another country.
   b. a dictator who protects the people.
   c. Cape Colony.
   d. a peasant uprising.

   ANS: A DIF: E

2. The Suez Canal
   a. was paid for with German funds.
   b. was built by French workers.
   c. was opened in 1869.
   d. was opened in 1889.

   ANS: C DIF: C

3. The Boers were
   a. Africans.
   b. Dutch farmers in South Africa.
   c. French merchants.
   d. British.

   ANS: B DIF: E

4. Which of the following was NOT true of Angola?
   a. It was the oldest colony in Africa.
   b. It was founded in 1648.
   c. It was a part of Southeast Asia.
   d. It was founded by the Portuguese.

   ANS: C DIF: A

5. By 1914, which two areas in Africa remained independent?
   a. Togoland and the Cameroons
   b. Angola and Mozambique
   c. Nigeria and Rhodesia
   d. Liberia and Ethiopia

   ANS: D DIF: A

MATCHING

Match each item with the correct statement below.
a. David Livingstone
b. Henry Stanley
c. Leopold II
d. Cecil Rhodes
e. Menelik II

1. newspaper reporter
2. Scottish medical missionary
3. Ethiopian king
4. king of Belgium
5. prime minister of the Cape Colony

1. ANS: B DIF: A
2. ANS: A DIF: A
3. ANS: E DIF: A
4. ANS: C DIF: A
5. ANS: D DIF: A

SHORT ANSWER

1. Before the Age of Imperialism, why had most Europeans only explored Africa's coasts?

   ANS:
   Europeans believed they were safer from disease and other dangers if they stayed along Africa's coasts.

   DIF: A

2. What two groups of people opened up Africa's interior?

   ANS:
   missionaries and explorers

   DIF: A

3. How did Stanley and Leopold of Belgium trick African chiefs in the Congo Basin?

   ANS:
   They had them sign contracts which they could not read.

   DIF: A

4. How did Great Britain and France gain control of Egypt?

   ANS:
   They took over Egypt's finances.

   DIF: A

5. Which were the only two African countries that were not conquered by European powers?

   ANS:
   Liberia and Ethiopia

   DIF: A

SECTION QUIZ 36-3—ASIA

MULTIPLE CHOICE

1. The Seven Years' War is also known as
   a. the Boxer Rebellion.
   b. the Boer War.
   c. the French and Indian War.
   d. the Sepoy Mutiny.

   ANS: C DIF: E

2. The Opium War was fought between
   a. China and the United States.
   b. China and Great Britain.
   c. China and Japan.
   d. Japan and Great Britain.

   ANS: B DIF: A

3. In 1842, the British took possession of
   a. China.
   b. India.
   c. Hong Kong.
   d. Togoland.

   ANS: C DIF: C

4. The Boxer Rebellion
   a. ended in 1913.
   b. began in Great Britain as a result of the Open Door Policy.
   c. began in 1913.
   d. was started by a Chinese secret society called the Boxers.

   ANS: D DIF: A

5. Which of the following was NOT true of Japan?
   a. It was fully industrialized by the end of the 1800s.
   b. Its first constitution was written in 1889.
   c. It became a world power.
   d. It annexed the Philippines.

   ANS: D DIF: C

MATCHING

Match each item with the correct statement below.

a. Boxer Rebellion
b. *zaibatsu*
c. Open Door Policy
d. concessions
e. sepoys

1. special rights
2. anti-foreigner movement
3. rich, powerful families
4. Indian soldiers
5. equal trade rights in China

1. ANS: D DIF: A
2. ANS: A DIF: A
3. ANS: B DIF: A
4. ANS: E DIF: A
5. ANS: C DIF: A

SHORT ANSWER

1. What country took over France's trading posts in India?

ANS:
Great Britain

DIF: A

2. Why were many Indians unhappy with British rule?

ANS:
They thought Great Britain was trying to change their culture.

DIF: A

3. How were the foreign policies of Japan and China alike?

ANS:
Both countries allowed only limited trade with Western countries.

DIF: C

4. Why did China finally come under the control of imperialistic countries?

ANS:
It lost the war to drive out foreign powers.

DIF: A

5. Why did Western imperialist countries fail to conquer Japan?

ANS:
Japan modernized.

DIF: A

SECTION QUIZ 36-4—LATIN AMERICA

MULTIPLE CHOICE

1. The Monroe Doctrine
   a. was issued by President James Monroe.
   b. was issued by a shipping merchant, Robert Monroe.
   c. was one result of the Spanish-American War.
   d. gave the United States Puerto Rico and Guam.

   ANS: A DIF: E

2. The Cubans revolted in
   a. 1799.
   b. 1865 and 1895.
   c. 1898.
   d. 1910 and 1918.

   ANS: B DIF: A

3. As a result of the Spanish-American War,
   a. Cuba became an American protectorate.
   b. Spain took possession of Cuba.
   c. the United States gave Puerto Rico to Cuba.
   d. the Monroe Doctrine was issued.

   ANS: A DIF: A

4. In 1903, the United States supported a revolution in
   a. Colombia.
   b. Cuba.
   c. Guam.
   d. Panama.

   ANS: D DIF: A

5. Between 1912 and 1916, the United States sent soldiers to
   a. Cuba, Puerto Rico, and Panama.
   b. Mexico, Costa Rica, and Spain.
   c. Nicaragua, the Dominican Republic, and Haiti.
   d. the Philippines and France.

   ANS: C DIF: C

MATCHING

Match each item with the correct statement below.

a. Prince Maximilian of Austria
b. Monroe Doctrine
c. Havana
d. Cuba
e. Panama Canal

1. city in Cuba
2. emperor of Mexico
3. issued in 1823
4. opened in 1914
5. American protectorate

1. ANS: C DIF: A
2. ANS: A DIF: A
3. ANS: B DIF: A
4. ANS: E DIF: A
5. ANS: D DIF: A

SHORT ANSWER

1. Which country supported the United States and the Monroe Doctrine?

   ANS:
   Great Britain

   DIF: A

2. To which country did Cuba and Puerto Rico belong?

   ANS:
   Spain

   DIF: E

3. How did the United States acquire territory in Latin America?

   ANS:
   by winning the Spanish-American War

   DIF: A

4. Why did the United States send American troops to several Latin American countries between 1912 and 1916?

   ANS:
   to protect American business interests

   DIF: A

SECTION QUIZ 36-5—EFFECTS OF IMPERIALISM

MULTIPLE CHOICE

1. Which of the following was NOT an effect of imperialism?
   a. Orderly governments were set up.
   b. Many local wars were stopped
   c. Communication improved.
   d. Railroad shipping stopped.

   ANS: D DIF: A

2. Colonists were seldom allowed to
   a. hold jobs in the armed forces.
   b. speak their native language.
   c. marry before the age of 30.
   d. leave their city of origin.

   ANS: A DIF: C

3. Communication became easier because
   a. the telephone was invented.
   b. French and English were spoken in most parts of the world.
   c. German became the international trade language.
   d. the colonists ran their own newspapers.

   ANS: B DIF: A

4. Communication brought about
   a. local wars.
   b. the spread of ideas about democracy and individual rights.
   c. an international trade language.
   d. bitter feelings among the colonists.

   ANS: B DIF: A

5. The colonists disliked the colonizers for
   a. making German the official international trade language.
   b. causing the failure of the railroads.
   c. beginning competition among the colonial powers.
   d. trying to change their customs, languages, and religions.

   ANS: D DIF: A

MATCHING

Match each item with the correct statement below.

a. nationalism
b. 85
c. colonists
d. sanitation
e. competition

1. improved under imperialism
2. colonies' response to colonial rule
3. led to disputes among colonial powers
4. colonial rule percentage by 1914
5. people who lived in the colonies

1. ANS: D DIF: A
2. ANS: A DIF: A
3. ANS: E DIF: A
4. ANS: B DIF: A
5. ANS: C DIF: A

SHORT ANSWER

1. What situation existed among the nations that colonized?

   ANS:
   competition for colonies

   DIF: A

2. What did the competition for colonies lead to?

   ANS:
   bitter feelings and nationalism

   DIF: A

3. What did the disputes among colonial powers ultimately cause?

   ANS:
   wars

   DIF: E

CHAPTER 37—CONFLICT AND CHANGE

MULTIPLE CHOICE

1. World War I was different from earlier wars because
   a. submarines were used.
   b. it ended with an armistice.
   c. civilians were attacked.
   d. the countries all had navies.

   ANS: C DIF: A

2. Under the Treaty of Versailles
   a. Germany lost more territory than Russia did.
   b. Russia lost more territory than Germany did.
   c. India won its independence from Great Britain.
   d. Austria-Hungary was split up.

   ANS: B DIF: C

3. Which country suffered the most casualties in World War I?
   a. Germany
   b. Sarajevo
   c. Austria-Hungary
   d. Russia

   ANS: D DIF: A

4. After World War I, several countries became dictatorships. The first was
   a. Italy.
   b. Germany.
   c. Russia.
   d. Poland.

   ANS: A DIF: A

5. The goal of the New Deal program in the United States was
   a. to mobilize people in support of World War I.
   b. to help the country recover from the Great Depression.
   c. to encourage membership in the League of Nations.
   d. to rebuild the economy after World War II.

   ANS: B DIF: E

6. The actions of which countries began to threaten world peace in the 1930s?
   a. Germany, Japan, Russia
   b. France, Russia, Germany
   c. Germany, Italy, Japan
   d. Manchuria, Japan, Russia

   ANS: C DIF: C

7. Which country was the greatest industrial power in the world at the beginning of World War II?
   a. Germany
   b. Russia
   c. the United States
   d. Japan

   ANS: C DIF: E

8. The end of World War II in the Pacific was brought about by
   a. the use of the atomic bomb against Japanese cities.
   b. the Allied invasion of Normandy on D-Day.
   c. an Allied air-sea victory at Midway Island.
   d. the scorched-earth tactics of Soviet troops.

   ANS: A DIF: A

9. After World War II, 50 countries joined together to form an organization to prevent war and support poor countries. What is that organization?
   a. League of Nations
   b. United Nations
   c. Allied powers
   d. New Deal

   ANS: B DIF: E

10. After World War II, which country was divided into zones occupied by the major Allied powers?
    a. Russia
    b. Japan
    c. Poland
    d. Germany

    ANS: D DIF: A

11. Atomic bombs were dropped on the Japanese cities of Hiroshima and
    a. Berlin
    b. Normandy
    c. Nagasaki
    d. Pearl Harbor

    ANS: C DIF: A

12. Which of the following was **not** a result of the U.S. occupation of Japan after World War II?
    a. Women were given the right to vote.
    b. Japan concentrated on rebuilding its military.
    c. The secret police was abolished.
    d. Large farms were divided and sold to farm workers at low prices.

    ANS: B DIF: C

MATCHING

Match each item with the correct statement below.

a. isolationist
b. armaments
c. Holocaust
d. Fourteen Points
e. Treaty of Versailles
f. Franklin D. Roosevelt
g. Peter the Great
h. depression
i. armistice
j. garrison

1. Peace program developed by United States President Woodrow Wilson
2. Country that stays out of other countries' affairs
3. Peace treaty signed by Germany after World War I
4. Equipment for war
5. Period of a slowdown in business
6. A stop in the fighting of a war
7. United States President who set up the New Deal program
8. A group of soldiers stationed in a certain area

9. The Nazis' program for killing Jews in Europe
10. Great Russian ruler who named the country Russia and reformed it

1. ANS: D DIF: A
2. ANS: A DIF: A
3. ANS: E DIF: A
4. ANS: B DIF: A
5. ANS: H DIF: A
6. ANS: I DIF: A
7. ANS: F DIF: A
8. ANS: J DIF: A
9. ANS: C DIF: A
10. ANS: G DIF: A

SHORT ANSWER

1. Why do you think the United States has never become a dictatorship?

   ANS:
   Answers will vary, but could include: the Constitution protects the United States from becoming a dictatorship; the country's history and Declaration of Independence make it unlikely that its citizens would allow a dictatorship to develop.

   DIF: A

SECTION QUIZ 37-1—WORLD WAR 1

MULTIPLE CHOICE

1. The spark for World War I was
   a. Russian industrialization.
   b. the shooting of Archduke Franz Ferdinand.
   c. the Fourteen Points.
   d. objections to the Treaty of Versailles.

   ANS: B DIF: E

2. World War I was the first war in which
   a. an archduke was killed.
   b. several nations fought against one another.
   c. civilians were attacked.
   d. Great Britain was involved in the fighting.

   ANS: C DIF: A

3. President Wilson drew up a peace plan called
   a. the Treaty of Versailles.
   b. the Fourteen Points.
   c. the Allied Treaty.
   d. the Isolationist Mandate.

   ANS: B DIF: A

4. The Central Powers consisted of
   a. Germany, Austria-Hungary, the Ottoman Empire, and Bulgaria.
   b. Russia, Germany, and Serbia.
   c. the United States, Great Britain, and France.
   d. Italy, Germany, and Russia.

   ANS: A DIF: A

5. Germany and its allies agreed to an armistice on
   a. November 11, 1941.
   b. December 7, 1941.
   c. November 11, 1918.
   d. June 6, 1921.

   ANS: C DIF: A

COMPLETION

1. By the early 1900s, ____________________ among European nations was causing tensions.

   ANS: rivalry DIF: A

2. European countries built up their ____________________.

   ANS: armed forces DIF: A

3. European countries made ____________________ with each other to give military aid in case of attack.

   ANS: alliances DIF: A

4. Land battles in World War I happened mostly in Europe, the Middle East, and North Africa, but naval battles took place all over ____________________.

   ANS: the world DIF: E

5. The Treaty of Versailles was an attempt by Allied countries to make ____________________ pay for the losses during World War I.

   ANS: Germany DIF: A

MATCHING

Match each item with the correct statement below.

a. mobilize
b. armaments
c. mandate
d. armistice
e. artillery

1. call up troops
2. right to rule
3. mounted gun
4. a stop in fighting
5. equipment for war

1. ANS: A DIF: A
2. ANS: C DIF: A
3. ANS: E DIF: A
4. ANS: D DIF: A
5. ANS: B DIF: A

SECTION QUIZ 37-2—BETWEEN THE WARS

MULTIPLE CHOICE

1. Which of the following was NOT true of Vladimir Lenin?
   a. He was the leader of the Bolsheviks.
   b. He signed a peace treaty with Russia during World War I.
   c. He created the Mensheviks.
   d. The city of Petrograd was renamed Leningrad in his honor.

   ANS: C DIF: C

2. The major goal of the Soviet Union's Five-Year Plans was
   a. to bring the Mensheviks to power.
   b. to build up heavy industry.
   c. to raise workers' wages.
   d. to end the country's famine.

   ANS: B DIF: A

3. A worldwide depression began in
   a. 1899.
   b. 1918.
   c. 1929.
   d. 1939.

   ANS: C DIF: A

4. U.S. social security laws provided money for
   a. war veterans.
   b. homeless people.
   c. elderly people and orphaned children.
   d. enslaved people.

   ANS: C DIF: E

5. Which of the following was NOT true of Adolf Hitler?
   a. He became chancellor of Germany in 1933.
   b. He called himself *Der Swastika*.
   c. He was supported by a violent political group called the Nazis.
   d. He blamed many of Germany's problems on the Jews and others.

   ANS: B DIF: A

COMPLETION

1. Few changes in Russia during the 1800s helped the ____________________ whose work supported the Russian nobles and clergy.

   ANS: peasants DIF: A

2. During World War I, more soldiers from Russia died than from any other nation because Russia did not have enough ____________________ producing guns and ammunition or ____________________ to get food and supplies to the battlefront.

   ANS: factories; railroads DIF: A

3. The Russian Revolution overthrew the ____________________ and put the ____________________ in power.

   ANS: czar; Bolsheviks DIF: A

4. During the Great Depression, ____________________ came to power in Italy and Germany.

   ANS: dictators DIF: E

5. In 1937, the Southeast Asian nation of ____________________ signed an alliance with Italy and Germany.

   ANS: Japan DIF: C

MATCHING

Match each item with the correct statement below.

a. soviets
b. dictatorship
c. chancellor
d. garrison
e. depression

1. ruled by one absolute power
2. military group
3. sudden slowdown in business
4. prime minister
5. worker-representative committees

1. ANS: B DIF: A
2. ANS: D DIF: A
3. ANS: E DIF: A
4. ANS: C DIF: A
5. ANS: A DIF: A

SECTION QUIZ 37-3—WORLD WAR II

MULTIPLE CHOICE

1. On December 7, 1941,
   a. the Germans invaded Great Britain.
   b. the Japanese bombed Pearl Harbor.
   c. the United States celebrated D-Day.
   d. Adolf Hitler killed himself.

   ANS: B DIF: A

2. The battle that changed the course of the war in favor of the Allies was
   a. fought at Pearl Harbor.
   b. fought in Poland.
   c. fought at Midway Island.
   d. fought at the Elbe River.

   ANS: C DIF: C

3. Winston Churchill was
   a. the American president.
   b. the king of Great Britain.
   c. the prime minister of Great Britain.
   d. an American general.

   ANS: C DIF: E

4. In 1943, the Russian Red Army
   a. surrendered to German forces at Stalingrad.
   b. surrendered to German forces at Leningrad.
   c. forced the Germans to surrender at Stalingrad.
   d. forced the Germans to surrender at Leningrad.

   ANS: A DIF: A

5. One result of World War II was
   a. the formation of the United Nations.
   b. the formation of the League of Nations.
   c. the formation of the Peace Corps.
   d. the end of imperialism.

   ANS: A DIF: E

COMPLETION

1. Japan attacked the United States because the U.S. had military ____________________ in the Pacific.

   ANS: bases DIF: A

2. The United States was able to help the Allies win the war because it could ____________________ huge amounts of battle equipment and supplies.

   ANS: manufacture DIF: A

3. In 1944, German armies got caught between ____________________ troops on their eastern front and American, British, French, and Canadian troops on their ____________________ front.

   ANS: Russian; western DIF: A

4. After the Battle of Midway in 1942, Allied forces moved from island to island, pushing back ____________________ troops.

   ANS: Japanese DIF: A

5. At the end of World War II, the Allies divided Germany into four ____________________, and Japan was occupied and run by ____________________.

   ANS: zones; the United States DIF: A

MATCHING

Match each item with the correct statement below.

a. Pearl Harbor
b. D-Day
c. cremation ovens
d. genocide
e. blitzkrieg

1. "lightning war"
2. American naval base
3. found in concentration camps
4. June 6, 1944
5. the mass murder of a people

1. ANS: E DIF: A
2. ANS: A DIF: A
3. ANS: C DIF: A
4. ANS: B DIF: A
5. ANS: D DIF: A

CHAPTER 38—THE COLD WAR ERA

MULTIPLE CHOICE

1. The leader who improved China's economy and the position of women there was
   a. Chiang Kai-shek.
   b. Ho Chi Minh.
   c. Mao Zedong.
   d. Sun Yat-sen.

   ANS: C DIF: A

2. The economic system in which most production is privately owned is called
   a. capitalism.
   b. communism.
   c. *glasnost.*
   d. common market.

   ANS: A DIF: E

3. Countries that have little industry and whose people mostly make their living from the land are
   a. Communist.
   b. independent.
   c. partitioned.
   d. developing nations.

   ANS: D DIF: E

4. How do most African people make their living?
   a. Manufacturing
   b. Farming
   c. In government
   d. Mining

   ANS: B DIF: E

5. Why was 1960 called the "Year of Africa"?
   a. because so many African countries started civil wars
   b. because life in Africa began to change then
   c. because 17 African countries became independent
   d. because Africans began to boycott goods

   ANS: C DIF: A

6. During the occupation of Berlin, the aim of the Soviet Union was
   a. to reunite Germany.
   b. to end the cold war.
   c. to control the whole city.
   d. to divide Germany.

   ANS: C DIF: A

7. Which of the following countries took an active role with military support for the government of South Vietnam during the Vietnam War?
   a. United States
   b. Soviet Union
   c. China
   d. Cuba

   ANS: A DIF: A

8. In Africa, strong feelings of nationalism developed after
   a. the French Revolution.
   b. World War I.
   c. World War II.
   d. 1960, the "Year of Africa."

   ANS: C DIF: A

9. In twentieth-century Latin America, feelings of nationalism often have been directed against
   a. colonial powers.
   b. foreign investors.
   c. *campesinos.*
   d. *haciendas.*

   ANS: B DIF: C

10. Many Latin Americans want to change the farming system so that
    a. farms will be larger and more efficient.
    b. peasant farmers will own land.
    c. more foreign money will be invested in agriculture.
    d. people will be able to import more food.

    ANS: B DIF: C

MATCHING

Match each item with the correct statement below.

a. NATO
b. *perestroika*
c. European Common Market
d. subsistence farmers
e. civil disobedience
f. Mohandas Gandhi
g. satellite nations
h. cold war
i. Warsaw Pact
j. Marshall Plan

1. United States program to help rebuild Europe
2. Soviet policy of restructuring
3. Indian leader who led peaceful protests against British rule
4. Organization of Communist countries formed during the cold war
5. Hostility without actual fighting
6. Countries controlled by a stronger neighboring country
7. Economic union of several countries
8. Grow only enough food for their families
9. Organization of western non-Communist countries formed during the cold war
10. Refusal to obey laws considered unjust

1. ANS: J DIF: A
2. ANS: B DIF: A
3. ANS: F DIF: A
4. ANS: I DIF: A
5. ANS: H DIF: A
6. ANS: G DIF: A
7. ANS: C DIF: A
8. ANS: D DIF: A
9. ANS: A DIF: A
10. ANS: E DIF: A

SHORT ANSWER

1. How do the problems of developing nations affect the United States?

   ANS:
   Answers will vary, but could include: developing nations do not support themselves; therefore, they must buy food and other necessities from countries like the United States; their internal problems and population growth often affect the rest of the world in terms of their use of scarce resources without the industry to contribute to their replacement. United States industries have located plants in many of these countries to take advantage of inexpensive labor.

   DIF: C

2. How was the Korean conflict resolved?

   ANS:
   with a truce

   DIF: A

3. How did the Vietnam War end?

   ANS:
   with an agreement between North Vietnam, South Vietnam, and the United States

   DIF: A

4. What happened to South Vietnam after the war?

   ANS:
   It came under Communist rule.

   DIF: E

5. What fear about the Chinese people prompted Mao to order purges?

   ANS:
   Mao feared the people had lost their revolutionary spirit.

   DIF: A

6. How did Chinese leaders handle the protesters at Tianenman Square?

   ANS:
   They sent soldiers in, and the soldiers opened fire.

   DIF: A

7. What improvement was the main objective of the Communist reformers in the Soviet Union?

   ANS:
   economic improvement

   DIF: A

8. What effect do rapidly growing populations have on the food supply in developing nations?

   ANS:
   The nations cannot produce enough food to feed all the people.

   DIF: A

9. Because developing nations must often spend much of their money on food, what areas of well-being are not fully provided for?

   ANS:
   decent housing, health care, and education

   DIF: A

SECTION QUIZ 38-1—AN UNEASY PEACE

MULTIPLE CHOICE

1. The loan program that was started in 1948 was
   a. the Monroe Doctrine.
   b. the North Atlantic Treaty Organization.
   c. the Marshall Plan.
   d. the Airlift Plan.

   ANS: C DIF: E

2. Fidel Castro overthrew dictator Fulgencio Batista in
   a. 1949.
   b. 1955.
   c. 1959.
   d. 1963.

   ANS: C DIF: C

3. In 1953 North and South Korea
   a. went to war.
   b. were absorbed by Japan.
   c. fought together against Vietnam.
   d. signed a truce.

   ANS: D DIF: A

4. The U.S. president during the Korean War was
   a. Harry S Truman.
   b. Douglas MacArthur.
   c. Theodore Roosevelt.
   d. James Monroe.

   ANS: A DIF: E

5. Which of the following was NOT true of the Berlin Wall?
   a. It was built in 1961.
   b. It was built between East and West Berlin.
   c. It symbolized the split between Communists and non-Communists.
   d. It was guarded by U.S. soldiers.

   ANS: D DIF: A

MATCHING

Match each item with the correct statement below.

a. airlift
b. satellite nations
c. Neil Armstrong
d. blockaded
e. Douglas MacArthur

1. delivering supplies by plane
2. first person to walk on the moon
3. closed off
4. United Nations commander
5. controlled by stronger countries

1. ANS: A DIF: A
2. ANS: C DIF: A
3. ANS: D DIF: A
4. ANS: E DIF: A
5. ANS: B DIF: A

SHORT ANSWER

1. How did the European Common Market change life in the countries that belonged to it?

   ANS:
   Trade among the countries increased and living conditions improved.

   DIF: A

2. What is a cold war?

   ANS:
   a non-fighting state of hostility between countries

   DIF: A

3. What are three countries where the United States and the Soviet Union supported opposing forces?

   ANS:
   Korea, Cuba, and Vietnam

   DIF: C

4. How did the Soviet Union and the United States carry the cold war into space?

   ANS:
   by becoming involved in a space race

   DIF: A

SECTION QUIZ 38-2—COMMUNIST POWERS

MULTIPLE CHOICE

1. Communist hard-liners
   a. wanted to bring capitalism to the Soviet Union.
   b. wanted to bring Leonid Brezhnev to power.
   c. wanted to stick to Stalin's rules.
   d. gave Puerto Rico and Guam to the United States.

   ANS: C DIF: A

2. Which of the following was NOT true of Sun Yat-sen?
   a. He led a revolt and overturned the government of China.
   b. He formed the Nationalist party.
   c. He was ousted and Chinese warlords ruled the country.
   d. He formed the People's Republic of China.

   ANS: D DIF: A

3. Mao Zedong
   a. organized the Nationalist party.
   b. purged China's intellectuals.
   c. died in 1961.
   d. ruled China before Sun Yat-sen.

   ANS: B DIF: A

4. Which of the following was NOT true of Nikita Khrushchev?
   a. He came to power in 1942.
   b. He began a program of de-Stalinization.
   c. He shut down labor camps.
   d. Under his leadership, the secret police became less violent.

   ANS: A DIF: A

5. Gorbachev changed the structure of the Soviet government
   a. with his policy of *perestroika*.
   b. with his policy of *glasnost*.
   c. by listening to the hard-liners.
   d. by breaking up the Soviet Union.

   ANS: A   DIF: C

MATCHING

Match each item with the correct statement below.

a. purges
b. *glasnost*
c. capitalism
d. *perestroika*
e. intellectuals

1. privately owned production
2. openness
3. restructuring
4. scholars
5. removals of undesirable members

1. ANS: C   DIF: A
2. ANS: B   DIF: A
3. ANS: D   DIF: A
4. ANS: E   DIF: A
5. ANS: A   DIF: A

SHORT ANSWER

1. How did the Communist Chinese gain control of the Chinese government?

   ANS:
   The Communist Chinese forced the Chinese Nationalists out of China.

   DIF: A

2. Where did the Nationalist Chinese set up a government after they left mainland China?

   ANS:
   on the island of Taiwan

   DIF: A

3. Why did economic conditions improve in China?

   ANS:
   Communist leaders put a number of economic plans into force.

   DIF: A

4. What rights do Chinese leaders refuse to acknowledge?

   ANS:
   human rights

   DIF: A

5. What two goals did Soviet leaders begin working toward in the 1980s?

   ANS:
   openness so that Russian people could have freedom of speech; government restructuring

   DIF: A

SECTION QUIZ 38-3—DEVELOPING NATIONS

MULTIPLE CHOICE

1. Which of the following was NOT true of Mohandas Gandhi?
   a. He was a member of the upper class.
   b. He used violent tactics against British rule.
   c. He began a protest movement against British rule.
   d. He was called Mahatma, which means "Great Soul."

   ANS: B   DIF: E

2. In 1950, India
   a. joined with the Communist party.
   b. fought a civil war.
   c. adopted a democratic constitution.
   d. elected Gandhi prime minister.

   ANS: C   DIF: A

3. The first African ever to receive the Nobel Peace Prize was
   a. Leonid Brezhnev.
   b. Albert John Lutuli.
   c. Mohandas Gandhi.
   d. Jawaharlal Nehru.

   ANS: B   DIF: E

4. The economies of Latin American countries depend on
   a. heavy industry.
   b. farming.
   c. foreigners.
   d. the United States.

   ANS: B   DIF: A

5. The *hacienda* system
   a. encourages economic progress.
   b. holds back economic progress.
   c. is run by the *campesinos*.
   d. is made up of small farming units.

   ANS: B DIF: C

MATCHING

Match each item with the correct statement below.

a. *campesinos*
b. subsistence farmers
c. cash crops
d. civil disobedience
e. *haciendas*

1. large ranches
2. peasants
3. sold to world markets
4. produced only food for family
5. refusing to obey unjust laws

1. ANS: E DIF: A
2. ANS: A DIF: A
3. ANS: C DIF: A
4. ANS: B DIF: A
5. ANS: D DIF: A

SHORT ANSWER

1. How do about three-fourths of the people in India make a living?

   ANS:
   farming

   DIF: E

2. How has India's government worked to improve economic conditions?

   ANS:
   It has supported the introduction of industry.

   DIF: A

3. How has Malaysia's location helped it to become prosperous?

   ANS:
   It lies in a major crossroads for trade and shipping.

   DIF: A

4. Why have many Africans moved to the cities?

   ANS:
   to get jobs, education, and better housing

   DIF: A

5. What groups often oppose land reform in Latin American countries?

   ANS:
   governments and wealthy land owners

   DIF: A

CHAPTER 39—THE WORLD SINCE 1989

MULTIPLE CHOICE

1. What caused Eastern Europe and the former Soviet Union to go through major changes beginning in the late 1980s?
   a. Communism collapsed.
   b. Gorbachev introduced reforms.
   c. Yeltsin quit the Communist party.
   d. The Soviet Union was dead.

   ANS: A DIF: C

2. Who was the first Russian head of state elected by the people?
   a. Gorbachev
   b. Honecker
   c. Ceausescu
   d. Yeltsin

   ANS: D DIF: E

3. When goods are scarce
   a. government controls are lifted.
   b. wages go up.
   c. prices go up.
   d. workers often strike.

   ANS: C DIF: C

4. The most valuable product of the Middle Eastern countries is
   a. oil.
   b. iron ore.
   c. wheat.
   d. beef cattle.

   ANS: A DIF: E

5. In the 1990s, the major problem in northeast Africa that has often led to war is
   a. hunger.
   b. need for medicine.
   c. violent clans.
   d. people moving away.

   ANS: A DIF: A

6. What percentage of the world's population goes to bed hungry every night?
   a. One-half
   b. Two-thirds
   c. One-tenth
   d. One-fifth

   ANS: D DIF: C

7. The biggest threat to the natural environment is
   a. the greenhouse effect.
   b. human activities.
   c. the tropical rain forest.
   d. carbon dioxide.

   ANS: B DIF: A

8. Communicable diseases are
   a. a problem in developing countries.
   b. a problem in industrial countries.
   c. completely wiped out.
   d. resistant to all known medicines.

   ANS: A DIF: A

9. Most countries today are part of a network of international trade because
   a. their populations are too large.
   b. there are many multinational companies.
   c. they can't make all the goods they need.
   d. they need to balance their economies.

   ANS: C DIF: A

10. Creating ways to balance economic development with the needs of the environment was the major concern of
    a. the Earth Summit.
    b. United States President George Bush.
    c. the World Health Organization.
    d. the United Nations.

    ANS: A DIF: A

MATCHING

Match each item with the correct statement below.

a. Saddam Hussein
b. Israel
c. privatize
d. Yugoslavia
e. habitat
f. apartheid
g. Solidarity
h. Egypt
i. Saudi Arabia
j. Gorbachev

1. Allow private citizens to own businesses
2. Soviet leader who introduced reforms in the late 1980s
3. Country that dissolved into six republics
4. Jewish country formed in 1948 from part of Palestine
5. Polish labor union whose calls for reform led to the fall of communism there
6. Only Arab country that recognized Israel before 1993
7. Dwelling place for humans, animals, or plants
8. Iraqi ruler who began the Gulf War by invading Kuwait
9. Source of the world's largest known oil reserves
10. Policy of strict separation of races in South Africa

1. ANS: C DIF: A
2. ANS: J DIF: A
3. ANS: D DIF: A
4. ANS: B DIF: A
5. ANS: G DIF: A
6. ANS: H DIF: A
7. ANS: E DIF: A
8. ANS: A DIF: A
9. ANS: I DIF: A
10. ANS: F DIF: A

SHORT ANSWER

1. What will life be like in the year 2100? Describe food production, protecting the environment, or health care as you predict it will be.

   ANS:
   Answers will vary, but could include: students may feel that scientific advancements will contribute to solutions to the problems of not enough food for the world population, protection for the environment, and more universal health care.

   DIF: A

2. Why were peaceful elections in Russia in March 2000 a hopeful sign for that country?

   ANS:
   They indicated a changed political climate that worked through peaceful transfer of power from government to government.

   DIF: A

3. What positive turning point took place in Arab-Israeli relations as a result of the 1990 Gulf War?

   ANS:
   Arabs and Israelis agreed to let their negotiators talk directly with one another.

   DIF: A

4. What happened to the city of Hong Kong in 1997?

   ANS:
   It came under the rule of Communist China.

   DIF: A

5. Why are residents of Hong Kong apprehensive?

   ANS:
   They are worried about their political future.

   DIF: A

6. Why do people in Nationalist China (Taiwan) fear uniting with Communist China?

   ANS:
   They fear that Communist China will take away their political and economic freedoms.

   DIF: A

7. Which African country has made remarkable strides toward freedom and equality for all its citizens?

   ANS:
   South Africa

   DIF: A

8. What will create change in cultures in the years to come?

   ANS:
   travel and communication among the peoples of the world

   DIF: A

9. Why do some experts say that today's teenagers have the best chance at working together to solve the earth's problems?

   ANS:
   because no other generation has had the freedom and exposure to global conditions that today's teens have

   DIF: A

10. Study the map below. How would the loss of the satellite countries affect Russia's population? Control of bodies of water? Access to European ports?

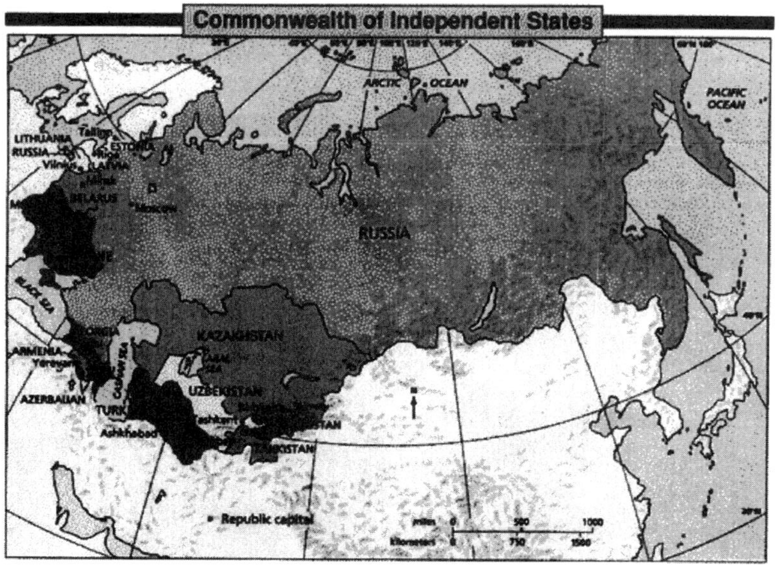

ANS:
Losing the satellite countries means that Russia loses many people. The country also loses some control of the Aral, Caspian, and Black Seas. Russia's access to European ports is decreased as well.

DIF: C

SECTION QUIZ 39-1—THE END OF THE COLD WAR

MULTIPLE CHOICE

1. In January 1989, the Polish government
   a. took down the Berlin Wall.
   b. executed Nicolae Ceausescu and his wife.
   c. lifted its ban on Solidarity.
   d. surrendered to Soviet soldiers.

   ANS: C DIF: E

2. Which of the following was NOT true of Boris Yeltsin?
   a. He was a reformer.
   b. He was elected president of Russia in May 1990.
   c. He quit the Communist party.
   d. He masterminded *perestroika*.

   ANS: D DIF: A

3. By the end of 1991, 12 of the former Soviet republics
   a. formed the Commonwealth of Independent States.
   b. became one nation.
   c. were at war.
   d. voted President Yeltsin out of office.

   ANS: A DIF: E

4. Which of the following is NOT true?
   a. On January 1, 1993, Czechoslovakia became two countries.
   b. On October 3, 1990, East and West Germany became one nation.
   c. By 1993, the Russian economy had grown strong.
   d. By December 1990, the Berlin Wall had been completely torn down.

   ANS: C DIF: C

5. Lithuania declared its independence from the Soviet Union in
   a. 1956.
   b. March 1968.
   c. March 1989.
   d. March 1991.

   ANS: D DIF: C

MATCHING

Match each item with the correct statement below.
a. Nicolae Ceausescu
b. coalition
c. privatize
d. Erich Honeker
e. Boris Yeltsin

1. Russian president
2. East German leader
3. combination
4. Romanian dictator
5. allow citizen ownership

1. ANS: E DIF: A
2. ANS: D DIF: A
3. ANS: B DIF: A
4. ANS: A DIF: A
5. ANS: C DIF: A

SHORT ANSWER

1. How did Soviet leader Mikhail Gorbachev differ from earlier Soviet leaders?

   ANS:
   He publicly discussed problems facing the government.

   DIF: A

2. Why did Gorbachev resign?

   ANS:
   The Soviet Union broke up, and he had no country to lead.

   DIF: A

3. Why had Communist leaders neglected economic development in Russia and other Commonwealth countries?

   ANS:
   They had put all energy and resources into winning the cold war.

   DIF: A

4. What kind of economic "inheritance" did the new democracies have?

   ANS:
   outdated industries and shortages of food

   DIF: A

5. What two major resources were the new governments lacking to run competitive businesses?

   ANS:
   money and experience

   DIF: A

SECTION QUIZ 39-2—WORLD CHALLENGES

MULTIPLE CHOICE

1. On August 2, 1990, Iraq
   a. declared war on the United States.
   b. lost 100,000 soldiers during U.S. air strikes.
   c. invaded Kuwait.
   d. surrendered to the United Nations.

   ANS: C DIF: C

2. Although Iraq lost the Gulf War,
   a. it kept control of Kuwait.
   b. the United States lost thousands of military personnel.
   c. Saddam Hussein remained in power.
   d. the Iraqi death toll was less than 300.

   ANS: C DIF: A

3. The most violent fighting in the former Yugoslavia occurred in
   a. Croatia.
   b. Bosnia-Herzegovina.
   c. Slovenia.
   d. Macedonia.

   ANS: B DIF: A

4. Which of the following was NOT true of Northeast Africa in the 1990s?
   a. A famine threatened Sudan.
   b. The United Nations sent peacekeepers to Somalia.
   c. Eritrea achieved independence.
   d. Rainfall helped keep crops growing well.

   ANS: D DIF: E

5. In South Africa in 1989,
   a. Frederick W. de Klerk became president.
   b. Nelson Mandela was released.
   c. most laws that defined apartheid were thrown out.
   d. the Inkatha Freedom Party elected a Zulu chief.

   ANS: A DIF: A

MATCHING

Match each item with the correct statement below.
a. Sarajevo
b. Palestine Liberation Organization
c. apartheid
d. Kuwait
e. Kurds

1. oil-rich country
2. led by Yasir Arafat

3. a people in northern Iraq
4. capital of Bosnia-Herzegovina
5. separation of the races

1. ANS: D DIF: A
2. ANS: B DIF: A
3. ANS: E DIF: A
4. ANS: A DIF: A
5. ANS: C DIF: A

SHORT ANSWER

1. What conditions began to cause violence and confusion in countries around the world in the 1990s?

   ANS:
   long-standing ethnic and national tensions

   DIF: A

2. What unstable situation exists in the area of the Persian Gulf?

   ANS:
   a stand-off between the Iraqi government and the United Nations

   DIF: A

3. What ongoing problems concern the peoples in Bosnia-Herzogovina?

   ANS:
   ethnic hatred and violence among the region's groups

   DIF: A

4. What ethnic groups are involved in trying to live peacefully in the Middle East?

   ANS:
   Israelis and Arabs

   DIF: A

5. What was the major cause of authoritarian governments coming to power in African nations?

   ANS:
   lack of experience in self-government

   DIF: A

SECTION QUIZ 39-3—THE WORLD TODAY

MULTIPLE CHOICE

1. Multinational companies are
   a. companies that operate across national boundaries.
   b. companies that hire ethnically diverse employees.
   c. companies that hire more women than men.
   d. companies in the European Community.

   ANS: A DIF: E

2. According to the World Health Organization, by the year 2000,
   a. about 40 million people will die of cholera.
   b. about 40 million people will carry the HIV virus.
   c. the world's population will reach 40 million.
   d. malaria will be the number one cause of death worldwide.

   ANS: B DIF: A

3. Which of the following was NOT true of the Earth Summit?
   a. Delegates from 178 nations attended.
   b. It was held in Argentina.
   c. Nations pledged to take steps to limit global warming.
   d. Nations discussed balancing economic with environmental concerns.

   ANS: B DIF: A

4. Rain forests
   a. have the thickest concentration of plants on land.
   b. cover most of the earth.
   c. make the earth warmer.
   d. are being flooded.

   ANS: A DIF: A

5. The present world population is about
   a. 40 million. c. 5.4 billion.
   b. 200 million. d. 50 billion.

   ANS: C DIF: C

MATCHING

Match each item with the correct statement below.

a. habitats
b. Earth Summit
c. European Community
d. communicable diseases
e. greenhouse effect

1. historic 1992 meeting
2. illnesses passed among people

3. Common Market
4. dwelling places
5. makes the earth warmer

1. ANS: B DIF: A
2. ANS: D DIF: A
3. ANS: C DIF: A
4. ANS: A DIF: A
5. ANS: E DIF: A

SHORT ANSWER

1. What is the major problem facing Cuba and North Korea today?

   ANS:
   economic ruin

   DIF: A

2. How do renegade nations pose a threat to the world at large?

   ANS:
   They refuse to reduce the weapons of war and use violent tactics to achieve their goals.

   DIF: A

3. What are the three major causes of the world population explosion of the 1900s?

   ANS:
   increased food production; improved medical care; better living conditions

   DIF: A

4. Why does progress in the 21st century depend on cooperation and communication?

   ANS:
   because contemporary problems cut across national boundaries, involve more than one nation, and cannot be solved by one nation alone

   DIF: A